THE
EVERYTHING®
NONPROFIT
TOOLKIT

Dear Reader,

From the title of the book you are holding in your hands, you would think it's only a toolkit to guide you through the process of forming and operating a nonprofit organization. It is obviously that, but actually so much more!

   This book is about organizing your community group, your garden club, or your performance venue. It's about bringing people in your neighborhood together, even in these challenging economic times, to make their lives and their world a better place. It is about working collectively to understand the confusing layers of detail that are necessary to make sure that your club or community group has the proper systems and groundwork in place. It is about learning to collaborate and to have a good time in the process.

   I've worked with groups all over the country, and I've seen many people with wonderful ideas become frustrated with the legalese and archaic terminology so often used in nonprofit organizing. *The Everything® Nonprofit Toolkit* is intended to reduce that chatter and to help you and your group gain the confidence and tools necessary to organize a successful nonprofit organization.

   Organizing your community and forming a nonprofit organization is a wonderful, exciting process that few people ever experience. I hope this book will help you continue the good work you are doing.

   Cheers!

Jim Goettler

Welcome to the EVERYTHING® Series!

These handy, accessible books give you all you need to tackle a difficult project, gain a new hobby, comprehend a fascinating topic, prepare for an exam, or even brush up on something you learned back in school but have since forgotten.

You can choose to read an Everything® book from cover to cover or just pick out the information you want from our four useful boxes: e-questions, e-facts, e-alerts, and e-ssentials.

We give you everything you need to know on the subject, but throw in a lot of fun stuff along the way, too.

We now have more than 400 Everything® books in print, spanning such wide-ranging categories as weddings, pregnancy, cooking, music instruction, foreign language, crafts, pets, New Age, and so much more. When you're done reading them all, you can finally say you know Everything®!

QUESTION

Answers to
common questions

FACT

Important snippets
of information

ALERT

Urgent
warnings

ESSENTIAL

Quick
handy tips

PUBLISHER Karen Cooper

DIRECTOR OF ACQUISITIONS AND INNOVATION Paula Munier

MANAGING EDITOR, EVERYTHING® SERIES Lisa Laing

COPY CHIEF Casey Ebert

ASSISTANT PRODUCTION EDITOR Melanie Cordova

ACQUISITIONS EDITOR Kate Powers

ASSOCIATE DEVELOPMENT EDITOR Hillary Thompson

EDITORIAL ASSISTANT Matthew Kane

EVERYTHING® SERIES COVER DESIGNER Erin Alexander

LAYOUT DESIGNERS Erin Dawson, Michelle Roy Kelly, Elisabeth Lariviere

Visit the entire Everything® series at *www.everything.com*

THE
EVERYTHING®
NONPROFIT
TOOLKIT

The all-in-one resource for establishing
a nonprofit that will grow, thrive, and succeed

Jim Goettler, Author of *The Everything® Guide
to Starting and Running a Nonprofit*

Aadamsmedia
Avon, Massachusetts

This book is dedicated to every person who looks around his or her community of like-minded individuals and picks up the phone, sends an e-mail, or sends a quick text message suggesting that they get together to talk about starting a nonprofit organization. To each of you and to the people with whom you are working, Welcome.

An Everything® Series Book.
Everything® and everything.com® are registered trademarks of F+W Media, Inc.

Published by Adams Media, a division of F+W Media, Inc.
57 Littlefield Street, Avon, MA 02322 U.S.A.
www.adamsmedia.com

Yew Dell Precase Final and Yew Dell Gardens Long Form of Yew Dell Gardens
of Crestwood, Kentucky, which appear in Appendix A, are used with permission
from Goettler Associates, Inc.

Contains material adapted and abridged from *The Everything® Guide to Starting
and Running a Nonprofit* by Jim Goettler, copyright © 2010 by F+W Media, Inc.,
ISBN 10: 1-4405-0015-0, ISBN 13: 978-1-4405-0015-2.

ISBN 10: 1-4405-3878-6
ISBN 13: 978-1-4405-3878-0
eISBN 10: 1-4405-3897-2
eISBN 13: 978-1-4405-3897-1

Printed in the United States of America.

10 9 8 7 6 5 4 3 2 1

Library of Congress Cataloging-in-Publication Data
is available from the publisher.

This publication is designed to provide accurate and authoritative information with regard to the subject matter covered. It is sold with the understanding that the publisher is not engaged in rendering legal, accounting, or other professional advice. If legal advice or other expert assistance is required, the services of a competent professional person should be sought.

—From a *Declaration of Principles* jointly adopted by a Committee of the
American Bar Association and a Committee of Publishers and Associations

Many of the designations used by manufacturers and sellers to distinguish their products are claimed as trademarks. Where those designations appear in this book and Adams Media was aware of a trademark claim, the designations have been printed with initial capital letters.

*This book is available at quantity discounts for bulk purchases.
For information, please call 1-800-289-0963.*

Contents

Acknowledgments

A huge thank-you to a number of people without whom the original *The Everything® Guide to Starting and Running a Nonprofit*, and now *The Everything® Nonprofit Toolkit* would never have come together. First, Verna Dreisbach of Dreisbach Literary Management for sending me a note one fine day asking me if I'd like to write a book on nonprofit organizing! Little did I know what an amazing adventure I was agreeing to. Thanks must also go to an excellent copyeditor/proofreader, Jeanine Paquin, who managed to get my tangents cleaned up and the word counts close to target before the folks at Adams Media went to work on the final manuscript that became the book you are now reading. Thank you to copyeditor Robin Witkin for your excellent work. Finally, a thank-you to Goettler Associates in Columbus, Ohio, for kindly sharing a case study of a successful fundraising campaign, which appears in Appendix A of this second edition.

The Top 10 Things Every Organizer
of a Nonprofit Must Remember

1. Be very careful about the money. Where it comes from and how it is spent will rank among the most important details in your life.

2. Never, ever forget why you decided to organize as a nonprofit! Everything in this book is designed to help you do your work—not to become your work.

3. Nonprofits are not the magic key to gaining outside funding. In reality, grants are few and far between, and the competition for them is intense.

4. The vast majority of new nonprofit organizations fail within two years. This is a simple fact.

5. Your board of directors is responsible for the organization. They may not always agree with you, even if you did help start it.

6. Nonprofits make communities stronger by bringing people together for a common goal. They can empower communities and all the people working in them.

7. A state nonprofit is *not* the same as a federal nonprofit! If you have not filed for federal tax exemption, you are simply incorporated in your state.

8. Never imply you have federal tax exemption or that contributions are tax deductible if you only have state incorporation papers. It just confuses everyone and will cause trouble down the road.

9. On the first read, the rules established by the IRS may seem very difficult to understand and follow. However, when you become familiar with them, they will actually help you remember why a nonprofit is different than a for-profit business and will remind you of the wonderful position nonprofits hold in our society.

10. If it isn't on paper, it doesn't exist! Record keeping, from the first meeting of your group to all communication with the IRS, must be documented.

Introduction

IN 1831, ALEXIS DE TOCQUEVILLE wrote *Democracy in America* after a nine-month visit to a fledgling nation, the United States. He wrote about the uniquely American phenomenon of forming "associations" of all types, including professional, social, civil, and political groups.

Today, even in times of economic uncertainty, people continue to organize groups around common interests or professions. The exact makeup of these groups will be as different as their members, but they all share a common characteristic: that is, people coming together to collaborate. The purpose of this book is to provide a solid foundation, indeed a toolkit, for community organizers who work with groups that may be considering formal incorporation in their state or possibly becoming a federally recognized nonprofit.

Nonprofits often take on responsibilities that were once the domain of government agencies. As a result, nonprofits are assuming an exciting and dynamic role throughout the country exactly as they did during the Great Depression in the last century. It has become even more important that people understand the basic requirements of organizing within their communities so that their group can remain viable and sustainable long after the original founders have moved on.

This book begins with the assumption that the reader is in some way connected to a small organization in its early formative stage. You may have heard the term *nonprofit organization,* but you probably have never had to apply for federal nonprofit status.

Because every state has developed its own system and process for incorporation, each state has different forms—and a few states don't have standard forms at all. If you live in a state that requires you to create forms, use the sample Articles of Incorporation—you are welcome to modify it to suit your needs.

This book will guide you through the process of organizing, starting with those early meetings, working through the maze of local and state forms, and finally building the application for federal tax exemption. Becoming a nonprofit is not a magical path to financial wealth. It is, however, a way for an organization to remain true to its principles of community service while conducting basic business functions, such as having a bank account, signing contracts, hiring staff, and owning property.

Becoming a nonprofit organization is one of the best ways to guarantee that your club or organization will be able to continue its business well into the future. Organizing a group to prepare for incorporating and eventually applying for nonprofit status is a lot of work. It will require a clear understanding of what a nonprofit organization can and cannot do, based on the simple, yet precise requirements of the Internal Revenue Service.

This guide will help you understand the core requirements for every nonprofit. It involves a lot of common sense, and as you will see, it is not that difficult. However, it is impossible to cover every possible detail related to forming and operating a nonprofit organization in one book, so in some instances there will be recommendations to seek advice from either a legal or nonprofit tax professional. Nonprofit regulations can and do change with amazing frequency.

Forming a nonprofit is an exciting process from beginning to end. You will work closely with many people in your community you might never have met as you take your ideals and your effort and pour them into an entity that will guarantee that work can continue forever. The aim of this guide is to help you do your good work.

CHAPTER 1

Organizer to Organizer—Let's Talk!

The essence of creating a successful nonprofit organization is to understand your community's needs and to navigate with the daunting federal tax-exempt status, perhaps for the first time in your life. As an individual or one of a group of people whose passion is your organization, focusing on your community is the first step. This chapter will help you understand the community your organization intends to serve.

Living in Interesting Times

There is a very old expression: "May you live in interesting times." Together, we are living through the most serious financial crisis of our lifetimes. Interesting times indeed! Banks are closing, families are losing their homes to foreclosure, and while the employment picture will improve, it is a multiyear process with few guarantees. Each day, more details of the challenges facing our communities are presented, the tax base continues to erode, and essential services are eliminated.

Although we face challenging times for global, national, state, and local economies, it is a very exciting time for the careful, deliberate, and focused organizer of a nonprofit organization. This is a time to re-examine exactly who you are as an organization and what you want to do, ever-mindful of an economic environment unlikely to improve for a number of years.

It is a time to study the history of the world's economies during and after the Great Depression of the early 1900s, and understand that in that time, just as now, the government was simply unable to fund many of society's most basic needs. It was during that earlier set of interesting times when the soup lines and missions, now remembered through the remarkable photography of the period, were often set up by "private charities" to simply provide the basic food and shelter needs the government was unable to meet. Likewise, many community improvement groups, established to maintain parks or gardens, or enhance through art and music, filled the void created by a government essentially out of money.

That financial crisis of the 1930s led to the boom in the nonprofit sector, as community groups were established to assume those core responsibilities, and in exchange the federal government recognized those efforts by relieving organizations meeting basic standards of their tax liability. If you look around any city in the country, you will see evidence of that earlier time. Many of the lodges and fraternal orders now known for their aging structures in many inner cities were the centers of life and culture at a time when money was scarce and people had to rely on one another to survive.

Core Values and Purpose

Although the regulations governing every aspect of forming and operating a nonprofit organization have become terribly complex over the years, and many people become focused solely on those regulations and reams of fine print, the core values and purpose of your mission will determine whether you and your organization are going to make it through this sour economy—exactly as it did in the last century.

FACT

In 2009, as the economy was well into the current crisis, more than 46,000 new nonprofit organizations were registered with the Internal Revenue Service. This clearly shows that many people are seeing an urgent need in their communities and setting about to create solutions!

Small Nonprofits Are Vital, Too

According to one school of thought, in times of economic hardship, the smaller nonprofits should step aside in favor of the larger, more established organizations able to utilize contributions more efficiently. This terribly shortsighted approach effectively eliminates the huge need that exists and is growing in every community.

Many of the people who are starting nonprofit organizations for the first time are people coming out of the corporate world, bringing the same drive and energy to their new organization they once contributed in business. They are seeing a need and putting to good use their many years of experience in the private sector—or doing exactly what people more than sixty years ago were doing during the Great Depression, an earlier "interesting time."

We're Not All MBAs

Many people act as community organizers. Along the journey, organizers decide there is a need to bring together like-minded people. For any group of individuals to survive beyond the first burst of excitement, some type of recognized structure must exist that will enable them to raise the necessary money to actually do the work over the long term.

Most people have heard the term *nonprofit organization* in one context or another. They often don't truly understand what it means or what the process entails, but they know intuitively that a nonprofit is the route to go.

The Passion That Drives Us

You may not think of your group as businesspeople; you probably see yourselves as members of a community who share a passion to make things happen. You are certainly not involved in organizing for any personal gain, so the usual profit motive does not come into play. Instead, you are looking at taking on the huge task of forming an organization to serve a purpose that is important to you. It is a passion ultimately for and about the community in which you live and work. Because of that passion, it makes sense to form a legal entity in which all profits are returned to the organization and the community it serves, rather than to any individual or group.

ALERT

Throughout this book, the terms *nonprofit organization* and *nonprofit corporation* will be used interchangeably. All state and federal legal filings will refer to nonprofit corporations. As the organizer working in your community, however, it is perfectly acceptable to refer to your group as an organization, society, or whatever terminology you have been using.

Unlike many of their for-profit counterparts, the majority of the thousands of nonprofit organizations that start every year have their roots in a core group of activists in their home communities. They are formed by friends or neighbors who share a common interest. To a large degree, the founders of nonprofit organizations do not come from the business community, but they care so deeply about their cause that they decide that they must organize. Although a formal business education or background is expected when starting a for-profit corporation, it has been acceptable not to have that background when starting a nonprofit since the earliest days of public charities.

In Perspective

When public charities first came into being, the government was relieved of some of its responsibilities to the community. No one questions the need for many of the services that nonprofits or charities assume as necessary for healthy, vibrant communities, so the government grants a lot of leeway in recognition of the sacrifices that individuals involved in nonprofits are willing to make. The government understands that nonprofits exist because their members are passionate about a cause. As a result, the lack of business skills is occasionally overlooked.

A growing cottage industry of business professionals are stepping up to offer their assistance to start-up nonprofits. Although you may not have a background in business, don't worry. There is an entire support system of MBAs to show you the ropes.

A master's in business administration (MBA) is generally awarded after completing two years of graduate-level study at an accredited business school. In the commercial business world, MBAs are valued for their training and understanding of how markets and businesses function.

As you move forward, you may find it helpful to engage businesspeople for their advice or to enroll in business courses to become a better organizer.

The Political Atmosphere

You must consider the political atmosphere in your community from the very beginning, and it must remain part of your strategic, long-range planning. Even if you don't think your mission and planned area of service will be controversial, the fact that you are interested in becoming a public charity and will be seeking donations to carry out your mission will invite scrutiny. Although nonprofit corporations pay fees and taxes (other than corporate income tax), as do their for-profit counterparts, the perception remains that nonprofits have a free ride.

Pay Attention to Any Pending Tax Law Changes

Every adjustment to state or federal tax codes can bring the entire concept of the nonprofit corporation to the forefront, which becomes a highly charged political issue. You need to stay on top of these potential changes. It is a good idea to connect with and join affiliated organizations that are able to effectively track legislation or ordinances that might affect your ability to carry out your mission.

Build Alliances

If your mission may be seen as controversial for any reason, build the necessary alliances that will help you organize and continue your work from the beginning. Although you may think that addressing the major problems in our society such as homelessness, substance abuse, hunger, violence, or accessible health care may not be controversial, the way you address those issues may bring you attention you never expected. You need to be prepared before that attention focuses on your nonprofit.

Exactly how you enter into this public discourse is determined by whether you apply for and receive a 501(c)(3) or a 501(c)(4) determination from the IRS. That difference may well affect how involved you become in the political process and what you may (or may not do) to affect that process.

ESSENTIAL

Meet the neighbors—literally! Invite your immediate neighbors over for lunch or a casual meeting so they understand what you are planning to do and exactly who they can contact if there is trouble or if they have any concerns, no matter how minor. Being proactive now will save untold aggravation later.

Neighbors

Where and how you choose to set up your organization's office and operations may affect your neighbors. You may never have given traffic and parking a second thought until now, but they are issues every organization with public or walk-in traffic comes to know well. Parking is, without question, the biggest source of problems in neighborhoods where a new organization sets up.

Every time you hold a meeting or a public event, your attendees will take up parking on the street or park in a spot that was "reserved." If you have access to off-street parking, you are well ahead of the game, but the vast majority of groups do not have that option. Reaching out to engage the immediate community so that everyone understands what you are planning to do will help neutralize much of the opposition and fear of the unknown that plagues many nonprofits.

Meeting with City Hall

Meeting with local political leaders and introducing yourself to personnel in your city and county administrative offices before you need them shows everyone that you are willing to work with the community, even those who may have reservations about your plans. This is an area where your skill as an organizer who is comfortable meeting with strangers is going to help in many ways.

So much of organizing a nonprofit comes down to establishing and building relationships with not only those people who are supportive of your plans but also those who oppose your organization. If your plans involve zoning or occupancy regulations, all your skills as an organizer and negotiator will come into play. By working with—rather than confronting—local review boards or citizen groups, you should be fine.

The Citizens United Ruling—How It Affects Nonprofits

In January 2008, at the height of Hillary Clinton's presidential campaign, Citizens United, a nonprofit organization, released a ninety-minute documentary titled *Hillary*. The movie expressed opinions about whether Senator Clinton, a candidate for the Democratic presidential nomination, was fit for the presidency. The nonprofit produced advertisements promoting the film and wanted to show them on broadcast and cable television and video-on-demand. To pay for the video-on-demand distribution and the advertisements, Citizens United planned to use its general treasury funds. This became very important in regard to ramifications of this court decision.

Until this time, federal law prohibited corporations and unions from spending their general treasury funds on "electioneering communications" or on speech that expressly advocated the election or defeat of a candidate close to an election, which everyone agreed this video did. Concerned that spending money in support of the production and distribution of the movie close to an election day might be found to be illegal, Citizens United sued the Federal Communications Commission (FCC) to prevent it from enforcing this law.

Although suing a federal agency to stop it from enforcing what is considered an unlawful rule is unusual, it does happen from time to time. The high profile nature of this case made it almost certain to move quickly through the federal court system.

The case finally made its way to the U.S. Supreme Court in January 2010. In a 5–4 decision, the Court ruled that corporations and unions have the same political speech rights as individuals under the First Amendment. It found no reason to prohibit corporations and unions from using their general treasury funds to make election-related independent expenditures close to an election or at any time they chose. Thus, it struck down the McCain-Feingold law banning this practice. The federal law had been named for the two senators, John McCain (R-Arizona) and Russ Feingold (D-Wisconsin), who drafted it.

Citizens United and 501(c)(3)s

The Citizens United ruling does not impact a 501(c)(3) nonprofit. Regardless of the changes in election law, the federal tax law that prohibits 501(c)

(3)s from supporting or opposing candidates still applies. A 501(c)(3) still cannot endorse candidates or make independent expenditures suggesting who is the "better" candidate.

What the ruling will do, however, is complicate the environment in which many nonprofits operate by opening the doors to corporate interests whose policies may be at odds with those of the nonprofit. As an example, if a nonprofit organization conducts nature classes for school children in a nearby forest, or develops programs to teach about water quality, and the surrounding lands are part of a larger land use debate, the unlimited corporate money that can now be spent in that debate may mean the forest or watershed will be changed, as well as the curriculum of the educational organization.

Political Advocacy

The Citizens United decision does allow nonprofit, issue-based 501(c)(4) or 501(c)(6) organizations to make independent expenditures furthering political advocacy using the organization's general funds to support or oppose candidates for the U.S. House, the U.S. Senate, and the presidency. By extension, this decision will allow the same opportunities at state and local levels. Previously, these independent expenditures for political purposes had to be made through Political Action Committees (PACs) using voluntary donations, rather than general treasury funds.

FACT

An independent expenditure for the purposes of this situation is a communication that urges someone to vote for or against a candidate. This type of communication typically includes words like *support*, *oppose*, *elect*, *defeat*, or *vote for* a candidate. It is the type of communication that floods your mailbox and television during every election cycle. Everyone has seen them.

Electioneering Communications

The Citizens United decision allows organizations—in our case, nonprofit organizations other than those determined to be 501(c)(3) organizations—to make "electioneering communications." This type of communication is defined as a broadcast ad that refers to a federal candidate and is distributed within thirty days of a primary or convention and within sixty days of a general election—as well as throughout the year.

Great News for Nonprofit Advocacy Groups!

Any landmark Supreme Court decision gives rise to a variety of opinions. The Citizens United decision opens up tremendous opportunities for nonprofit advocacy organizations—those groups that do not have the 501(c)(3) determination—to become more actively involved in the political life of their communities. This decision may in fact help further the overall mission of many nonprofit organizations as well as increase the direct, positive impact of your group on your community. How you and your organization decide to avail yourselves of this opportunity will require careful thought and deliberation, but the fundamental rules regarding political financing have changed forever.

ALERT

It is important to understand that even with the Citizens United decision, nonprofit corporations remain subject to federal tax law, including a primary purpose restriction, namely that political activities cannot be the primary purpose of a nonprofit organization. Further, all reporting requirements not only remained unchanged; they were reinforced through the wording of the decision.

Reaction to the Citizens United Decision

It is difficult to say what steps, if any, are going to be taken with respect to this controversial opinion. A number of national organizations are planning to prepare methods that range from legislation to a constitutional amendment to reverse what some people consider an unsettling decision. How any of these plans materialize remains to be seen over the next few years, but every nonprofit organization or even a group planning to file for federal recognition would do well to keep an eye on developments that occur as this story evolves.

Evaluating Your Capacity Honestly

Capacity, when used in the context of a nonprofit organization, is used to describe the ability of a group to accomplish the work it has set out to do. When people are accustomed to a traditional business approach, including relying on capital to finance the production of items for sale, having to adjust to not having that capital presents a real challenge. Newer nonprofit organizations, especially those driven by a more traditional business focus, often have mission statements and other materials that lay out tremendous plans but actually end up requiring more time, energy, and resources than are available. If you are not aware of your actual capacity or you pretend it is greater than it really is, expect frustration among the group members. Try to avoid this situation at all costs.

Approaching the matter from a community organizer's perspective may help. Community organizers must develop relationships that are not financial, so many of the capacity-building issues melt away.

FACT

Nonfinancial relationships include in-kind contributors, or people who have a unique skill the group would otherwise lack. This also includes venue managers and arts commissioners if yours is a cultural organization, other school administrators if you are in the education field, or professional service providers if you are filling a gap in health care delivery.

It's about Your People

The ongoing task will be to develop internal capacity by selecting people within your group to maintain the organization as well as develop and execute your projects and programs. During the formative stages, much of the work will fall on the board of directors. They will need to determine what tasks they can realistically assume and see through to their conclusion.

Growing Slowly Is Perfectly Okay

Helping the group develop a realistic multiyear work plan and allowing the internal capacity to build slowly to the point where more and more ambitious projects can be undertaken will also greatly reduce the frustration of not being able to do everything at once.

The topic of capacity building will invariably come up in any conversation among members of different nonprofits. It is an extremely important element in your planning.

Time Commitment

One of the overlooked elements involved in starting a nonprofit organization, especially a community-based one that will rely in large part on volunteers, is the time commitment for everyone involved. In a mature organization with paid staff, everyone has a set time to start work and a set time to leave. When you are relying on volunteers, the scheduling depends on the other things in everyone's lives. The time people can commit to the organization will by necessity take a lower priority, with a combination of planning and compassion, however, your people will find a good mix of personal and organization time. Of course, if you are one of the main organizers or a member of the board of directors, the new organization will become your constant mental companion during every waking hour.

Delegate, Delegate, Delegate!

There are a number of tricks you can employ to avoid letting the organization take over your life and make you a far less effective organizer. Many of the tricks involve delegating responsibilities. As much as you may think you can do everything, you can't! You will need to become comfortable asking other people to take on more responsibilities once you believe they are up-to-speed on whatever task they're doing.

Running on Empty Is Not an Option

Many organizations suffer as the lead organizers try to do too much, become run down in the process, and grow less and less effective. Such a situation hurts the individuals involved and can cripple the organization. As the organization grows and more people become involved, it is essential to ensure that members step back when they are overworked and are no longer fully engaged. Encourage yourself or others to take time to recharge the batteries and return fully refreshed and able to handle the responsibilities of the group.

Looking Over the Horizon

Looking into the future and trying to predict what will happen in the political or economic environment is always a tricky exercise, made more so by the unsettled economic conditions in the United States and around the world. Most economic forecasts point to a difficult but steady recovery over the next few years. For you and your nonprofit organization, this means it is a perfect time to re-evaluate your entire operation and adjust your long-range plans in line with the larger economic picture.

Watch the Market

Although it is perhaps counterintuitive for a nonprofit organization to carefully monitor the stock markets, keep in mind that while some people invest in the markets with an eye toward short-term benefits, many others look toward long-term investments in companies considered safe in the short term, and, more important, highly productive in the future.

Try to understand the philanthropic interests of the companies recognized as having long-term stability, whose internal forecasting has them weathering the current economic storm. You should not change your mission or operational plans to satisfy a potential donor, but it is beneficial to gain an understanding of trends that may affect your own fundraising in the future.

Make Friends!

Use this period of economic uncertainty to develop relationships that are not based solely on asking for money. Let's face it—too many people see someone involved at the core level of a nonprofit organization coming toward them, and they are prepared for the plea, prepared for the ask, prepared for that little business reply envelope to be pressed into their hand.

Surprise them! Use this unsettled time to do more than ask for money. Get to know your future supporters on a deeper level. Attend their meetings, show up at their public events, and help them understand you are more than the person who always asks for money for your group. Sure, you need to maintain your basic revenue streams, but it is difficult for everyone right now, and those who come out stronger in the end made a point of developing real relationships and strong strategic partnerships.

Identify Corporations with Like Values or Useful Product Lines

Use this time not only to identify possible funders—those within your community or extended network able to help financially—but also to join the e-mailing lists of corporations whose values are closely aligned with your own, or whose product lines indicate that *they* might benefit from a relationship with your organization.

If your group is involved in building homes for the homeless, for example, learn all you can about the companies that manufacture the tools you use; or if you are giving performances for shut-ins, learn about the hospital equipment they might use. Remember, the companies you are interested in approaching also want to get their names and good deeds out into the communities they serve, so it makes perfect sense (and has proven to be a very successful method!) to initiate communication with them.

Prepare for Recovery

Many organizations are having a rough time. Those in the best position to weather this recession will remain true to their mission while adapting to both the current economic environment and to the one that will present itself as the recovery continues.

The truly successful organizations will foresee how their unique communities are going to look as more people find employment, the housing market stabilizes, and the revenue streams once taken for granted begin to re-emerge. They will see new communities being built and understand the needs those communities will have for service a nonprofit might provide.

They will see the need for educational and cultural programming that the tax base may not support but that people will want to make their lives complete.

Watch Politics!

Although as a nonprofit you are not permitted to be directly involved in the political process, you can and must watch everything that is happening at both the federal and state levels. Watch for any proposed changes in tax law; even if the words *nonprofit organization* are never mentioned, much of the money contributed to nonprofits comes as a direct result of the tax code. Terms such as *payroll tax,* or *capital gains,* or *inheritance* take on a special meaning if your organization's fundraising plan includes targeting the very people whose net worth (and by extension disposable income) is determined by changes in tax law. Most tax law takes months, if not a year, to take effect, which means your organization must follow what is happening in that arena now in order to devise practical plans well into the future.

CHAPTER 2

Networking Within Your Community

Before we begin to focus on your organization, let's take a look at how the broader community works. Understanding the people, businesses, and relationships within your community is an essential step toward developing a successful nonprofit organization. Once you've identified these key factors, you should utilize every resource available to connect to your community, including the latest social media outlets. Read on to discover the best networking options for your nonprofit.

Evaluating Your Broader Community

As someone who is interested in starting an organization that will be supported by the community, looking for and understanding elements that are under the radar just makes sense, and in our current economic environment, this knowledge is essential.

Looking at the Media

Begin by looking at the traditional forms of local media: the radio, the daily newspaper, and the local television, including any cable access channels. Are there writers at the paper who are sympathetic to your project? How about radio personalities? Is there a nonprofit station that not only accepts community groups but actively encourages them with free airtime or production assistance for public service announcements?

Public service announcements (PSAs) are prerecorded spots, generally between thirty and sixty seconds in length, produced by radio or television stations for later broadcast at no charge to you. Every station has a set policy for accepting and broadcasting PSAs for nonprofit organizations in their service area.

Audacity

A tremendous tool for use in producing PSAs is a freely available software program called Audacity. When downloaded from the Internet and installed on your computer, Audacity turns your computer into a mini-recording studio, able to produce broadcast-quality audio files. Although very sophisticated, Audacity is remarkably intuitive and can be used with only a little practice; the same can be said as well for other basic recording/editing programs.

Get Your Press List Together

If you don't already have a local media list, consider putting one together that includes all the outlets, their general contact information, and a rough tracking of both supportive and critical articles they have put out over the past year. You want to get a good sense of where you will find both support and criticism. With that understanding, you will be able to better present the pros and cons of incorporating as a nonprofit.

Looking at the Neighborhood

Although it might seem like an odd thing to assess, how are the roads? Are they in good repair, or is it obvious the local government is strapped for cash and has neglected the infrastructure? How about the parks? Are they well maintained or are they showing signs of trouble? This becomes very important when you seek funding. When money is tight, you'll need to expend extra effort and far more creativity to raise your operating capital. Roads and parks are too often the first indicators that money is either tight or the political will to maintain them does not currently exist. As time passes and your organization begins to seek funding, you may be in direct competition for limited funds with long-established groups. If the roads are in need of repair and parks are going without maintenance and upkeep, local discretionary funds might run out before you have a chance to request them. Even if your group is not directly affected by the condition of the local infrastructure, the individuals or businesses you will be approaching for financial assistance, generally referred to as your "funders," may well be impacted by the same economy that stripped the roads or parks of funding. You need to be aware of your funders' current situation and to understand the financial stresses they might be facing as you develop your organization.

Looking at the Economy

Now let's look at jobs and the overall employment picture. Are people working or has unemployment become a crisis? People who are unable to meet basic living expenses are unlikely to be in any position to contribute cash to a nonprofit regardless of how supportive they might be. This means you may have to think of ways to utilize in-kind contributions, as opposed to cash donations, more than you otherwise would.

By the same token, what is working well? Are housing starts and the overall real-estate market holding their own or improving? Are elementary and high school enrollments up? Are social groups thriving? Are the parks well maintained and being used by families? These indicators mean people are hopeful about the future and will be far more likely to support a nonprofit organization if they connect with your mission.

Urgent Needs Facing Communities

While an understanding of how the roads and parks and schools are doing in the current economy is very important, so too is maintaining an understanding of the basic needs facing your neighbors and your community. It may be time to dig deeper into your community to assess the core needs of food and shelter that represent the historical origins of nonprofit organizations in this country—of neighbors helping neighbors when no one else could do so. The tax-exempt status enjoyed by nonprofits today was an outgrowth of the value placed by the federal government on those organizations that did the work it could not afford to do.

FACT

As early as the Tariff Act of 1894, there was a clear understanding that in exchange for an organization's good work, a tax exemption would be provided, with language similar to the current regulations used today: "Nothing herein contained shall apply to . . . corporations, companies, or associations organized and conducted solely for charitable, religious, or educational purposes."

Food

Nothing is more basic than having enough food to eat, yet nonprofit organizations are being formed throughout the country to raise private funds and help meet the gaps created between government-financed food distribution and the amount that families can provide for themselves.

Community food banks are often the first organization people think of when looking into basic needs, but do not let your organization stop there. Across the United States, community gardens are coming back, often operated through partnerships between cities that may own the properties and nonprofits that are in the best position to manage the day-to-day operations of the gardens.

People are establishing culinary schools as a way to educate their students and to develop ways to make the best use of the existing food supply. Many of these schools are providing the necessary education to help people gain entry-level employment in food service and related industries.

Look beyond the obvious surface of your community to understand its needs. Then, through the mission of your nonprofit organization, you can contribute significantly to that community in these times of extreme challenges.

Shelter

Whereas some people in your region might only understand the housing crisis in America in terms of what they see on television, a nonprofit organization can be actively involved in addressing the problem by providing tangible resources and solutions. A nonprofit organization focused on assisting with the construction, operations, or maintenance of basic housing in your community can be established to meet the stringent requirements for federal recognition as a nonprofit organization and become a tremendous asset to your community.

Organizations such as Habitat for Humanity have led the way on the national level by marshaling the human, equipment, and material resources in communities to build safe homes for people in crisis or in transition. However, they cannot do it all! Many nonprofits are pitching in to manage new construction projects and to tackle the extensive remodeling/upgrading of existing buildings to make once-vacant structures habitable.

Nonprofits whose mission addresses the broad field of housing are usually in a favorable position to secure the needed financing to bring older buildings up to code, and to offer the newly refurbished dwellings at a fair price to people needing a good place to live. Such a project generates a positive revenue stream, enhances the organization's standing in the community, offers numerous opportunities for partnerships and collaborations with other nonprofits, and most important, provides a family a home.

Employment

Carefully analyze the current employment situation in your community because it will directly affect the levels of disposable income that may be readily available to your organization. On the other hand, nonprofits are uniquely positioned to assist people in transition to learn necessary job skills to allow them to re-enter the job market, even as our economy is facing an extended period of uncertainty. Consider incorporating a well-developed vocational education component into your existing mission as a way of helping your organization as well as the community.

ALERT

Although state and some local governments have taken the lead in providing vocational training and assistance with job placement, the economic reality facing those entities is requiring them to close some of these services, just as the need is expanding.

A small arts venue might offer classes in sound engineering, or a garden club hands-on training in landscape design or horticulture. The idea is to take the organization's mission and passion and expand it to meet very real needs in the current economic climate.

Local Networking

Now that you are getting a sense of how your community looks, it is time to begin to network. You'll start with the people you know in the community and then branch out to others to whom you will need an introduction.

Don't Be Shy! Meet the Local Media

If there is indeed a community radio, introduce yourself to the station manager and news director as soon as it is practical. Without the tremendous start-up funding necessary to personally contact every individual in your area, learning to work with the media will be your best alternative and will provide a direct means of communicating with your supporters throughout the region. Keep in mind that the people who work in community media need you to help provide content for their programming just as much as you need them to help publicize your activities.

If your organization is statewide or even nationwide in scope, the local broadcast and print outlets can provide direct access to a national audience with the flip of a switch. Over the past decade, new networks serving millions of people have been established; these are networks you need to become acquainted with and plan to use.

As you access available resources that exist under the large umbrella of the media, don't overlook the multitude of Internet mailing lists commonly called *listservs,* some of which undoubtedly include whatever your focus might be. Now is the time to document every media resource and develop a unique file listing every element they have that is applicable to your needs.

ESSENTIAL

Consider preparing a "one page" that introduces you to the general community. A "one page" is a one-page open letter printed on your organization's letterhead in which you briefly let people know of your group and its plans, and how to contact you for further information or to attend a meeting. Write the letter in a friendly, inviting tone, and be sure it's double-spaced.

Introducing Yourself to the Business Community

Introduce yourself to the local chamber of commerce and other business groups. News of your organization has probably already been circulating, so take the initiative and request an informal meeting with these groups. This meeting will help you position yourself very well for future cooperation. Turn the "one page" into a simple brochure or trifold by using a desktop publishing program. Have it available at every meeting you attend, and your crucial first impression as a well-planned, successful venture will be a positive one.

Don't overlook the importance of taking the initiative and offering to meet with local businesses. You will meet people in your community you never would have otherwise, which will allow you to form potentially advantageous relationships.

ALERT

Think about how you approach these introductory meetings. It may be good to have two board members attend as well to encourage an easier flow of conversation. Remember, you are not asking for anything; rather, you are seeking to establish a solid relationship that will be mutually beneficial.

Social Media Networking

In the past few years, social media have completely transformed online communication, and their potential uses are continuing to expand. Users can directly contact hundreds—if not thousands—of people with an immediacy never seen before. Fortunately, the most popular systems have been designed to allow users with minimal technical know-how to enter and make use of the environment fairly quickly.

Apart from the actual technical details of using the new media, there are a number of overarching reasons to consider these communication tools as a part of your overall outreach program. Although six major systems are in use, we will focus on a few networks that serve very different purposes, yet create an excellent tool when strategically utilized by a nonprofit. It is useful to understand what these systems are, as well as what they are not.

Facebook

The largest social media system in the world is unquestionably Facebook (*www.facebook.com*).

Facebook is an extremely user-friendly system that, once set up, allows the user to freely interact with others via a blog (posting on users' "walls"), in which posts on any topic can be posted to be read later, or as a real-time communication tool through the use of a chat system. While there are many more uses for Facebook, and more being created on a regular basis, the intention here is to identify how a nonprofit organization can quickly and efficiently use this tool.

In addition to providing a means for people to stay in touch, Facebook also allows an organization to have a very public, free presentation on the web with a potential worldwide viewership. The viewership is determined by how aggressive and active as friends the group's other individuals or organizations are. As friends become part of that group's network, potential visits can increase exponentially within days or weeks.

Keep in mind that unless people have their memberships set to receive updates via e-mail or text, they must actually go to your Facebook page to see what activities you are posting. As many people are simply unable to track everything going on within their many groups and many friends, cross-promotion becomes very important.

FACT

As the name suggests, *cross-promotion* involves telling people about what you are doing in other media, such as your website or brochures. Cross-promotion reaches people who may not be thinking about a Facebook page, until they see it in a seemingly unrelated situation, and decide to check it out. It is a very effective method of outreach. Use it!

Twitter

Whereas Facebook relies on overlapping, interconnected circles of associates or acquaintances to create the huge networks that are the basis of that system (and it is an excellent tool when used for that purpose), Twitter (*www.twitter.com*) allows a lot of people to be alerted simultaneously to the same event.

ALERT

Using social media can take a lot of time to fully understand, and then use appropriately. Consider identifying one or two people within your organization who are already comfortable using these systems to provide this essential service for any nonprofit organization. They can be the same individuals who manage your overall web presence, but they don't need to be. The general aptitude and skill sets needed to run social media sites are unique. An additional benefit of identifying these people to assist with an information technology (IT) position is that you are involving people who might not otherwise feel welcome in an organization.

The people who are "following" you can be notified of a special event you are presenting, meetings they may want to attend, or anything else the organization feels necessary to communicate to its membership and followers. You can also use your "tweets," the very brief, 140-character messages transmitted via the Twitter network, to drive traffic to your Facebook page or to your website.

Although Twitter is usually associated with usage by cell phones that have a data plan, it can also be accessed from any computer, making communication directly to your membership an easy process.

LinkedIn

The third system that should form the core of your social media activities is LinkedIn (*www.linkedin.com*). LinkedIn was not designed for the massive volume represented by Facebook, or the immediacy of Twitter, but rather as a networking tool for use by professionals interested in connecting with others in their field.

LinkedIn is not limited to any one profession or area of interest, which makes it a terrific tool for the organizer of a nonprofit. As users indicate their general areas of expertise, locating other people with either a shared interest, or professionals you may need for consulting purposes, is but a few clicks away.

In addition to the actual networking LinkedIn provides, it is also a good means of gathering ideas and unique perspectives presented by other users who regularly post what they are doing and why they are doing it. The system provides both direct and indirect e-mail exchanges through their e-mail relay service.

ESSENTIAL

Maintaining privacy is always a concern when using any of the social media platforms. Each system discussed in this chapter has levels of privacy that the account holder can set. These levels range from completely open to anyone who finds you or your site to increased levels of security and limits on who has access to specific types of information, including photographs and files. It is a good idea to check and verify your security settings regularly.

People who sign up and use LinkedIn regularly welcome communication. Feel free to send a note to individuals sharing your interest and to those with whom you feel collaboration may be possible.

Flickr

If your organization's activities are visually appealing, or if you have any number of photographers at every event you present, consider using a social media site expressly designed to both store and show photographs—Flickr (*www.flickr.com*). Flickr is a project of Yahoo! and will require a separate account to use, but as with all the other major social media platforms, it allows and encourages logging in from other accounts (i.e., Facebook or Twitter). In turn, this makes it easy to reference back to those sites, as well as have your homepage clearly visible with an active link.

Flickr is not a site for detailed explanations of your organization or a place to publicize the minutes of your last board meeting. It is a place to share photographs of volunteers working on a project, or your table at a neighborhood street fair, or anything you feel presents your group in the best possible light for all to see. The general public—and in particular, potential donors—always appreciates seeing photographs of your activities as they consider helping you further your mission.

As with the other forms of social media, a basic account is free. The systems receive their income from advertising revenue, not from their user base.

Branding Your Organization

Branding your organization on the Internet is one of the valuable secondary benefits of using any number of the social media platforms. With so many new nonprofits being formed, it is very important to consider how you are branding your group in the eyes of the general public, as well as others in the nonprofit community

FACT

Branding represents the entire experience anyone has with your organization, conveyed in a matter of moments. It represents your mission, your personality, your volunteers, your promises, and your ability to see those promises through. Your brand will constantly remind everyone exactly who you are, what you do, and why they should support the work you are doing.

YouTube

While not generally thought of as social media, YouTube (*www.youtube.com*) is a must-have tool for your online activities. Producing videos for YouTube does not require any more equipment than is generally included in newer computers (namely, a webcam and a microphone). As your interest and finances allow, you may get more sophisticated equipment, but is it is not necessary to get started; in fact, many individuals and organizations never progress past that simple stock equipment.

Your organization can create its own channel and begin to upload the videos you have created of your volunteers sharing their stories, your special events, your meetings, and anything else you think is important. When your nonprofit is cross-promoted though the other online services, people will understand your entire story and begin to share the passion necessary for them to want to participate. As with the other forms of social media, consider using the videos for general outreach and to share information, but also to drive traffic back to your website and that ever-important donation button.

Similar Groups

Unless you are in a small town or live in a rural area where you may be the only organization of your type, it is likely that there are other organizations in the general region working on similar issues. Some of the organizations may simply be informal associations. Some may be incorporated as state nonprofits, and others may have obtained their federal nonprofit status. Regardless of their legal status or exactly how they have chosen to organize themselves, they may be doing similar work and may be of tremendous help to you and your organization.

The Win-Win Approach

When setting out to meet the directors or board members of similar groups, be sure to plan ahead and strategize about exactly what you hope to get out of the meeting and what you are able to offer. Especially when discretionary funds in a community are tight, you need to be willing to collaborate to eliminate any fear of competition.

Just as many professions and skilled trades have formed unique associations and guilds over the years, so too have nonprofit organizations joined forces to share resources and general support. Seek out these organizations well before you have formally incorporated or applied for your nonprofit status. Many of these organizations—whether they are arts, cultural, or social service groups—will have publications and websites for their members as well as more general information for nonmembers.

QUESTION

How do we actually locate these organizations?
Using any Internet search engine, type in "directory <your general field> <your state or city>". This search will produce a variety of groups and organizations that maintain databases of the very organizations you need to locate.

Music societies customarily offer reciprocal newsletter subscriptions, in both hard copy and via e-mail, to other organizations in their area or around the world. Any music organization or society may send out dozens upon dozens of such mailings every month, which publicize their activities as well as keep all the groups in casual contact with current addresses and e-mail for the main people.

There are often guest memberships available for new organizations. Taking advantage of this avenue allows you to get a sense of what these organizations can offer and what your peers are doing.

CHAPTER 3

Understanding Organizations and Corporations

To move forward, you will need to understand the definitions of corporation and organization, as well as exactly what a nonprofit organization (NPO) is and what it isn't. You will also need to understand the differences between a state-recognized nonprofit organization and one recognized by the federal government. This chapter will also discuss when to seek outside advice to be certain that you and your group are on the right track.

The For-Profit Corporation

To understand fully what a nonprofit corporation is, it helps first to understand what a for-profit corporation is. A corporation, either nonprofit or for-profit, is a unique legal entity recognized by state and federal governments as completely separate from the people who own it. The one exception is the sole proprietor, which will be addressed in the next section. Otherwise, corporations are viewed essentially as though they were people, with many of the same rights and privileges, although technically they only exist on paper.

Corporations as People

If you find this concept a little difficult to understand, you are in good company. The debate over the rights of a corporation as a separate entity has been raging in the United States since before there even was a United States. The names of two of the earliest corporations are known by every schoolchild: the Massachusetts Bay Company and the Hudson Bay Company. What you may not realize is that these for-profit corporations were chartered by the British government, claiming equal rights and privileges as the people of the colonies!

FACT

In the 1886 *Santa Clara County v. Southern Pacific Railroad* case, the U.S. Supreme Court deemed that a private corporation, Southern Pacific Railroad, was a "natural person" under the Constitution and was therefore entitled to protection under the Bill of Rights. With that decision, which holds to this day, the Supreme Court declared that corporations have the same rights as people.

Since the Southern Pacific Railroad ruling, the Supreme Court has continued to maintain that corporations of almost every type are indeed artificial people with most of the basic rights held by "normal" people, including the right to own property, take on debt, and sue or be sued.

The Five Basic Elements of the For-Profit Corporation

For-profit corporations have five essential components:

1. They may have "limited liability," meaning investors in the corporation can only lose (or are only liable for) the amount of money they have invested, rather than potentially losing everything they own.
2. They maintain a "continuity of existence," which means that the corporation can literally exist forever or well beyond the lifetimes of the founders or current owners.
3. They offer an "ease of ownership transfer" through the sale of shares, rather than selling the actual business.
4. They have the ability to raise money or capital through expanded ownership. In other words, if more shares are sold or more partners are brought in, there is no limit to the amount of money that can be raised—and of course, lost.
5. They offer shareholders the ability to profit from the growth of the business through the increased value of their shares, when shares are sold on the open market, or through the payment of dividends based on the profit the corporation has generated.

Types of For-Profit Corporations

For-profit corporations generally fall into two categories: private corporations owned and operated by a closed group of people, and corporations that allow the public to own shares. Both in theory and in practice, shareholders can exercise control of the business's affairs by casting votes on major issues that come before them, generally based on the number of shares they own. A person who owns 5 shares of a corporation might get 5 votes; a person who owns 100 shares would be able to cast 100 votes.

When planning to organize as a nonprofit corporation, familiarity with a few basic types of for-profit organizations can be useful since many of the practices developed for these groups can be adapted to the nonprofit world as well.

It would be impractical to discuss every type of for-profit corporation. There are many volumes, and indeed entire universities, devoted to nothing else. Rather, what follows are three examples of common types of for-profits.

FACT

This simplified overview of for-profit corporations is designed to give you, as an organizer of a nonprofit, a basic understanding of the environment you are entering. It is not meant to be an all-inclusive analysis.

Sole Proprietorships

A sole proprietorship is the most basic, elemental, and, quite possibly, the oldest form of formally recognized corporation. It consists of one person, and it provides the only exception to the notion of a corporation as a separate and unique entity. In a sole proprietorship, the person is the business; she is responsible for everything that takes place within the business, including any debts or legal liability.

General Corporations

A general corporation is the most common type of for-profit company. In these situations, the corporation is a separate, unique legal entity that is owned by any number of stockholders who may receive dividends and buy and sell their shares for a profit or a loss. A stockholder's personal liability is generally limited to the amount of his investment in the corporation. A slight variation of the general corporation is called a closed corporation, which is different only in that there are a limited number of shares involved.

Limited Liability Corporations

Limited liability corporations (LLCs) have become all the rage among people interested in forming a simple for-profit corporation. The partners are protected by the limited liability from losses, they maintain direct control of the activities, and they are recognized by the state in which they incorporate as a corporation. From a tax perspective, the owners or partners file the profits as part of their personal income tax.

The Nonprofit Organization

Nonprofit corporations share many of the same characteristics as for-profits, particularly since they are also separate from the actual human beings involved and so, for the most part, shield the individuals from direct liability. The larger issues relating to liability insurance for a nonprofit organization are discussed later.

The Core Element of a Nonprofit Organization

Unlike for-profit corporations, in which individual owners, partners, or shareholders may personally benefit from the organization, in a nonprofit corporation, no individual may directly benefit from any "profit" generated by the organization. Rather, the money generally considered to be "profit" must be turned back into the organization to continue its work. This effectively eliminates the profit motive and makes it truly a public organization.

QUESTION

What is meant by the term *profit motive*?
Profit motive describes the chance of generating a surplus of revenue over all costs; it is the reason most people start and remain in a traditional for-profit business. The profit motive is the exact opposite of philanthropy, or giving for the common good, one of the foundations of nonprofit organizations.

The Origins of Nonprofits

The laws behind nonprofit organizations were formulated at the very beginning of the United States. Before formal government agencies and departments were created to handle the many tasks necessary for the smooth running of a government, people often formed small groups or societies to take care of issues themselves.

When the first regulations establishing an income tax were drafted, exemptions were made for community-based charitable groups. These exemptions allowed them to undertake necessary work that would never be profitable from a financial perspective, while relieving the government of the task.

ESSENTIAL

Any organization seeking recognition under IRS section 501(c)(3) must exist for "purposes which are charitable, religious, educational, scientific, literary, involve testing for public safety, fostering national or international amateur sports competition, and preventing cruelty to children or animals." This definition comes from the IRS Form 1023, which you will need to complete and submit to apply for tax-exempt status.

The federal government recognizes close to thirty distinct types of nonprofit organizations. Although this book will focus only on one—the 501(c)(3) and its slight variation, the 501(c)(4)—familiarity with the other types will help you and your organization understand where you fit in the larger scope of things. Each of these categories has its own set of rules and regulations.

Nonprofits Can and Do Make Money

Nonprofit organizations can and do make money, but funds in excess of the organization's operating costs must be returned to the organization and may never be divided among investors, staff, or board members. By the same token, nonprofits may hire staff, engage private consultants, and operate as does any other corporation; the important distinction is that salaries or fees must be established as set amounts. A sliding-scale compensation structure that depends on the success of the organization would place the individual in the position of directly benefiting from the organization, which would run contrary to the tax code and in all probability cause the nonprofit to lose its tax-exempt status.

State Versus Federal Nonprofits

Well before you ever get to the stage of making an application to the IRS to obtain tax-exempt status, the federal government requires your organization to be incorporated in the state in which you intend to do business. Every state and territory has forms, generally issued by the state's secretary of state or other designated state office, to make incorporation an easy, straightforward process.

Some states walk you through a short questionnaire. Others simply ask for a copy of your articles of incorporation. All states will ask you to identify the type of corporation you intend to form. The answer is a "state nonprofit corporation."

FACT

Incorporating as a nonprofit corporation in your state has no bearing on your federal tax-exempt status. Unless you obtain a federal tax exemption, your organization remains completely liable for federal taxes. State tax liability is a separate situation that is determined by state law and is beyond the scope of this book.

Stopping with State Nonprofit Incorporation

Many organizations choose to stop at this stage and operate as a state nonprofit, which is a perfectly fine way to go. However, that status presents limitations to your organization and to members of the public who wish to donate funds. If you are in a state with a corporate income tax, check with the revenue office to verify exactly what your tax liability is and how obtaining your federal tax exemption affects your situation.

With federal nonprofit status, your organization does not have to pay corporate income tax to the federal government. If you have obtained the 501(c)(3) status, people who contribute money to your organization can deduct those contributions from their tax liability with certain restrictions. This status also opens the door to funding opportunities that may be limited to federally recognized nonprofits.

In addition to the many financial requirements you must follow to remain in compliance with state and federal laws, remember that you are doing your work for the community in which you live and are employed.

State Secretaries of State as a Resource

This toolkit contains a link to the National Association of Secretaries of State (NASS), which in turn has the addresses, telephone numbers, and e-mails for all fifty state secretaries of state. You will also find the current roster. The individual officeholders will change with election cycles, but the contact information will remain the same. Contact these offices with any specific questions you may have with respect to how best to incorporate as a nonprofit in your state.

Types of Nonprofit Organizations

Just as there are countless variations of for-profit organizations, there are a few—three, to be exact—main categories of nonprofit corporations. Under these three categories fall the more-familiar subcategories:

1. The public benefit corporation includes the generally understood charitable organizations and social welfare organizations such as those with a 501(c)(3) or a 501(c)(4) classification.
2. The mutual benefit corporation, which is not public, might include groups such as homeowners' associations and private foundations.
3. The great "other," which includes fraternal societies, labor organizations, farm bureaus, social clubs, veteran's organizations, cemetery companies, credit unions, and the many other organizations listed under the 501(c) code of the Internal Revenue Service.

The Difference Between a 501(c)(3) and a 501(c)(4) Organization

If you are directly involved in the incorporation process or work on an organization's application for federal nonprofit status, it's important to understand how the two primary types of nonprofits—501(c)(3)s and 501(c)(4)s—are similar and how they are different.

The Similarities

A few basic elements apply to both types of organizations. Both are exempt from paying federal income tax, must be operated as nonprofits, and are restricted from allowing any individual or shareholder to benefit financially from the work of the organization. In fact, because those particular rules are so similar, any organization that qualifies for 501(c)(3) status also qualifies for 501(c)(4) status.

The Differences

First of all, a 501(c)(4) is defined by the IRS as meeting three criteria:

1. The group must be a civic league or organization that is not organized for profit but is operated exclusively for the promotion of social welfare.
2. The group is a local association of employees, the membership of which is limited to the employees of a designated person or persons in a particular municipality.
3. The net earnings of the group are devoted exclusively to charitable, educational, or recreational purposes.

You'll note some immediate similarities to the requirements for the 501(c)(3) status—in particular that the group is, in fact, operating as a not-for-profit. The big differences involve what types of activities the groups plan to undertake, with particular focus on political activities.

Whereas a 501(c)(3) is not permitted to advocate for a political candidate or ballot initiative, a 501(c)(4) may do so all it wants, as long as the activities fall within its primary purpose. The tradeoff is that contributions to a 501(c)(4) are deductible only if the organization is a government agency or is involved in public service. Otherwise, contributions may not be deducted from the personal income tax of the contributor.

If you meet all the other requirements pertaining to both classifications, are not planning to be directly involved in political campaigns, will not be lobbying to a large degree, and plan to solicit tax-deductible donations, consider applying for the 501(c)(3) status.

If, on the other hand, you meet all the other requirements pertaining to both classifications but *do* plan on being actively involved in political campaigns, will be conducting extensive lobbying, and understand that your contributors will generally not be able to deduct those contributions, then consider the 501(c)(4). Some groups have actually formed two separate tax-exempt organizations—a 501(c)(3) and a 501(c)(4), allowing one part of their organization (the c-3) to fully comply with the lobbying and campaigning restrictions and focus solely on the educational component, while the other (the c-4) conducts political outreach and activities.

The Federal Nonprofit Categories

Each category in the following table has precise rules governing how funds may be collected, whether contributors may also claim tax deductions for their donations, who may or may not participate in the organization, how money may be spent, and exactly what kinds of reporting are required to maintain nonprofit status. Some of the classifications are more entertaining than practical for the vast majority of people planning to form a nonprofit corporation and apply for a 501(c)(3). Look at them solely as a reference point in your planning.

▼ **TYPES OF NONPROFIT ORGANIZATIONS**

Section of IRS Code	Type of Organization
501(c)(1)	Corporations organized under an act of Congress
501(c)(2)	Title-holding companies
501(c)(3)	Religious, charitable, educational groups
501(c)(4)	Groups that promote social welfare
501(c)(5)	Labor, agriculture associations
501(c)(6)	Business leagues
501(c)(7)	Social and recreational clubs
501(c)(8)	Fraternal beneficiary societies
501(c)(9)	Voluntary employee beneficial societies
501(c)(10)	Domestic fraternal societies
501(c)(11)	Teachers' retirement funds
501(c)(12)	Benevolent life insurance companies
501(c)(13)	Cemetery companies
501(c)(14)	Credit unions (not established by Congress)

Section of IRS Code	Type of Organization
501(c)(15)	Mutual insurance companies
501(c)(16)	Corporations to finance crop operations
501(c)(17)	Supplemental unemployment benefit trusts
501(c)(18)	Employee-funded pension trusts
501(c)(19)	War veterans' organizations
501(c)(20)	Legal services organizations
501(c)(21)	Black lung trusts
501(c)(22)	Withdrawal liability payment fund
501(c)(23)	Veterans' organizations (created before 1880)
501(c)(24)	Only one organization, Spring Prairie Hutterian Brethren Inc., in Hawley, Minnesota, is registered as a 501(c)(24) entity as a special trust under the Employee Retirement Income Security Act of 1974.
501(c)(25)	Title-holding corporations or trusts with multiple parents
501(c)(26)	State-sponsored organizations providing health coverage for high-risk individuals
501(c)(27)	State-sponsored workers' compensation reinsurance organizations
501(d)	Religious and apostolic associations
501(e)	Cooperative hospital service organizations
501(f)	Cooperative service organizations of operating educational organizations
501(k)	Child-care organizations
501(n)	Charitable risk pools
521	Farmers' cooperatives
527	Political organizations

Needless to say, most organizers planning to form a 501(c)(3) or 501(c)(4) nonprofit will probably not need all the information in this table. However, there may be situations where it may be advantageous to apply for another determination in addition to a primary classification. As your organization grows to maturity and everyone involved becomes comfortable with the opportunities and the limitations of your tax-exempt status—or if you find your operations are expanding beyond your original mission—it may be advisable to seek other exemptions, or perhaps form another unique organization.

Consulting a Tax Lawyer

When combining ever-changing state and federal nonprofit tax laws with start-up nonprofit corporations, the need to develop a long-term relationship with a lawyer who understands your organization and stays up to date with changes in tax law is essential. Be sure to evaluate your planning from a legal perspective so both your organization and the lawyer you choose make the best use of everyone's time. Unless you are in one of the American territories, where legal assistance when forming a nonprofit corporation is required by law, there is no such requirement in any of the fifty states or in the District of Columbia.

Not Any Lawyer Will Do

As with many professions, the practice of law has developed specialties over the years, allowing lawyers to refine their expertise and provide the most assistance in specific areas. Many law firms, particularly those with numerous lawyers sharing office facilities, will have a specialist in business and tax law on staff. She will be able to assist you at any stage of the process. Seek referrals from other small nonprofit organizations in your immediate area to find a tax lawyer you can trust.

ALERT

Remember that lawyers are experts in matters of law. They are not accountants or social workers, although some may be comfortable in those fields as well. Keeping your questions and concerns to legal issues will lead to more productive sessions and less wasted time (and money) in the lawyer's office.

Working with a lawyer who understands the entire process yet is removed from your organization can be an excellent experience.

The Process

After locating a lawyer, make a preliminary phone call to ensure she is comfortable with nonprofit business law and to make an appointment to discuss your needs. Most lawyers working in this field offer a brief consultation visit for a minimal charge, which enables both parties to gauge if everyone's needs will be met.

Limit the attendees at the initial meeting to people who really need to be there. Bring any documents you have completed or anything still in development so you can refer to them. Take careful notes so that you can give a detailed report later to your board members or pertinent staff. In all likelihood, the lawyer will ask for a summary of your plans, what your organization intends to do, where in the incorporation process you are, and where she can be of assistance.

Lawyers generally have set fees for services. Some attorneys handle all elements of your incorporation with the state; others stay with you to apply for tax-exempt status. Of course, the more you ask her to do, the more expensive it is going to be. The trick is to find a middle ground. Do as much of the basic work as you can, and then seek legal advice to review the final packages before they are submitted.

FACT

The job of a good lawyer is to keep you and your organization out of the courtroom. Once you have an agreement for legal services, her complete responsibility is to keep you in full compliance with the law. If she seems overly cautions, it is with good reason. You may accept or reject any advice you receive, but you do so at your peril.

After your organization has become established, and the activities you undertake become more complex, check in with your lawyer to verify any tax issues long before they become problems. Normal legal issues are to be expected, and legal advice might prove helpful. You may have questions about activities that are incidental to your mission that may involve a tax liability or about how to handle income from ticket sales for a fundraiser—or even questions about the fundraiser! These situations are hardly a cause for alarm, but you may rest easier knowing you can just call your lawyer to be certain everything is good to go.

You may never need to utilize the services of a lawyer until your organization enters into contracts or purchases property. Many tax questions can be handled by an accountant who is familiar with nonprofit filings, but having a lawyer you can contact when something isn't looking right or you are faced with a real problem will give you, your board, and your organization incredible peace of mind.

CHAPTER 4

The First Organizing Meeting

The first meeting is always one of the most exciting times for any organization. At this meeting, the ideas that you have circulated informally come into the open so you can make plans to move forward. This is also when you begin to think and act like a nonprofit and decide who will take on what specific tasks.

Meeting Basics

Your group is probably composed of friends, neighbors, and casual acquaintances who share a common interest. Through word of mouth, you learned of each other's desire or interest in forming a nonprofit organization.

Your initial meeting will probably not be a board meeting, because you don't have a formal organization. Instead, this meeting is an opportunity for a group of people to finally get together and decide if they want to form an organization.

Meeting Location

The location you choose for your first meeting will set the tone for the organization, so select an appropriate meeting space. Try to pick a neutral setting where everyone will feel comfortable. Schools, community centers, and libraries often have rooms available at little or no cost. Consider the ease of public transportation and parking when selecting your location. Never select a room that is too large; it will feel empty, even if everyone invited shows up. Public cafés can suffice, if you make advance arrangements to have an area reserved for your use. However, think ahead if you consider to use a public café during normal business hours. If it's too crowded or noisy, no one will hear anything, and maintaining focus during the meeting will prove impossible. Espresso machines are noisy!

Should You Publicize the Meeting?

Avoid publicizing an initial meeting. It is far better to make personal invitations by telephone or e-mail to people who have already expressed an interest in working together. There will be plenty of time to invite the community into the organization once your group is a little more established.

Arrive Early to Set Up

If possible, arrive ten to fifteen minutes early to turn on the lights, arrange chairs, set out snacks, and get ready to welcome invitees. Consider printing a sign-in sheet with spaces for names, telephone numbers, and e-mail addresses. If you are drawing from a larger geographic area, leave space for a mailing address so you know where people live, even though you'll probably communicate almost exclusively by e-mail. This sign-in sheet can help the person taking minutes remember who said what, and it will also serve as the beginnings of a contact sheet, the core of your organization's database.

If the meeting space does not have a chalkboard, bring a portable easel and a large paper tablet or whiteboard. Print out copies of any background information that was sent out earlier, including a draft agenda if one was prepared. Try to schedule the meeting for early evening and let everyone know it will last no longer than two hours.

ESSENTIAL

As soon as everyone is ready to begin, the group needs to select a facilitator, or someone willing to help set the agenda and lead the meeting. Another person should take minutes, or accurate notes of the discussion. Taking notes on a laptop makes it easier to e-mail them later.

Approach the first meeting with an open mind. Even though the attendees have probably been making plans based on their notions of how the group should function, the purpose of an initial meeting is to encourage the discussion of everyone's ideas.

Introductions

To determine who is attending and what they might bring to an organization, encourage each person to take a minute to say why he is interested in the group, how he learned of the meeting, and how he makes a living. This is a not-too-subtle way of finding out what each person might bring to the organization.

Defining What You Want to Do

The facilitator should guide the discussion as the group works through what the attendees want to see happen. You can base your agenda on the headings in this chapter. Create a plan of action so you can follow up after the meeting. This plan should outline the steps that everyone chooses for moving forward and designate people to take on specific tasks. The facilitator may have to ask for volunteers or ask attendees to take on certain tasks.

Discussion of the Ground Rules

The discussion can be as freeform as you would like. As ideas are brought forth, write them on the whiteboard or in a place where everyone can see them. The only real ground rule should be to withhold criticism or back-and-forth discussion for the time being. Allow the conversation to continue long enough for everyone to have a turn and to add any follow-up contributions. You want to get as many ideas as possible, including ones that may not sound plausible, out on the table.

FACT

Facilitating, or leading a group of people in a discussion, is not as easy as experienced facilitators make it look. The trick is to encourage everyone to have a turn while keeping the discussion to your agenda and within any time constraints. Until you have made formal arrangements for offices, try rotating the job of facilitator so everyone has a chance to improve his or her skill.

Since the purpose of this initial meeting is to flesh out ideas, everyone should feel free to make suggestions. This exercise can and should be a lot of fun; it gives everyone a chance to dream about what he wants the group to be and do.

Prioritize Ideas

After at most thirty to forty-five minutes, the facilitator should begin to guide the discussion toward prioritizing ideas. Don't eliminate anything, but get everyone to come to a general agreement on what is important and comfortable for the group.

Do You Really Want to Be a Nonprofit?

While this question may seem out of place in a book about forming a nonprofit organization, it is a very important question and is entirely appropriate to bring up at your first meeting. There are numerous misconceptions about what a nonprofit organization is, and this is the time to clear them up. Too many groups jump right into the application process without understanding the full scope.

You Can Leave at Any Time

Depending upon what your organization wants to do, the 501(c)(3) might not be the ideal option, especially if you are intending to be involved politically. If the 501(c)(4) classification is more appropriate or if it makes sense for your group not to apply for federal tax exemption for the time being, discuss this option honestly. You may need to reread the different nonprofit classifications discussed earlier. You have twenty-seven months from the time you incorporate to apply for the tax exemption. That clock begins ticking when you are formally incorporated within your state.

Forget Any Personal Gain

Everyone in the room must understand that if you decide to apply to become a federally recognized nonprofit corporation, the group will become a public organization. No one can ever take a financial gain because there will be no shares or dividends. Furthermore, anyone who agrees to serve on the board will most likely do so as a volunteer and only their actual expenses will be reimbursed. The organization's annual financial report will be open to public inspection.

Needless to say, the work involved and the restrictions and duties of maintaining a federal tax-exempt status are unique responsibilities. It is vital that groups seriously consider every option before determining their course of action.

Reality Check

There are many advantages to incorporating as a nonprofit in your state and applying for federal tax-exempt status, but there are also disadvantages.

Very High Failure Rates

The vast majority of all new corporations fail within three years of incorporation. Nonprofit organizations also fail at an alarming rate for a number of reasons, not the least of which is that they are often started by well-meaning people who have limited business experience.

ALERT

Among newly formed arts organizations in some states, the failure rate in the first year of operation is 75 percent. This means that funders will need to be certain of the group's long-range planning and overall strategies before considering a partnership.

Slow Down

All too often, groups try to rush through the preliminary organizational steps and attempt to file their tax-exemption application as quickly as possible. A tax lawyer can generally file all the necessary paperwork in a few weeks, but it's much better if he takes his time to discuss the paperwork thoroughly with you. Furthermore, if the groundwork has not been established, the chance that the organization will survive more than a few years is low. In addition, simple oversight and carelessness can result in failure as well.

Limitations and Ongoing Reporting Requirements

Your first organizing meeting is an excellent time to discuss the limitations of applying for nonprofit status and the requirements involved in annual reporting to the IRS and to your state. Everyone concerned with the actual organizing must understand the ramifications of becoming a nonprofit and how it may directly affect him or her. The law prohibits any personal gain from nonprofit work. This means monetary compensation cannot depend on a sliding-scale model that would make payment directly contingent on the success of the organization. Similarly, the core organizers may want to be compensated for eventual work they do. But such work must be compensated at the fair market value; organizers should not be paid simply for being on the board. Board members may be reimbursed for travel or miscellaneous expenses related to their attendance at board meetings.

These limitations are quite different from how for-profit organizations operate, and misunderstandings cause many groups unnecessary problems. Organizers need to be honest if your group agrees to move forward. Everyone must understand exactly what they will and won't be permitted to do.

Limits on Activities Outside of Your Purpose

A nonprofit is restricted to its purpose in everything it does. Taxes may result if the group chooses to undertake an activity that falls outside of its tax-exempt purpose. For example, an organization may decide to sell trinkets as part of its fundraising program, but the group will incur a tax liability if it sells the items for more than they cost. The group is in the nonprofit business, not the commercial trinket business. The best advice here is to let an accountant figure it out. This activity will need to be reported to the IRS in the group's annual statement if it is to remain in compliance.

FACT

Sloppy reporting of financial activities is the way most organizations get into trouble. It's one thing to mistakenly conduct activities outside your purpose or outside the strict rules governing tax exemption. Failure to report those mistakes and pay any taxes owed is a much more serious offense.

Reporting Requirements

The other major element that many start-up nonprofits fail to consider is the ongoing requirement to file annual financial reports with a number of public and private entities. Although as a federally recognized tax-exempt organization you do not have to pay federal income tax, you do have to make a detailed financial report to the IRS using Form 990. These forms are public record, and anyone can see exactly what funds your organization garnered over the past year and where that money went.

Most states also have a requirement that all corporations submit a report of their annual meeting. These reports are not complicated, but they must be sent in every year for the entire life of the organization.

Failure to submit the state or federal reports will cause real trouble for your organization. In extreme cases, your tax-exempt status may be revoked and your corporation formally closed. A recent decision by the IRS determined that any organization that fails to submit its Form 990 for three years in a row will have its nonprofit status revoked. They are serious about the reporting requirements and you should be as well.

At your initial meeting, you need to decide if you are prepared to take on the long-term responsibility that comes with filing for tax-exempt status.

The 20 Percent Rule for Political Activities

For many organizations considering whether to apply for federal tax-exempt status, the rule strictly governing the political activities of a 501(c)(3) non-profit can be a huge issue. Even organizations that might never consider themselves "political" in any traditional sense must be aware of the rules and go out of their way to adhere to them. There are many situations in which candidates for public office, ballot initiatives, or pending legislation might directly affect your organization and its mission, so this will always be an area that needs attention.

ALERT

To quote the instructions for the tax-exemption application (IRS Form 557), "the organization will not, as a substantial part of its activities, attempt to influence legislation or participate to any extent in a political campaign for or against any candidate for public office." In other words, just don't do it!

As part of becoming a 501(c)(3) organization, you agreed not to participate directly in political campaigns. Be careful that your organization does not appear to be directly involved in any political campaign. If this occurs, your status will be in jeopardy very quickly.

With this said, there is the 20 percent rule, which allows a 501(c)(3) nonprofit to spend up to 20 percent of its tax-exempt operating budget on lobbying efforts, although never on advocacy for a particular candidate or ballot initiative. These restrictions do not limit the individuals within your organization. They can work for candidates or campaign for initiatives, but as a 501(c)(3) organization, you agreed not to involve yourselves with any campaign for office or any ballot issue. However, as an organization, you may be involved in general voter education about issues that are relevant to your group, as long as all points of view are presented. You can host forums with candidates or initiative sponsors or opponents, but you may not advocate for one side.

QUESTION

How can an advocacy group holding a 501(c)(3) tax exemption be involved in the community and not place its nonprofit status in jeopardy?
Conducting voter education on the broader issue will not jeopardize an organization's nonprofit status. For example, instead of advocating for a particular park department levy, a group could educate its community about the general advantages of parks and open space.

Political Rules for 501(c)(4) Organizations

A 501(c)(4) organization adheres to a different set of rules when it comes to political activity. Although there is not a prohibition on advocating for any particular candidate or ballot initiative, a group may only do so if the advocacy is not the group's primary purpose. A 501(c)(4) may, however, spend unlimited funds on general lobbying efforts without jeopardizing its tax-exempt status. It is not bound by the 20 percent rule, but the money spent on direct political campaigning (as opposed to lobbying) may become taxable.

To a casual observer, the difference may not be apparent, but it is actually substantial. As a publicly supported charity that receives contributions that are tax-deductible, a 501(c)(3) is held to the highest standard with regard to interference in the political process. A 501(c)(4) is still exempt from federal corporate taxes, but contributors do not deduct the money they donate from their income taxes, so advocacy for a cause or issue is permitted.

If an organization obtains its 501(c)(3) status and then violates the restriction on lobbying activities or involvement in political activities and loses its status, it will not be able to qualify later for the 501(c)(4) status. These rules are serious, so avoid taking chances that might result in losing your exemption status.

FACT

Groups operating under Section 527, or 527s, exist solely to advocate for a political cause or issue. They may not expressly advocate for a candidate, only for an issue (which may be remarkably close to a candidate). There can be no coordination between any political campaign and the activities of a 527. These groups are tax-exempt.

These distinctions are important to understand for you to decide exactly what route you want your group to follow. The choice you make now will affect how your organization will operate from this moment forward.

Acting and Thinking As a Nonprofit Organization

Let's say your group decides to incorporate as a state nonprofit and to apply for a federal tax exemption as a 501(c)(3) or a 501(c)(4) organization. The process for federal recognition is designed to take months as organizations slowly build the necessary community support, learn to function as a viable business, and get their internal affairs in order so they can prepare a successful application.

The Twenty-Seven-Month Rule

You can incorporate as soon as your organizational documents are ready and you identify the board of directors, which can happen soon after your initial meeting. However, there is a built-in window of twenty-seven months from the time you incorporate until you need to file your IRS Form 1023, the application for tax-exempt status. During this period, your organization should take form, both internally and within your community. Use the time to identify potential contributors and establish all programs and outreach elements. Start getting media coverage, establishing various committees, and operating as a fully functioning corporation. Before you receive federal recognition, you will be liable for any federal corporate taxes if you generate a level of income requiring it.

Plan to Use This Time Wisely

The time between your formal incorporation and application for tax-exempt status is designed to allow your organization to come into its own. Acquaint your community or service area with your planned work and answer any questions they have. Use this time to gear up to your full potential; don't hold off on your operations until you apply for a tax exemption. Make use of the people who gathered for your initial meeting. You can generate media coverage, contact major sponsors, and do everything a nonprofit would do.

QUESTION

May we accept contributions before we have our federal tax-exempt status?
Of course! However, you must let all contributors know that although you are applying for tax-exempt status, you do not currently have it. Contributors may take the deduction retroactively to your incorporation date. Until you receive that determination letter, you do not have tax exemption, you may not imply that you do, and you may not suggest that contributors deduct donations on their next tax return.

Your corporate tax exemption will be retroactive to the time of your formal incorporation, but during the window between incorporation and the receipt of your determination letter granting tax-exempt status, you may be responsible for federal taxes. You may want to seek the advice of a tax professional to determine how best to proceed in your unique situation.

CHAPTER 5

The Initial Board of Directors

The driving force as your organization applies for federal nonprofit status will be the initial board of directors, which should be comprised of the most committed people in your group. The board will also guide your new organization in its mission and activities. After that, the board will become your group's public face and will assume the responsibility for overseeing everything the organization does.

The Initial/Founding Members of the Board

The people who agree to become the founding board will have worked together through the early stages of organization and will have a good understanding of the personalities involved. Many start-up nonprofit organizations are, by their very nature, driven as much by personalities as by an official mission, so it's important that board members understand and get along with each other.

The founding board's responsibility is to keep the details surrounding incorporation in place by remaining above the fray. They need to transform an informal group into one that is formally incorporated and ready to do good work.

QUESTION

How many people are necessary on the initial board?
Many states specify the minimum number of board members, and the respective incorporation documents will indicate this number. Generally, on the initial board, three people will be sufficient. Remember to specify that number as the minimum number of board members in your by-laws.

Begin by staggering the terms of service. If you decide to have three initial board members, each person should agree to a different-length term, so members will not rotate at the same time. One person should agree to a one-year term, the next to a two-year term, and so forth.

Qualities of the Initial Board

Unlike any carefully contemplated plan for board development, there are no firm criteria to apply to the initial board of directors. However, there are a few basic needs that can be met with some advance thought. To some extent, a significant portion of your initial board is going to be decided for you, since it will generally be the people at the center of the organizing process.

In addition to the general responsibilities any new organization has to handle, board members must be willing and able to deal with the ever-present need to raise money. At the very least, they must show a willingness to learn how to raise money. Although a passion for the mission of the group is very important, the first question for an initial board member should always be "How do we pay for it?"

Therefore, it is entirely appropriate to include individuals who have expressed a willingness to help financially. As the organizer, be prepared to have serious discussions with people who are in a position to be of financial assistance. Be honest about the needs of the organization as you understand them, and then seek the counsel of those who have offered to help. If you need to offer a board seat to an individual with networks in the philanthropic community, then do so.

Prima Donnas Need Not Apply

Work on an initial board is not glamorous. Your organization likely won't have any staff, so board members are going to have to lead by example. Board members can't be afraid to suffer a few paper cuts stuffing envelopes for your organization's first fundraising effort.

Dealing with Personal Agendas

Board members should not have their own agendas nor should they use their positions on your initial board to advance their careers. This situation is not uncommon, particularly in cultural and artistic organizations where people whose qualifications make them suited for programming or operations instead seek board appointments. Sadly, they often realize too late that board responsibilities are much more difficult than they had envisioned. Such bad appointments are also hard to undo once the organization has incorporated and formal by-laws are adopted.

People who may not be suited for the fairly narrow needs of the board should be encouraged to consider a seat on the advisory committee, which exists precisely to allow people in the community to make a significant contribution even if their talents are outside the business needs of the board. Your organization will need their ideas and contacts, so the trick is to keep them involved at a level more appropriate to their skills.

Attempt to Meet Immediate Needs

In addition to the board's core responsibilities, which focus on finances and policy, there are many other areas the board will eventually address. You will need to find members who are comfortable with the following:

- Articulating and writing long-range plans
- Handling human resources
- Creating graphic designs
- Writing press releases

If individuals with these skills are interested in sitting on your initial board and becoming an officer, you have a clear advantage over most start-up nonprofits.

Choosing the Initial Officers

Even if your initial board is no larger than the minimum suggested, select the officers of the corporation from the board. Anyone who assumes one of the leadership positions should be willing and able to carry out the responsibilities. Some states have articles of incorporation that request specific officers; even if your state does not, it is wise to do so. Using a separate sheet if necessary, list the offices and the people on the board who have agreed to take those seats. There is no rule that prohibits offices from being shared, but it is not advisable.

ALERT

Your board officers should reflect the community you serve, in terms of life experiences and in racial, ethnic, or religious makeup. How you present yourself to the public is very important, and how the public perceives you is crucial to the long-term success of your organization.

Even if the initial board is chosen essentially by self-selection, give serious thought to who among the core group already has the specific skills to do the work required of each position. Time commitment is another issue.

The time required will be far greater than that of other board members and certainly more than other volunteers.

The First Year Will Be Rough

While the idea of missing dinner at home for the greater cause may have a romantic ring to it, multiple evening meetings each week can be very difficult on personal lives. This element should be factored into any discussion around board-level commitments. The first year of any nonprofit organization's existence is the most stressful, and anyone who is considering participating at the board level needs to be aware of that fact.

The Board as the Inspiration

The board has additional responsibilities that rarely appear on lists of accomplishments. These responsibilities, which are equally important, if not more so, than the others, involve inspiring the organization, the other board members, and volunteers to do good work. Many problems that besiege nonprofits could be avoided if board members regularly reminded everyone in the group why they came together to work on a mission they all share.

Responsibilities of the Officers

The general duties of the officers of a nonprofit organization are similar to those of a for-profit corporation. If you decide to use the accepted offices, the responsibilities for each can apply to almost any organization. It is a good idea for the initial board to adopt clear definitions of the officers' roles so they become the standard. You can refine the roles to suit your needs, and the responsibilities of each position should be spelled out in your by-laws so future boards and their officers can follow your guidance and your example.

President

The board president is responsible for much more than facilitating the meetings of the board of directors. She will become the public face of the organization, the contact person for every question anyone in the community may want to ask. She will also be the main advocate for everything your organization is trying to do, from attending early-morning business break-fasts to arranging lines of credit to overseeing programming issues to facilitating board and community meetings. It is common for the board president to be one of the organization's check-signers. Although she won't manage the financial data, she should always have access to it.

Meetings may be conducted in any manner the group agrees to, from consensus all the way to strict adherence to *Robert's Rules of Order*. Unless everyone on the board can recite *Robert's Rules* from memory, a modified consensus is the best option. In other words, a formal recorded vote is taken only if general agreement without a formal vote (consensus) cannot be reached.

As the organization grows and more people join at a decision-making level, either as staff or committee members, many of the initial board president's roles will diminish. In the beginning, however, the initial board president should be called upon to do many tasks.

Vice President

The official role of a vice president is to be available when the president is temporarily unable to fulfill her responsibilities or to be readily available as a permanent replacement should the president need to step down. On a volunteer board, the responsibilities go much further.

The vice president needs to be aware of everything that goes on in the organization, from knowing what the committees are working on to being familiar with the status of any programming. He must be able to work in partnership with the president when needed. The vice president also needs to be available to take on special projects such as chairing a committee on short notice.

Secretary

There are actually two independent roles the secretary needs to assume. The internal role, often referred to as a recording secretary, involves generating and filing all of the group's corporate documents, the minutes of meetings, general mailing lists, and databases in a safe place. The secretary takes accurate minutes during every board or public meeting and collects the minutes from the committee meetings. The secretary is also responsible for cleaning up rough meeting notes that will become part of the permanent record of the organization.

ESSENTIAL

A standardized template for recording board or committee meeting minutes will make the secretary's job much easier. Taking minutes on a laptop is generally acceptable, and having a template eliminates the need for repetitive writing.

The second role, which can certainly be filled by the same person, is external and is often referred to as a correspondence secretary. Her ongoing task is to handle all the official correspondence of the organization. These tasks have greatly expanded in the electronic age to include monitoring all e-mail traffic, keeping the organization's website current, and anything else that involves communication between the group and the broader community. The board member who assumes this role must be comfortable with e-mail and writing in general and will need to create reports within a regular time frame.

Treasurer

The office of treasurer in a nonprofit also has more than one role. First, the person should maintain the group's financial books, which involves basic checkbook balancing and bill paying. The treasurer is generally one of the official check-signers and has access to any bank accounts or investments held by the group.

In consultation with the board president and the financial committee, the treasurer is responsible for preparing the yearly financial report for the IRS once the tax exemption (IRS Form 990) is obtained or for paying any federal corporate taxes if the tax exemption has not yet been received. The treasurer also makes sure that all local fees and taxes are paid.

The second role is to assist in developing the yearly operating budget. If projected budgets are necessary to qualify for funding opportunities or at the early stage for the application for nonprofit status, the treasurer should be directly involved in developing these documents for presentation to the full board and outside entities as necessary.

The third role for the treasurer, especially in the early stages of the organization's formation, is to oversee fundraising efforts. This role is not limited to making requests (though every board member needs to learn to do that). Rather, it is an opportunity to work on a long-term development strategy for long-term sustainability.

The treasurer needs to be comfortable handling money and working with numbers. Although there are numerous software programs available to help with budget development and bookkeeping, it is helpful to understand the basics.

Maintaining a Separation of Responsibilities

It is not by chance that the responsibilities of the officers rarely overlap. This separation intentionally provides a minimal level of checks and balances within the organization. The board of directors must assume roles that are similar to the legislative, executive, and judicial branches of government. However, within nonprofit boards, a much simpler structure has evolved over time that incorporates separation without such stark divisions.

As an example, the person who is responsible for the finances does not facilitate meetings where operational decisions might be made. In turn, the president, who essentially has executive authority, does not handle corporate record keeping.

The importance of this separation will become clearer as your organization develops working committees. Even as all the committees work to further your organization, they may develop competing interests, usually over allocation of limited resources. Setting up your board to separate the needs of programming and operations from your financial and legal elements will create a more productive organization.

To Pay or Not to Pay the Board

The members of the initial board of directors have to decide whether to pay themselves. That decision may be written into the by-laws if they so choose. The common assumption is that nonprofit boards are always voluntary, and this book supports the all-volunteer board.

The excess benefit tax is levied if a payment is viewed as exceeding a fair market value. Such a payment would run counter to the basic requirement that no one may benefit from the work of the organization. It is a slippery slope that no start-up nonprofit organization should test.

Checking with the Law

As with everything else that governs nonprofits, there is an emotional side, but there is still the actual law as it applies to your group and nonprofit organizations in general. There is no law expressly prohibiting a nonprofit board from being paid, as long as that payment is considered "reasonable."

That said, your board is venturing into dangerous territory if they choose to pay themselves. Not only will they run the risk of being liable for the excess benefit tax, they will also raise questions within the organization and the broader community about exactly how scarce funds are being spent.

Generally, about 5 percent of nonprofit organizations in the country compensate board members. If you decide as an organization to pay board members, seek legal advice from an attorney well versed in nonprofit law to avoid inadvertently crossing dangerous lines and placing your tax-exempt status in peril.

Reimbursement for Board Expenses

Your board may be reimbursed for reasonable expenses directly related to their activities as board members as long as there is a full and complete accounting for those costs. It is a good practice to submit estimates of the items well before the money is spent and to set limits on reimbursable expenses. These decisions can be handled through simple motions of the board at any regular meeting. Use the law and common sense as your guide.

Acceptance of Corporate Documents

Unlike the first meeting of the organization, which can be an opportunity for brainstorming and general planning, the first meeting of the board of directors represents the beginning of your organization as a legal entity. It is also the time when your newly seated board needs to formally accept the documents necessary for incorporation, elect the officers, agree to move forward with the application for federal nonprofit status, open a bank account, and authorize a method for paying expenses. Additional housekeeping decisions will need to be made, but at the initial meeting, you need to authorize the most important details to be open for business.

QUESTION

What is meant by formally accepting documents?
Formally refers to the fact that it will take place at an official meeting of your board, with minutes being taken and any votes or agreements by consensus recorded. Informal agreements are fine for casual groups, but incorporation requires more formality.

The most important thing to keep in mind is that you are not only establishing an organization for the present, you are establishing a legal corporation that will survive past your personal involvement.

It becomes even more important that each document you helped write meets all of your needs as well as every need mandated by the group, the state, and the IRS, if you plan to pursue federal tax exemption.

ALERT

Once the board has formally accepted the incorporation document and initial set of by-laws that will be sent to the state office responsible for incorporation, delegate the responsibility for assembling all the other documents you will want to file. Although these forms will not require formal board action, having one member of the board oversee the process will make certain it all gets done.

The Fiduciary Responsibility of the Board

The most important, lasting legacy the initial board of directors can pass on is the recognition that the work they do on behalf of the organization is held to a higher level than anything else.

The Financial Part of Fiduciary Responsibility

From a financial standpoint, it is the board's responsibility to keep the funds the group raises safe from risk. The board must make sure that all operational decisions are based on sound financial analysis. Maintaining the organization's financial integrity is the first thing associated with the word *fiduciary,* but the responsibility includes preserving the essence of the group for the present and the future.

Nonfinancial Fiduciary Responsibility

As the organization matures and the committees, staff, and community volunteers come into their own, the board must temper risky options that may be presented. The board will need to weigh proposals that may not appear to be financial in nature but could potentially affect the group's finances if mistakes are made or if there is a lapse in attention.

ESSENTIAL

Fiduciary responsibility also means "carrying the flame"—that is, being the soul and conscience of the organization at all times. It's hard, demanding, and, at times, uncomfortable work. It is also invaluable.

Examples of such issues include real-estate purchases; they may also include programs the group wants to present that may have a negative effect on parts of the community or on funding streams. Examine everything you consider doing in light of how it might affect the organization in the short term (attendance, positive media, etc.) and also how it might affect the group's financial well-being in the long term.

CHAPTER 6

Articles of Incorporation

Articles of incorporation tell the state and the general public about your organization. They state exactly who you are and how you operate. If you are planning to become a federally recognized nonprofit organization, articles of incorporation show that your organization complies with basic requirements. The articles also detail how the organization will be dissolved if necessary, including the disposition of any remaining funds.

Required Language

Articles of incorporation tend to be similar. The style, language, and overall appearance of the document have evolved over time. They often look archaic, using language you are not likely to hear on the street, but this language is intentional and precise.

The actual wording that each state requires is surprisingly basic and very similar. With few exceptions, every state supplies template articles containing the language it requires. Before going any further, be sure to read and fully understand what is being asked of you. The documents require you to print them, sign them, and mail them to the office identified on the form.

FACT

Some states are converting to paperless corporation filings, allowing or even requiring electronic submissions. If you are incorporating in a state that has converted to electronic filings, the template you will use is still included in this toolkit. Be sure to print, file, and retain an exact copy of the form you submit electronically.

State secretary of state offices usually handle nonprofit as well as for-profit corporate filings. Some states have authorized other offices to handle these documents. You can visit the National Association of Secretaries of State (NASS) website at *www.nass.org* for a list of office addresses.

Although each state has its own form and specific questions that you will have to answer, the questions in common are going to be discussed here to make the process less daunting. Some forms start with the articles of incorporation and offer little or no explanation. So here's a look at the form.

Name

The Name section may also be identified as Article 1. Enter the name exactly as you want it to appear on all subsequent legal documents. No one will edit or spell-check what you put on the form. Any abbreviations or punctuation you use will remain as the name, so take this element seriously. Remember, if you use the word *the*, as in "The XYZ School for the Performing Arts," it stays. The same holds true for abbreviations in parentheses, often used for longer names. If you put it on the form as your name—again, identifying our example of a performing arts school as "XYZSPA"—it stays. Carefully read the instructions for requirements regarding words such as *Incorporated* and *Company*.

ALERT

Once you have decided on a name that is unique, consider registering the name immediately as a future website domain so it will be available to you when your organization is ready to build a site. Securing a domain name has become the essential first step in establishing an organization's identity both on the web and in the general community.

Run an Internet search of the name you plan to use; this is the easiest way to verify that your name is unique. Some states allow you to reserve a name prior to filing for incorporation. These states will have forms available through the same office that handles the incorporation. States will not allow names that appear to be misleading or that they consider to be indecent or vulgar.

Term

The term of existence is more often than not going to be "perpetual," so check that box if it appears. This indicates that you are planning to be in existence forever, as opposed to simply existing for one project. Of course, if you are incorporating for the purpose of a short-term project as a state non-profit and have no plans to apply for federal tax exemption, indicate this on the form along with your projected date of dissolution.

Purpose

The purpose of your organization is discussed later because the IRS requires clear, specific language. If you do not plan to apply for federal tax exemption, you are not restricted in the language you use: You may explain your purpose as you like.

Addresses

Unless otherwise instructed, post office addresses are fine for the organization and the initial board of directors, but an actual street address must be listed for the registered agent.

NAICS

Some states require the North American Industry Classification System (NAICS), which was established by the census bureau. For an NAICS classification, refer to the website *www.census.gov/eos/www/naics* to locate the classification that is the closest to your mission.

QUESTION

What happens after the articles of incorporation are sent in?
Provided everything has been properly filled out and you included the required fee, you will receive a formal document, which is embossed with the state seal, from the state government office that handles corporate filings. This certified document, which will be date stamped, will be evidence of your incorporation status; be sure to make copies of it.

Some states require additional information, including plans for disposing of any leftover funds in the event the organization is dissolved. The IRS requires specific language that addresses dissolution, which will be discussed in greater detail later in this chapter in the section titled "Planning for the End—While Meeting IRS Standards!" Some states use the same form for nonprofit and for-profit corporations; groups registering as nonprofits are required to check a specific box. A few states ask you to indicate on the form that the organization is nonprofit. Be sure to read the instructions and forms thoroughly.

Covering the Basics

Once the state articles of incorporation have been filed with the secretary of state, you have met the most basic requirement for conducting business in your state. There are also local filings with your city or county for their respective business licenses.

Your state may require additional filings, so check the general instructions for the articles. There is no rule stating you need to apply for federal tax exemption, but there are time limits if you plan to do so. If you and your organization are satisfied with state incorporation and understand you will be responsible for federal corporate income taxes, you're good to go.

A General Overview of Suggested Language

If your organization intends to file with the IRS to obtain tax-exempt status, you must use precise language in your articles of incorporation. This language is required to show that, as an organization, you fully understand the ramifications of securing tax-exempt status and that you agree to adhere to some basic rules governing how you handle your organization's finances.

Making the Articles Your Own

The sample articles of incorporation provided by many states do not have extra space to include the wording necessary to meet the IRS requirements because the state and federal incorporation requirements are not the same. The easiest way to solve this problem is to include the articles you want to use, attaching additional sheets as necessary to the form, and send it all in together. On every attached sheet, be sure to write the name of the organization, the preparer's name and contact information, and the organization's Employment Identification Number (EIN). The people who review these state incorporation filings are used to seeing additional language, so there will not be a problem.

Don't Get Too Creative

Remember that these articles will show the state your intent to incorporate and the IRS your qualifications for tax-exempt status. For the most part, you must meet minimum standards and use required language. Anything too far beyond what everyone expects to see will raise more questions than answers.

Defining Your Purpose to Meet IRS Standards

How you define your purpose in terms of your articles of incorporation is much different than defining your purpose to your community. When you are talking in the community, you will define your purpose in terms of the projects you hope to take on and the good work you hope to do. You can and should talk about what really drives you and the organization, or what most people would immediately think of when discussing "purpose." Defining your purpose in the articles of incorporation follows a different set of rules.

The IRS is less interested in why you want to form an organization than it is in the legalities of incorporation. The nonprofit corporation must adhere to a set of rules governing its financial transactions. Following these rules allows your organization to continue and, in fact, succeed.

As far as the IRS is concerned, your purpose is defining and expressing exactly how you intend to operate from a financial standpoint. More to the point, you must inform the IRS that you intend to follow both the letter and spirit of the regulations regarding nonprofit organizations. The IRS wants specific language to be included.

Purpose

To meet IRS requirements, use this exact language in your articles of incorporation:

"The organization is organized exclusively for charitable, religious, educational, and scientific purposes under section 501(c)(3) of the Internal Revenue Code, or corresponding section of any future federal tax code."

You may also want to add the following language to explain your purpose further:

Notwithstanding any other provision of these articles, this corporation shall not, except to an insubstantial degree, engage in any activities, or exercise any powers not in furtherance of section 501(c) (3) purposes.

While this language may seem dry and archaic, it must be included so the IRS is comfortable knowing that you know the rules; in addition, it reminds future board members forever of the commitment they are making to the community. If you have already incorporated and did not have this language in your articles, you need to adjust them before you apply for tax-exempt status by filing an amendment with the same office you filed your original articles of incorporation.

Additional Language

The IRS encourages applicants to go into additional detail to define their purpose more narrowly. Keep any additional language succinct. Here is one example:

The XYZ Corporation, organized to teach home-building and remodeling skills to unemployed individuals, is organized exclusively for charitable, religious, educational, and scientific purposes under section 501(c)(3) of the Internal Revenue Code, or corresponding section of any future federal tax code.

Such a statement narrowly defines your purpose and clearly indicates that you will be carrying out that purpose within the restrictions of the IRS laws for tax exemption.

Planning for the End—While Meeting IRS Standards!

Although it may seem odd to plan for exactly how your organization will end just as you are preparing to begin, the IRS requires every applicant for tax-exempt status to include a clear plan for dissolution in its articles of incorporation. Everyone involved must understand how money or other assets will be handled if or when the organization decides to stop functioning and elects to dissolve. The underlying reasoning is to guarantee that any net earnings or assets held by a nonprofit organization will not benefit any individual or private shareholder; instead, these funds will be distributed to another organization that also has a 501(c)(3) status.

FACT

Not every state requires a dissolution clause in the articles of incorporation, but you are still going to need it to apply for the federal tax-exempt status. In addition, it's a good idea to plan for the eventuality.

Option A

You can indicate that upon dissolution of your organization, you will distribute any remaining assets to another 501(c)(3) organization that will not be identified until your organization formally dissolves. This option can be tricky because it leaves a very important decision to people you may not know, people who may choose to distribute funds in a way that is counter to the wishes of the current board. Further, if the organization does not formally dissolve but simply ceases operation, the last board may lose control of the remaining funds and a court will have to determine the final disposal.

Here is some sample dissolution language that meets IRS standards:

Upon the dissolution of this organization and after payment of all outstanding debts of the organization, assets shall be distributed for one or more exempt purposes within the meaning of section 501(c)(3) of the Internal Revenue Code, or corresponding section of any future federal tax code, or shall be distributed to the federal government, or to a state or local government, for a public purpose.

Option B

You may indicate that upon dissolution of your organization your funds will go to another organization that you name in your articles. The advantage here is that your organization can be certain that another nonprofit with a similar mission and overall approach will be the recipient of your assets and that the decision will be made when everyone is thinking clearly. You can include language to the effect that if that organization is no longer in existence or chooses not to accept the distribution, your board may then select another group.

ALERT

An organization may amend its articles of incorporation as often as it chooses, as long as the amendments do not stray outside the boundaries of what is legal for a nonprofit corporation to do in the state in which it is incorporated.

If your board would like to specify an organization that already has its federal tax-exempt status to receive any distribution of assets, possible language for your dissolution clause might be as follows:

Upon the dissolution of this organization and after payment of all outstanding debts of the organization, the remaining assets shall be distributed to the ABC Society for Good Deeds, of 123 Main St., Hometown, OK, a 501(c)(3) organization. If, however, the ABC Society for Good Deeds is not, at that time, in existence, is no longer exempt from federal income tax, or for any reason is unwilling or unable to accept the distribution, then the assets shall be distributed to an organization that has a current 501(c)(3) determination to be selected by the board of directors.

Amendments

It is entirely possible for an organization to change something in its articles of incorporation after they have been filed. In a perfect world, such changes would never be necessary, but fortunately everyone involved in the process realizes that mistakes happen and changes are required, so a smooth mechanism is available to amend your articles. Remember that because your organization is now a corporation recognized by the state and the articles are the legal basis for the corporation, any changes to those articles must be handled in a precise manner.

There are two separate and distinct parts to amending the articles of incorporation. First, your board must propose and pass the language, following the process spelled out in your by-laws to cover this exact situation. Second, you must file articles of amendment with the state secretary of state at the same address you filed the original incorporation documents. There is usually a small fee associated with the filing.

ESSENTIAL

Language that accurately defines your organization's purpose could be too precise or too vague to meet the guidelines of a particular funding organization or for grants issued by government agencies. For example, you may be working with patients living with a particular disease, but you may need to broaden your definitions to avoid any appearance of discrimination and to remain in contention for a grant. Filing an amendment to adjust wording can generally solve that problem.

Reasons to File Articles of Amendment

You may need to file amendments to your articles because of simple omissions in the initial filing or to adjust the exact wording for the federal tax-exemption application. The most common reason is to move from a nonmembership to a membership organization.

Be Careful When Filing Amendments

Do not make a habit of filing too many articles of amendment, but do use the option when necessary. Unlike your by-laws, which can be modified with little outside scrutiny, articles of amendment filed with your state become public record. Many groups hold off on changes as long as possible and then combine multiple amendments into one form to streamline the process.

The Registered Agent

The incorporation form in most states will have a line on which to identify your registered agent. This term also appears on forms provided by many local jurisdictions that require some form of permit or license to conduct business in their area.

QUESTION

Does the registered agent assume full responsibility and liability for the organization?
No, he or she simply agrees to be the real person willing to accept papers on behalf of the organization, list a street address for the legal record, and be identified on the incorporation or other licensing documents.

Once it is established, a corporation essentially becomes a person in the eyes of the state. It has many of the rights and privileges of a real person, but it is obviously not a person who can be contacted or served with legal papers should the need arise. Therefore, a real person must agree to accept legal filings on behalf of the organization.

The person who becomes your registered agent can be anyone of your choosing. He or she can be a board member, anyone in your organization, or anyone in the larger community who is trusted by the organization and agrees to assume this role. It is not unusual for the registered agent to be identified in the by-laws as the current president of the board of directors or the executive director, with a mailing address readily available. As part of your annual reporting, note any changes in the person holding that position.

Registered Agent or Incorporator

There is sometimes a bit of confusion over these two terms and just what each person does. While these roles can be handled by the same person, they are actually distinct. The role of registered agent continues as long as the organization exists. The person holding that role can obviously change over time, but the role remains.

The incorporator, on the other hand, literally prepares the articles of incorporation and delivers them to the state secretary of state. He or she agrees to be available by telephone or e-mail should questions come up. The incorporator might be your lawyer, a consultant you asked to assist with the process, or any member of your core group who agreed to manage the process. After the application has been approved and the certified copy with the stamp or seal of the secretary of state's office has been returned, the role of the incorporator is pretty much over—with your thanks!

CHAPTER 7

By-Laws

Whereas articles of incorporation describe your organization and your relationship to the state, by-laws tell people within your organization how you conduct your internal business and how members relate to one another. The by-laws describe who makes up your membership and the responsibilities of everyone involved in the group, from the board and committees to staff and volunteers. By-laws also outline the organization's commitment to fairness and nondiscrimination.

Organizational Details

By-laws provide you with the opportunity to create an ideal world. Within a generally accepted framework, your organization is free to decide how you will select future boards of directors, handle meetings, establish committees, hire staff, manage finances, and conduct business. As one of the earliest documents your organization will draft, by-laws are created before the stress of running an organization makes crafting a well-designed set more difficult.

Building the Document

The first few sections should cover housekeeping details. You need to state the formal name of the organization and the location where you conduct business. You can find sample by-laws included in this toolkit. Modify them as you see fit. After you cover the basics, it's time to detail the main parts of your organization's operation.

ESSENTIAL

As you develop the language for your organization, find a middle ground between being specific and allowing for necessary flexibility. Although the board may amend the by-laws as needed, it is good to have some give already built into the document to avoid changes that can waste time.

By-laws should follow a certain format so your mission is clear to three specific groups: staff, volunteers, and the board of directors; your donors; and the IRS. If you follow the examples in this toolkit, you will meet the needs for each group.

Operating the Organization as a Charity

You must state in your purpose that you are a charity. The language must be clear so your future financial supporters understand exactly what you are planning to do.

You must establish positive relationships with these people in order to meet the IRS requirements to become and remain a public charity. Your supporters will want to be assured that your commitment to certain core principles that appear in your by-laws aligns with their values as well. The philanthropic community will often evaluate these basic elements well before any consideration is given to actual requests for financial support. The funding community will want to know that your organization understands the meaning behind the words *public charity*.

Understanding What a Charity Means

The IRS looks at an organization's by-laws to determine whether it is operating as a public charity. By definition, a public charity must receive a substantial part of its support in the form of contributions from publicly supported organizations, governmental units, and/or the general public. In addition, no more than one-third of support can come from investment income, and more than one-third of support must come from contributions, membership fees, and gross receipts from activities related to its exempt functions.

Translated from IRS jargon, a membership-fee organization, such as an arts group with box office revenue, is a publicly supported charity because a large percentage of its revenue comes from public contributions.

QUESTION

Does the IRS require specific language in the by-laws?
The IRS does not require any specific language, but you must include a copy of your by-laws with the application for tax-exempt status. The IRS will review the by-laws to ensure there are no discrepancies in terms of your other material and to further document your intentions.

For your board and membership, by-laws tend to reinforce exactly what the organization is and intends to do. Whereas the language in your articles of incorporation is to a large degree mandated by state law or IRS regulations (especially if your organization is applying for federal tax-exempt status), your by-laws reflect who you are as an organization, where you want to go, and how you intend to get there.

Responsibilities of the Board

The first section or article in the by-laws is usually about the board of directors. This is a symbolic way of recognizing the importance of the board to the ongoing viability of a nonprofit organization.

1. The board must agree to carry out two primary tasks, each of which includes long lists of responsibilities.
2. The board must manage and oversee the board of directors, which includes its own meetings, meetings of any committees, elections, selection of officers, and other responsibilities.
3. The board must maintain management or oversight of the organization, which includes fundraising or financial management, staffing, legal issues, real estate, and programming.

Managing Board Business

The board is responsible for calling and then running its own meetings, which should be scheduled at regular intervals. All decisions that affect the organization are made at these meetings, and an accurate record (the minutes) should always be retained. The board is responsible for creating its committees and soliciting any outside advice it feels it needs to manage the organization.

FACT

In practice, as your board begins to work together, the clear line between its two distinct responsibilities—managing the organization's affairs and managing its internal business—will fade. However, these two management arenas will remain separate areas of focus; the best boards remember this fact and plan their agendas and overall activities accordingly.

Some boards find it advantageous to utilize an administrator to help manage the board's internal business. This selection is not a priority for the first stages of a start-up nonprofit; it is a decision that can be made later.

Managing the Organization

The board is also responsible for the group's financial management, and it is ultimately responsible for staffing, long-range planning, general policy decisions, and public perception. The board's fiduciary responsibilities will affect everything it does both within the organization and in the community. From both a legal and moral standpoint, how the board handles that responsibility will make or break the organization.

Membership Options

The type of membership structure will say a great deal about how you plan to relate to the broader community, so examining a number of options makes sense. Each option carries its own set of advantages and disadvantages. The by-laws presented in this toolkit give one option, but you are certainly not limited to that.

Membership Limited to the Board

This is an entirely valid option, in which the board is also the entire voting membership. It nominates itself into office and then determines, by whatever agreed-upon means, how the organization will operate. Particularly in the formative stages, this option limits outside distractions from diverting the board while allowing it to remain focused on the immediate work that needs to be done.

ALERT

Any decision the board makes regarding the type of membership to adopt, or for that matter any other decision appearing in the by-laws, can always be changed when the board of directors approves it. Changing membership requirements is a relatively common adjustment that many organizations make to their by-laws as they grow.

The disadvantage is simply the reverse. Since this option excludes participation at the decision-making level by members of the community, it may lead to feelings of resentment among those who are not able to vote. This is not to suggest that the public cannot be involved in the organization. Once board decisions have been made, the board members may invite anyone they want to implement those decisions. Those individuals, whether they are community volunteers or paid staff, are just not voting members of the board.

The board is always free to invite guests to any meeting to participate in discussions and offer expertise. Likewise, members of the community who are active in the organization may ask to be invited. The only limitation is that only board members participate in decision-making.

Membership Open to the Community

This option opens the membership to people outside the board of directors, using clearly established criteria. Membership may require nothing more than active participation. There may be different membership levels, ranging from those who can vote to those who are simply on a mailing list.

FACT

"Care" of the membership must be taken into consideration if you decide on an open-membership policy. While members can be a wonderful asset to the organization, there will be ongoing commitments such as mailings, possible elections, and other administrative tasks throughout the life of the organization. If you choose that route from the beginning, make sure you have the resources to maintain this work.

The advantage of an open-membership system is that your organization will appear more inclusive and not prone to claims of cliquishness among the leadership. The disadvantage is that it opens your organization to the possibility of political maneuvering by any determined group interested in forcing its agenda. This possibility can be mitigated by how board members are nominated, and the danger decreases as the organization matures, but it is something to keep in mind.

Mixing and Matching

The third option is to combine elements of the other options so that you and the organization can be inclusive and still able to conduct the necessary work for your group. You can establish levels of membership that range from being on your mailing list to active membership that may involve voting rights.

Even if you choose not to have members, a mailing list of active people in the community, regardless of their legal membership status, will become a useful fundraising tool. Such a list is tangible evidence of the necessary community support your organization has established.

Standing Committees

The by-laws identify the standing committees of the board and articulate their basic responsibilities. Membership on the committees is for the board to determine. At least one board member should be on every committee. Having only board members populate every committee is an option. In the beginning, it is normal for the committees to include only board members. In time though, as you begin looking for individuals whose skills may be beneficial to your organization, consider opening up committee memberships. You may mandate in the by-laws exactly how the committees are to function, or you may leave that to the actual committee to determine. At a minimum, committees should establish regular meeting times and always record minutes of the discussion.

The unique nature of your organization and the type of service you are involved in will determine the standing committees, but there are a few that every group should consider.

Finance or Budget Committee

After selecting the committee of the whole, which is a term for the entire board, establish the finance committee. Financial affairs are the sole purpose of this committee, which keeps these issues before the board and brings together the people best suited for the task. The finance committee should maintain oversight of fundraising activities and of all real and projected expenses. If these are not the people developing the working budget, they must have regular access to it.

Program Committee

The program committee is where the work of your organization is developed. This committee will analyze proposals from inside your organization or ones brought to you from the larger community for their suitability and appropriateness to your stated mission. The program committee may also become a portal into your organization for community members who want to take a larger role in the actual operations, making it an initial point of contact to your board.

ESSENTIAL

From the beginning, committees must remain in regular communication with one another, so everyone is aware of the activities of the whole board. This is critical when money is involved, requiring consultation with the finance committee or at least its chairperson.

Once the program committee evaluates projects, they may be proposed to the full board for action. There can, of course, be countless variations to the process, which may involve staff, volunteers, and other constituencies, but the standing committees exist to spread out the actual work of running the organization and preparing action items for the board to consider.

Proposed Committees

There is language in the by-laws that enables the board members to create committees that would help them do their work. Include some form of this language, even if the notion of also establishing committees at the early stage of the organization may not seem necessary.

Committees may be proposed at any time and for any reason that the board feels it needs more help to carry out its work. Committees may be proposed with a limited life span—for example, to investigate and secure a real-estate purchase or to hire an executive director. In other words, the committee only exists until it has completed its work and made its final report to the board.

Nominating Committee

Depending on how you have structured other parts of the organization, you may want to have a nominating committee. Its sole purpose would be to bring potential board members to a vote of the membership. One advantage is that the committee would have a high level of independence to solicit potential board candidates, to interview them well out of the public eye (in order to avoid embarrassment if they are not proposed as candidates), and most important, to vet the individual completely before presenting her to the board and/or the community.

FACT

In the context on a nonprofit board, vetting a person is a prudent exercise. Vetting generally refers to conducting a thorough evaluation of an individual's background to be certain that all potential conflicts of interest are disclosed and nothing in his personal or work history would negatively impact the organization.

Advisory Committee

Establishing an advisory committee is an excellent way to bring on board highly respected members of the community who support your mission but are too busy to commit to specific tasks. Advisory committee members are usually brought in through a personal invitation of a board member. They agree to be available to offer advice in their particular area of expertise, as well as open up their respective networks for periodic outreach and solicitations.

It is not too early, even in the formative stages, to begin thinking about who you would approach about joining the advisory committee. If personal relationships already exist between people in your organization and prospective advisory committee members, then you're well ahead of the game. If you decide to approach someone you do not know, determine where your networks and that person's networks intersect and approach her from that point. Keep in mind that well-known people are asked to lend their name and support to worthwhile organizations all the time. Carefully plan how to present yourself and the group in order to give yourself the best chance of creating a strong, respected advisory committee.

Other Committees

The specifics of your group's mission and operation will determine which committees may be helpful. If the group owns or rents property, a committee to oversee that element might be helpful. If there is a staff, or even plans to bring on a paid staff, a personnel committee will help considerably. Likewise, if there are ongoing legal issues, a legal committee will allow the board to obtain the best possible advice prior to making any decisions.

Nondiscrimination and a Statement of Ethics

The by-laws are an ideal place to remind yourselves, and the broader community you will be working with, that discrimination in any form will not be tolerated.

ALERT

While your organization may have come to terms long ago with issues of discrimination or maintaining ethical standards, many funding entities with a long history of supporting nonprofits hold these issues at the forefront of all they do.

As a public charity, your organization has a special responsibility to hold true to many ideals. You will be subjected to ongoing scrutiny, so having language in your core document outlining the organization's approach to discrimination will benefit all you do.

Need for a Statement of Ethics

Your by-laws should include specific language outlining the ethics by which your organization will operate. As with the nondiscrimination language, the purpose is twofold: to remind current and future board members

/ volunteers / staff of your core values, and to let external entities know what you believe in as an organization and that you are willing to put it on paper.

FACT

Many organizations print their nondiscrimination policy and their statement of ethics and distribute them to staff and volunteers. The underlying purpose is to constantly remind everyone of the special trust held by the organization. You want your people to know that you plan to do things a little differently and a little better than occurred before.

Underlying Reason for Including This Language

Much of the ongoing operations, including outreach and fundraising, will depend on the firmly established personal relationships your board develops with the larger community. Many new nonprofits are formed every year, and each attempts to establish itself within its area of service. A clear set of by-laws that details how your organization conducts itself internally and externally will be as powerful as any traditional outreach. This language in your by-laws will help meet that purpose. Elements to consider in your statement of ethics include:

- Avoid any perception of conflict of interest.
- Protect intellectual property.
- Always use restricted contributions for the purpose they were intended.
- Promptly direct any inquiries from the media to the designated representative of the board of directors.
- Prevent the organization from incurring indebtedness for other than trade payables incurred during the normal course of doing business.

The sample by-laws include a more complete statement of ethics and can be used as a model as you develop your own document.

Language for a Specific Audience

Your by-laws present a fine opportunity to let potential volunteers, potential funders, and general supporters know that you will be operating in a style and manner that meets your needs and theirs. This is particularly true as your organization enters into more precise activities where funding sources may need to identify closely with the organization through its by-laws. If, for example, you are planning to purchase property as soon as possible, having language requiring a real-estate committee will show the seriousness of that element to your board's overall agenda. If your organization has a cultural/arts focus, you need to have respected artists involved in a visible manner, and a programming committee where their talents will be most useful.

ESSENTIAL

Most grant-makers will ask you to include a copy of your governing document in your grant application so they can ensure that your operations and their interests line up well before any actual funding requests wind up on the table. It is, therefore, important that the organization is as prepared as possible for the many funding environments that will exist over the next five to seven years.

There is a fine line between being certain your by-laws accurately show how you plan to function internally so you can show external audiences that you are all on the same page and appearing to pander to a specific funding source. Remember all materials that have been developed since your founding will be examined, not simply one document. The best thing to keep in mind as you write your by-laws is to be honest and realistic.

CHAPTER 8

Filing Incorporation Documents

To legally conduct business, a new organization must become incorporated. This process involves filling out a number of forms so the organization officially exists in the community. This chapter presents the common licenses and permits needed for incorporation.

Local Government Offices

Legal operations require that you apply for and maintain an assortment of licenses and permits to conduct business in the city, county, township, or parish in which you are located. For the most part, you can obtain these documents by filling out a form and paying the fee. When compared to the intricacies of applying for a federal tax exemption, filing these forms may seem easy.

Check with your city or county government for specific details. Keep in mind that each jurisdiction and layer of administration is essentially independent, but they also rely on one another. If this sounds confusing and contradictory, it is. The city and county revenue offices may share a building or even a suite, but they are completely separate entities that may not be able to answer questions about each other.

ESSENTIAL

One person, ideally the incorporator, should visit the county or city offices and collect all the general business information. Check the appropriate website as well. Although the offices are independent, many municipalities have collaborated to provide a basic road map through the permit process. This information may include contact information and is generally free of charge.

At the start-up stage, you are trying to fulfill the minimum licensing requirements to open a business. Once you are up and running, there will be more details and documentation to tend to, but it is important that you have a solid foundation.

Location, Location, Location

As strange as it may seem, one of the first issues people often encounter at the city level is determining where the office is located. Some cities allow identifying post office boxes as a business address, but they also may require a street address.

If you use an address that is not zoned for business use, the city may raise concerns about your venture. Government employees are bound by the law and they must review your materials. All they will see is that you are a business and you have an office at a specific address. Keep in mind that all local government employees have to go on are the forms you have submitted and any corresponding land-use code.

FACT

Many organizations use the address of their incorporator, especially if their incorporator is a legal or tax professional. If the incorporator's office is already in an area zoned for business, using that address when your preferred address is impractical may be an easy, short-term solution. When you have your own office, make the needed address changes and you will be good to go.

If you find out that your office location is in a restricted area for any reason (usually involving zoning), ask the people in the office how to negotiate your way out of the problem. If your start-up office is simply someone's living room (a very normal circumstance), you may need to change addresses. If you have a building or are in the process of obtaining one, you may need to apply using a temporary address, pending your acquisition of necessary variances. This can be a long, complicated process, so seek professional advice from someone familiar with your situation.

Make New Friends

Visiting your local government offices in the early stages of setting up your organization is very important. You will gain a profound understanding of how your government actually functions on a day-to-day level. On the other side, the individuals who keep everything humming will also have a chance to meet you and to establish the human connection that's often missing from the process of obtaining permits and licenses.

Time to Ask Those Questions

As much as everyone uses the Internet, websites are only as useful as the webmasters intended them to be. Search engines do not always return satisfactory answers. Asking questions when you visit local government offices is the best way to resolve any outstanding questions. It is quite common for county and city offices to be in the same general area, so if you are in the wrong office, the correct one will often be nearby.

ALERT

When you visit local government offices, collect the business cards of every person you talk with or meet. In the unlikely event you run into problems, having the direct phone number or e-mail address of a person you met—even briefly—will help resolve small annoyances before they escalate.

Federal Tax ID Number

You need to obtain a federal tax number, also referred to an Employer Identification Number (EIN), as soon as possible. This is the number the federal government and many state and local government agencies use rather than one person's social security number. Most of the government forms you fill out request this number, so you might as well get it now and check that task off your to-do list.

The fact that you do not have employees has no bearing on your need for an EIN. Most of these systems are set up with the expectation that while you may not need everything in the beginning, you will be set when the need arises.

QUESTION

Who actually obtains the federal tax number?
Anyone directly associated with the organization. If the person acting as the incorporator is available, ask him or her to do it to keep things simple.

The Process

Obtaining a federal EIN is probably the easiest process. There are three options.

1. Call 1-800-829-4933 to make your application. You'll have a federal tax number before you hang up.
2. Download IRS Form #SS-4 from *www.irs.gov*. Fill it out and mail it in.
3. Apply online (*www.irs.gov/businesses/small/article/0,,id=98350,00 .html*); the confirmation letter will be e-mailed to you in about a week.

The person who applies for an EIN will need to use her personal social security number for reference. She will also need to have the organization's legal name and address with her. There is no liability incurred for using that social security number. The whole point of having the number is for standardized corporate record keeping.

FACT

The immediate benefit of getting an EIN as soon as possible is that you will no longer need to use a personal social security number on any public documents. In an age when identity theft is not uncommon, this offers an easy way to make your identification numbers too complicated for the casual criminal.

State Business License

All states require some form of license to conduct business. It is entirely separate from the incorporation.

The articles of incorporation establish your organization as a separate and unique legal entity. The business license allows you to conduct business in the state. Generally speaking, you must first incorporate before you can obtain a business license, but verify the preferred order in your state. The outstanding question deals with what registration numbers are required for each form. The articles of incorporation will remain on file with your secretary of state or corporations' office; the business license is handled through a department of licensing or department of revenue.

The purpose of the license is to facilitate your ability to collect taxes on behalf of the state and remit those taxes on an established schedule. The license will also enter your organization into the database for other state taxes, such as employment taxes, which you may be responsible for paying.

These taxes are unrelated to any federal tax exemption you may obtain. Your organization will be responsible for them whether or not you obtain tax exemption. State business licenses are generally valid for a specific time and then they must be renewed.

ESSENTIAL

If your organization plans to sell anything to the public in a state that has a sales tax, you must collect that sales tax and forward those funds to your state. You may be required to obtain a sales tax permit, which authorizes you to collect sales tax on behalf of the state. Your federal or state tax-exempt status will have nothing to do with this obligation.

Do not allow your business license to lapse. It will jeopardize your ability to conduct business and leave you open for criticism in the community, which will negatively affect your ability to maintain your revenue stream.

State Income Tax

If you are operating in a state that has a tax on corporate income, ask now about obtaining your exemption from that tax. More often than not, the state exemption will run in conjunction with the federal tax exemption, but you need to verify this with the office handling your state business license. In California, Montana, North Carolina, and Pennsylvania, you must make a separate application to your state to obtain a nonprofit tax exemption. Washington has a similar tax called a business and occupation (B&O) tax.

Where the Money Goes

States collect sales tax for a number of reasons; as a new nonprofit, it may be good to have a basic understanding of where you fit into the picture. Many states return some portion of the sales taxes they collect in a particular city or county to that jurisdiction. In other words, the money collected in City A returns to City A. As a business, you are obligated to collect those taxes, but much of that money will eventually come back to your community.

This is the reason communities suffer so terribly when major retailers or manufacturers leave the area. Not only do jobs vanish, but so does the revenue stream generated by the sales taxes.

A nonprofit organization might find itself trying to fill in the gaps for services the government can no longer offer, because the tax revenue to carry out those services is simply not there. For this reason, although as an organization you may not be paying some of these taxes, they do affect your ability to operate. Stay on top of any changes.

Local Business License

A local business license, usually issued by your city and often referred to as a tax registration certificate, allows you to operate in your city. If your city or other local jurisdiction has its own sales tax system, this certificate will also be your authorization to collect those taxes on behalf of the local government and forward that money on an established schedule, much as you do for the state.

FACT

It may seem as though you will be collecting taxes and fees every time you turn around, and that's probably not what you envisioned as part of operating a nonprofit organization. In reality, not every tax or license identified here will apply to you. Furthermore, you will slowly factor in these elements as your organization matures, making it simply a part of doing business.

There is an annual cost associated with a local business license. As with other assorted fees, permits, and licenses, plan to work it into your yearly budget as an operational expense.

The most difficult time for getting these licenses in place is during your start-up phase, when much of the work will fall to your treasurer. Once everything is established, these tasks will become a routine matter of maintaining and staying current with your yearly obligations.

The Combined Local Taxes

When you open your first tax bill, you may find things you never dreamed existed. Your nonprofit will have to pay for common city or county services such as public safety, emergency services, and many others. Once you have been in business for a year, these numbers will no longer be shocking and you will simply factor them into your budget.

The Local Improvement Districts

Local improvement districts (LIDs) are generally small parts of a city that share a common purpose and agree to tax themselves as a way of paying for services unique to their area. For example, many theaters and other cultural organizations are located in LIDs. This tax actually works to your advantage because you will have direct input into the level of taxation and how expenditures are determined.

The Twenty-Seven-Month Clock Begins

As you locate the many forms required by numerous jurisdictions to conduct business, keep in mind the time requirements to file your IRS Form 1023, the application for federal tax exemption. The IRS form will be the last in a long progression of material you will develop. You may note on any of the appropriate forms that you are intending to make that application, but until you have done so and obtained your determination letter from the IRS, do not imply that you have tax-exempt status.

From the date you submit the articles of incorporation with your state, you have twenty-seven months to file your IRS Form 1023. You may be able to secure an extension, but with careful planning that should not be necessary.

Requesting an Extension

If you do not file for federal tax exemption and do not obtain a further extension within twenty-seven months, it is highly unlikely you will receive a favorable determination. Your option will be to start all over again, which means redoing every state and local detail you've already completed. After the amount of work and valuable time expended to wade through the reams of permits and documentation, a failure to file in the allotted time is always a setback.

Schedule E: Your Final Life Preserver

If you need an extension, you must file a Schedule E in the Form 1023. You will need to prepare a statement explaining that you have been acting in good faith. Seek professional assistance in the preparation of this statement; it is your organization's final chance to obtain its 501(c)(3) tax-exempt status.

ALERT

Miracles have been known to happen. There are cases of organizations letting the twenty-seven-month clock run out, not filing a Schedule E, making a special request, and receiving a favorable determination. That said, don't count on or expect anything but a rejection if you go that route.

If, on the other hand, the goal is to obtain a 505(c)(4) determination, the rules are a little less stringent and your chances of prevailing are a bit better. Ideally, watch the calendar and do not allow your organization to get this far along without filing your Form 1023.

Miscellaneous Documents

Once you have submitted the basic forms with the necessary fees, you are essentially open for business. If you have incorporated as a state non-profit and are operating as a not-for-profit organization or have secured your federal tax exemption, there are additional forms and certifications you may want to look into. The following are a few examples. There may be other opportunities for your organization to decrease its operational expenses through a careful examination of every fee paid to every level of government.

Admission Tax Exemption

If your organization produces public events, and if your local municipality has an admission tax, you need to see under what circumstances you may be exempt.

FACT

Admission taxes are always administered at the city or county level. You should inquire at those offices about whether such taxes exist in your area and how to apply for an exemption. It often requires a federal tax exemption, but it may also be possible with only your state nonprofit incorporation documentation.

Nonprofit Mailing Permit

As you plan to apply for federal tax exemption, consider applying for a nonprofit mailing permit to reduce your annual postal costs. Even with the increased use of e-mail, postage continues to be one of the major budget items in every nonprofit organization, particularly if you send out periodic solicitation letters. The United States Postal Service (USPS) has its own set of rules and criteria for authorizing organizations to mail at its reduced nonprofit rates; the information is available on the USPS website at *http://pe.usps.com/businessmail101/rates/nonprofit.html*.

The criteria for authorization are similar in many respects to the requirements to obtain your tax-exempt status, but there are differences. While a determination letter from the IRS is one of the documents necessary to establish your status for the USPS, it is not the only one.

The application for nonprofit authorization, USPS Form 3624, is available for download at *http://pe.usps.com/text/pub417/pub417_appd.html*.

CHAPTER 9

Record-Keeping Systems

Determining the appropriate record-keeping system for a nonprofit organization is one of the most important early tasks. Your organization's ability to raise money, spend money, and record all internal deliberations for review will rely on your system. Good records can show that the organization remains true to the original mission and will be essential for regular reporting to the IRS to maintain your nonprofit status.

The Core of Any Nonprofit

Becoming a nonprofit and maintaining that status involve a great deal more than good intentions and providing a valuable service to your community. Although these are very important aspects and must always be kept in sight, they are only part of the task.

If your group is comfortable remaining an unincorporated association, which is a fine option, skip this chapter. However, if you are planning to pursue formal incorporation and apply for federal tax exemption, a good amount of your time will be devoted to record keeping, financial reporting, and adhering to a vast assortment of regulations buried in fine print.

One of the most common reasons for losing tax-exempt status is careless record keeping or, even worse, failing to maintain accurate corporate records at all. If everyone in a position of responsibility within your organization realizes the importance of record keeping and does not allow the organization to fall behind, you should not have any problem.

Assigning Responsibility

Basically, there are two categories of records. Financial records include bank statements, budgets, assorted fees for licenses, and permits—anything involving money. Then there is everything else—such as the minutes of meetings, media, material you have produced to further the general mission, solicitation letters, grant proposals—your organization has produced or that others have produced about your organization.

Assign the responsibility for the safekeeping of all financial records to the treasurer and the responsibility for all other records to the secretary. They may need to delegate as the volume grows over time. A clear separation of authority exists among the board officers due to their respective roles; that separation should continue to the organization's record keeping. A third area of record keeping, still fairly new, falls outside the traditional categories of financial and nonfinancial material; it is your website.

Your Website

What you put on your website is every bit as important as all your other records. Maintain current and historical website material with the same level of diligence. The responsibility for keeping this virtual environment accurate is a little different from keeping the minutes or maintaining the bank statements; responsibility for the website may be handled by your information technology person, and, in all likelihood, may be handled offsite.

ESSENTIAL

Building a website does not have to be an expensive undertaking. User-friendly, open-source systems are available to meet the needs of the nonprofit community. Some systems also supply document management capabilities; even with limited server capacity, this will help with the backup storage of your important organizational documents.

Many nonprofits whose websites are designed by volunteers run into problems if the original designers leave and never pass on the original server information. Have a system in place for tracking server information and other relevant data.

The technical details that went into setting up the initial website must be preserved so future webmasters will be able to pick up where the earlier one left off. Make certain all technical data are retained by the organization, not just by the designer.

Agendas and Minutes

Agendas and minutes are the basic records of your actual meetings. Keep the corrected minutes and make them available for future reference. Such referencing is essential if there is a question about who said what at a meeting or when you need the details of a particular vote. The minutes become the organization's legal documents. They need to be well preserved because they will become an excellent history of the organization as well. Be sure to include the minutes of your annual meeting, the only official meeting actually required by most states, in the required annual report to the state.

Agendas

An agenda is the list of topics to be covered at any meeting of the board—or of any committee of the board. The board may decide to adopt specific rules for putting items on an agenda. At this stage, however, follow a basic form and modify it when necessary.

FACT

Many organizations keep a copy of all their meeting agendas and minutes in a spiral notebook, available to anyone in the organization who wishes to read through or examine the events of past meetings. While an electronic record is useful, having a permanent hard copy of your group's history will provide an easily accessible record.

Standardized Forms

Using standardized forms to establish your agenda, either as hard copy or as a template on your word processor, makes the task much easier and more streamlined.

The standardized form does not need to be elaborate. It should have a place for the date and the normal parts of the meeting as headers. Then fill in the template with specific details and include items such as:

- Special announcements and introduction of guests
- Approval of the minutes of the last meeting
- Changes or adjustments to the agenda
- Input from the audience or anyone other than board members
- Officer and/or staff reports
- Committee reports
- The date for the next meeting

Strongly consider a space on your agenda template to insert times, in minutes, to denote how much time to devote to an agenda item. Select a timekeeper to watch the clock throughout the meeting and enforce the time limits agreed to in the agenda. He or she should be comfortable interrupting the proceedings, if necessary, when the allotted time is up. This action will move the meeting along and ensure that every topic is covered. Be sure that everyone agrees on the agenda before the meeting begins; encourage all board members to suggest additions or deletions, as well as times allotted for discussion.

Minutes

Unlike the agenda, the minutes of the meetings of an incorporated non-profit organization are actually legal documents. They are the record of how your public organization conducts its business. Although rare, there is the possibility that someone will ask to review the minutes, and you are obligated to permit him to do so. As with the agenda, many organizations design a basic form to make the task of recording the meeting a little easier on the secretary. Many groups often make an audio recording for their archives.

Financial Reporting to the Organization

By now, it should be obvious that a large amount of effort involved with forming and operating a nonprofit organization centers on money. Not only are funds necessary to fulfill your mission and do all the things in the community you set out to do, you will need money to run the organization. Even when enough funds are available for both internal operations and external programs, money will become the largest source of unnecessary strife if the organization does not have a clear financial-reporting system.

ALERT

Covering all of the requirements for setting up bookkeeping and financial-reporting requirements for a nonprofit organization would require an entire book. This information is being presented to help you set up your organization and get it started on the right track. Once you are established, consult with a tax specialist to see precisely what your group needs to do to remain in compliance.

The IRS has specific requirements for what must be included in the annual financial report, Form 990. Because every organization operating with a federally recognized tax exemption must file this form, structure your bookkeeping from the beginning to make reporting easier. Although you may not need the detail required in the form for every internal report, it is easier to delete something than to create required documents when you are busy with other tasks.

Regardless of who will ultimately be receiving your financial reports, make sure the basics are covered. Your main accounting must include the following:

- A basic income/revenue statement, with categories for salaries or consultant fees, office/postage expenses, and revenue specified in general terms
- A balance sheet, identifying particular categories such as accounts receivable and cash on hand
- A statement of earmarked expenses, in which your expenses are clearly allocated to program services (what you "do"), fundraising, operations, or the internal details of actually running the organization
- A statement of expenses broken out by the actual program service (i.e., educational mailings, a field trip, or a public lecture)
- A support schedule that describes your organization's sources of revenue (e.g., charitable donations, membership fees, or investment income)

FACT

The financial report for the board meeting is a quick overview or snapshot of the organization's health. It needs to have enough detail to give board members a clear sense of the current situation, but it does not need to be the entire operating budget.

Although most reporting will not call for this level of detail, the IRS does, so it makes sense to design your entire financial environment to meet the most stringent requirements you will face. You can always skip unneeded details.

Reporting to the Board

To maintain its legally required oversight, the board needs to be fully engaged and up-to-date on the financial health of the organization at all times. At every board meeting, the treasurer or her designee must present an accurate financial report. The report does not have to be all-inclusive, unless a full accounting is requested. At a minimum, the financial report needs to outline current cash on hand, current and known liabilities, and all expenses expected to come due in the next month. The expenses can be fully itemized, but it is unnecessary unless specifically requested.

If the organization owns stock or other investments, include a report on their status. The whole purpose of the report is to keep the board current on finances and provide an opportunity to have necessary discussions. Developing this monthly report should be the financial committee's ongoing responsibility.

ALERT

While it is best to consult your attorney for advice specific to your situation, consider keeping confidential any financial details surrounding current or potential litigation, real-estate transactions, or employment (other than general salary information). Details of these matters should only be available to board members and whomever they designate, such as senior staff.

However, a looming problem or a situation that may become a serious problem may call for a complete discussion beyond the brief report and may warrant an adjustment to the agenda.

Reporting to the Staff and Membership

Be certain the organization's financial status is accurately explained to paid and volunteer staff as well as to the membership. Nothing can create general lack of trust throughout an organization faster than a feeling that the board is not operating in a transparent manner regarding financial reporting. Other than the parts of your budget that require confidentiality, the best option is to make your finances as open as practical.

Allowing anyone to review the budget to satisfy any questions they might have will quickly eliminate lingering concerns over how funds are spent. A small notice in your printed newsletter or on your website indicating that people are welcome, with advance notice, to review the budgets or other corporate documents will help establish the organization as open and its inner workings as transparent. People do not like thinking there are secrets, so taking the extra step to open your process will reduce issues before they occur.

Financial Reporting to the State

Most states require an annual report from every corporation, for-profit or nonprofit. They use forms that have requirements similar to those used by the federal government, although states generally do not ask for as much detail. If you set up all your financial reporting to comply with the federal standards as used in the IRS Form 990, it will be easy to extract what you need to comply with the state requests. In the packet of information that came along with your business license (not your incorporation!), you will find all the information you will need to make these very important yearly or quarterly reports.

FACT

If your state offers the option of quarterly versus yearly reporting, make certain your gross revenues are within the parameters offered. You do not want to be declared delinquent on taxes because you checked the incorrect box.

If you have any questions about state reporting requirements, call the general information number in the packet. The number is very likely at the top of the business license itself.

Financial Reporting to the Federal Government

An organization holding a tax exemption from the federal government is relieved from paying any federal corporate income taxes but not from making annual reports detailing its financial situation. An organization must tell the federal government where its operating money came from and how it was spent. The completed form—Form 990—is considered a public document, open for examination by anyone at any time with no requirement to state a reason.

QUESTION

> **Must every nonprofit organization file a Form 990?**
> No. If your receipts for the year were less than $25,000, you do not have to file the complete form but must file Form 990-N, an electronic postcard accessible only through the IRS website (*www.irs.gov*). There is no hard-copy version of this form, so all filings must be done electronically.

This transparency is one of the tradeoffs your organization must accept in exchange for nonprofit status—your organization is now public in every sense of the word. The IRS website maintains a database open to the public. The site allows anyone to search for and read Form 990 or 990-N of any nonprofit in the country holding federal tax-exempt status.

The 990-N

Since most new nonprofits will have receipts in their first year well below the $25,000 threshold requiring them to file the complete Form 990, it is appropriate to include an explanation of Form 990-N here.

The process for filing is easy and straightforward. First, go to the IRS website, locate the Form 990-N link, and set up an E-Postcard account. Before you begin filling out the form, be sure you have the following necessary information at hand:

- Your Employer Identification Number
- Tax year (be careful not to insert the current calendar year)
- Legal name and mailing address of the organization
- Name and address of the principal officer (the name of your board president is sufficient)
- Any other names the organization uses (this enables cross-referencing by people conducting searches)
- Website address, if you have one
- Confirmation that annual gross receipts are normally $25,000 or less

- A statement that the organization has terminated or is terminating (going out of business), if applicable

ESSENTIAL

Consider purchasing a quality accounting package. Most of the major brands have programs specifically designed for nonprofits, including seamless integration with the federal reporting forms. Although they may be expensive for some groups, it is money well spent.

Organizations with gross receipts over $25,000 must file the complete Form 990. If you followed the basic guideline in setting up your books in line with the needs of that form, filling out the form and filing it should not present any trouble.

Recent Changes in Form 990

If your organization is filing the full Form 990, you need to be aware of a number of significant changes that have been made to the form and the level of detail required. Specifically, Part VI seeks information regarding the board of directors, and their family and/or business relationships to one another. If your organization is new and small enough not to be required to submit the longer Form 990, these requirements will not immediately affect you. However, these requirements will affect you in the future as your organization grows.

The new requirements seek detailed information about your board of directors, such as:

- Whether they or any of their family members engaged in any business transactions with the organization
- Whether entities (of which they or their families owned more than 35 percent) engaged in any business transactions with the organization
- Whether they do business, other than as a member of the general public, with another board member, officer, or key employee, or with an entity of which another board member, officer, or key employee is a director, officer, or owner of more than 35 percent

- Whether they have a family relationship with any other director, officer, or key employee of the organization
- Whether they are a director, officer, or owner of greater than 10 percent of an entity of which another of the organization's directors, officers, or key employees is a director, officer, or owner of greater than 10 percent

Identifying Conflicts of Interest

Clearly all of these questions, which at first glance may appear intrusive, are actually intended to increase overall transparency by identifying conflicts of interest within the organization. It then becomes the responsibility of the organization to develop and adopt internal standards to eliminate actual conflicts of interest as well as any appearance of those conflicts.

ESSENTIAL

Conflict of interest arises whenever the personal or professional interests of a board member are potentially at odds with the best interests of the nonprofit organization. Any loss of public confidence and a damaged reputation are the most likely results of a poorly managed conflict of interest. Because public confidence is important to all nonprofits, it is essential to take steps to avoid even the appearance of impropriety.

Increased Scrutiny of Allowable Activities

First of all, for the vast majority of start-up nonprofit organizations, there is nothing to worry about. However, in this very fragile economy, there are people who will try to game the system. Likewise, in response to political pressure, ongoing efforts are being made by the Internal Revenue Service and others to identify people who are taking advantage of loopholes in nonprofit law. This information is presented to alert newer organizations—or those still considering making their application for federal nonprofit status.

Suspicious Minds

Due in large part to the general economic conditions in the United States, there is an increased level of scrutiny on how nonprofit organizations are raising and spending money. This increased interest has come about because a few high-profile organizations have violated the basic trust between nonprofits and the community they serve, and as a direct result, even small start-up organizations (such as the one you may be working with) are subject to increased scrutiny.

Many people who are not involved with or interested in nonprofits may believe that these groups are somehow taking advantage of the system. Of course this belief is absurd and uninformed, but it has led to political rhetoric surrounding how nonprofits function. If not corrected, these misconceptions can severely damage even long-established, highly reputable organizations.

Once Again—It's about the Money!

It is impossible to overstate the hard rule that funds donated to your organization are intended to further the mission of the organization. If you are concerned about any expenditure that is not closely associated with the reason your organization exists, stop and reassess what you are doing. Seek the advice of a tax professional; such advice may seem expensive, but it is nowhere near the cost to the organization in both money and reputation that will accrue if you are in violation of this basic rule.

ALERT

Organizations need money to raise money. Although this is an understood aspect of doing business, it does occasionally involve paying for travel and meals for potential donors. In direct response to political pressure, the IRS is stepping up its scrutiny of these expenses, so take care. Study the regulations and make every effort to follow them. You have too much at stake to risk damaging your group's reputation due to the careless oversight of fairly simple rules.

In this unstable economy, the media will broadcast any question or hint of financial impropriety—even if the concerns are later shown to be completely false. The public will remember the sensationalized accounts of any misdeeds long after the relatively dry facts are published, and by then, the damage to reputations and the funding stream has been done.

Wages and Salaries

Executive directors of nonprofit organizations who receive inflated salaries that equal or exceed their counterparts in the for-profit world have been the subject of widely published articles that generate a lot of public anger. These situations, while actually rare, are often circulated by people interested in dismantling the nonprofit sector. Always remember, as a nonprofit, your community may exercise its right to examine the internal workings of your organization, so sensitivity to the general economic conditions should become part of your organization's overall culture.

Commercial Activities

On a related note, there is increased public interest in the donations of large contributors/sponsors. If your group is still at the stage of raising operating funds from friends, family, and business associates, this probably will not affect you, but organizations soliciting and receiving sponsorship funds are encouraged to pay close attention to the laws related to exactly how those sponsors may be recognized. You do not want to be seen as an advertising billboard, yet you do need the contributions. Try to work with your corporate sponsors so everyone can win.

Engaging in Commercial Activity

The IRS is also paying particular attention to the conduct, and that may generate unrelated business income (UBI). A nonprofit organization can, under limited circumstances, engage in commercial activity, provided it pays the Unrelated Business Income (UBI) tax. If your organization is considering this type of activity or planning to solicit or accept sponsorships, it is wise to consult a tax lawyer to make certain your plans line up with current law.

If you are using the Internet as an outreach tool and as a way to market goods and services, it is important that any items you offer on your website are clearly aligned with the mission of the group and do not enter the gray area of UBI.

Recording All Publicity

Although it may seem strange to include the recording of advertising and promotion with state and federal reporting requirements, the public comes to recognize your organization through the publicity your organization generates and any additional publicity from the media. You are a public organization, and as such, people must understand what you are doing and decide to support your efforts with their time or money. Much of their decision will depend on what is broadly defined as "publicity."

From the moment your organization establishes itself, develop a means to collect and retain any printed or broadcast articles, newsletters, web links, and videos that make it to the web. Collect and retain anything and everything that portrays your organization in a positive light.

Record of Publicity Needed for Your 1023

Your application for tax-exempt status, Form 1023, includes a section that asks for a narrative, or a description, of exactly what your organization does. As part of the narrative, you can attach newsletters, publicity, or other material that will support what you are saying. High-quality documentation will improve the look of your overall application. As soon as you have incorporated, you can and should begin collecting and saving everything that might show what you are doing and what you intend to do.

Record of Publicity Needed for Grants

Simply put, if you cannot show a potential grant-maker or other funder evidence of the work you are doing by the publicity you have generated, you are placing your organization at a severe disadvantage.

FACT

Earned media is the current catch phrase used to describe coverage your organization has earned; that is, some event so noteworthy that an element of the media decided to cover it. Showing potential funders your earned media is essential in securing their involvement.

Consider producing a package of self-produced and earned media to show to current and potential supporters. Everyone loves to see themselves and their projects on television or in the newspaper, so preparing a presentation of clips and video will be a fine way to store the material and show it off.

CHAPTER 10

Developing a Budget

Budget development should begin long before you actually apply for your federal nonprofit status. In fact, you should begin developing your budget as soon as you form as an organization and determine what projects you want to take, how much they will cost, and how you expect to pay for them. At this point, you understand what it means to be a charitable organization and can begin to look into ways to fund your planned projects and operations.

Be Realistic

Creating a budget for any type of project will determine what your organization can and cannot do. So much will ultimately come down to money, and the numbers represented in the budget will give you a lot of information. It is therefore a responsibility that requires great care. The trick in developing a budget is to merge the desires and dreams of the organization with the reality of securing the funds necessary to pay for them.

Under no circumstances should an organization—especially a new nonprofit—try to live beyond its means. Everyone must understand that the group can only do what it can pay for, so the budget must reflect realistic income projections as well as proposed expenses.

Initial budgets start out with estimates of what items will cost, especially if you don't know precise numbers. Likewise, until you truly know how your actual income will line up, you are in a fragile zone of uncertainty.

Do Your Research

Unless you are trying to reinvent the wheel, people within your community will be able to share with you the numbers you need to get your budget into a usable form. The real-dollar amounts that relate to the basic expenses associated with internal operations (office supplies, rent, and even miscellaneous permits) are straightforward and should be simple to collect.

It will be far more difficult to establish concrete income streams. For the purpose of developing your initial budget, you may have no choice but to enter speculative numbers and then be prepared to adjust them as your preliminary research bears results. Once you have identified your income streams, put them into your budget.

The main task at this stage is to create budget lines as placeholders. As hard numbers become apparent and the placeholders are filled in, you will be able to plan your programming and other operations while minimizing the risk of overextending yourself.

Think Conservatively

Even with all the planning you are doing, it is still going to be difficult to get through the first few years of your organization's existence. Taking an over-reaching budget to potential financial supporters will leave them scratching their heads.

ESSENTIAL

Always remember that grant-makers and others involved in philanthropy live in the same world you do. They are just as aware of the regional and global financial picture as everyone else. They also understand the value and role of the nonprofit sector in the broader community.

Until you are firmly established, you will face stiff competition for operational funding, so it will not be beneficial to show inflated numbers in your proposed income lines. Show honest expectations of revenue—such as conservative estimates of memberships, ticket sales, or projected revenue from fees for service—with the caveat that you are presenting preliminary plans, not hard numbers.

Budget Projections

As a brand-new organization with no financial history, you will have to use the available data you have to explain to a number of unique audiences where your organization wants to be in the future. If you were able simply to open your books and show a funder or the IRS what you have been doing, it would be easy. However, since you do not have a verifiable record of accomplishment, you will need to be creative.

Furthermore, once you are up and running, budget projections will continue to be part of your ever-evolving strategic planning. Strategic and business plans will always have a major financial component.

The First Audience: The IRS

To complete your application for tax exemption (Form 1023), you will need to provide a three-year budget. However, you may not have existed for three years, much less have three years of a budget, so take the budget for however many months you have been operating and multiply the numbers to show a three-year projection.

ALERT

Operate as though your organization is already an established non-profit. Have accurate records and financial accounting well before you apply for your nonprofit determination. You must establish a record of accomplishment to show that your clear intention is to comply with the nonprofit standards set by the IRS.

Where your money comes from is every bit as important as how you get it. Be sure to account for the sources of your projected income.

The Second Audience: Your Internal Organization

Although the IRS requires a three-year budget as part of its application, your board may want to see a five-year projection, which will become part of the organization's strategic plan and, in turn, your business plan. Thinking about and planning from a budgetary standpoint five years into the future will make sense when you begin to evaluate funding opportunities and understand the application cycles many funders use. Likewise, planning for major expenditures should not happen quickly. Major expenses must wait until the organization's revenue is at a level necessary to support those expenditures. Both the expenses and income projections must be included in your five-year plan.

Identifying Income Sources

Income sources are extremely important to identify in your budget, in large part because it will show the IRS that you are meeting the one-third test and are indeed a publicly supported organization. In the event you are unable to meet that threshold for public support, you may lose your status as a public charity, so understanding the requirement is very serious. As you put together a working budget, begin thinking in terms of the IRS requirements, so your group will be well prepared for the tax-exempt application and then remain in compliance.

As you become more familiar with the IRS regulations, you may find they actually help your organization function along the lines you originally intended. Most of the regulations exist to keep groups true to their original intention—with a lot of legal jargon thrown in for good measure.

Possible Revenue Sources

When you are developing your initial budget, few things are more difficult than identifying revenue sources. Everyone around you will find ways to spend money; to develop a budget, however, you must identify sources to raise funds. Most nonprofit organizations start out with barely enough money to rent a room to meet in, so the idea of looking beyond the immediate to attaining viability can be a challenge.

ESSENTIAL

The one-third support test requires any organization applying for or seeking to maintain its status as a public charity, such as a 505(c)(3), to receive at least one-third of its total support from government entities, from contributions made directly or indirectly by the general public, or from a combination of these sources.

Remember how important it was to evaluate your community and make contacts. Now is the time to use those fledgling relationships. The local business community, the media outlets, and the people you see every day may become your future individual or corporate sponsors, and you should include them as such in your budget.

Evaluate your membership options. If members pay dues, enter them as both current and projected income.

As you identify appropriate grants, include those sources as possible or projected income. Do not include these sources if the grant is something you have no chance of securing. This is not a time to live in a fantasy.

If you will be receiving a fee for services and are able to provide an estimate of the projected income through those fees, that is an income source; include it in your projected budget. The sales of any product that complies with the strict requirements regarding "unrelated business income" are also eligible for inclusion as projected income. Consult a professional tax advisor who is familiar with your situation before including any sales in your projected income.

Unrelated Business Income

Unrelated business income (UBI) can be tricky when developing your budget. If you have UBI, you must pay taxes on that income. If it becomes more than incidental in nature, you are risking your tax-exempt status.

There are three main criteria used to determine if your activities are UBI.

1. Would the activity generally be considered a trade or business?
2. Is the activity a regular, repeated occurrence as opposed to a one-time special situation?
3. Is the activity not substantially related to your organization's exempt purpose?

If you answered yes to any of these questions, the income source you may be considering may well be unrelated business income for which you will need to file a Form 990-T—and yes, the T stands for tax. You will then be obligated to pay the tax due.

Organizations are allowed UBI, but not to any substantial degree. If you are planning such activities, contact a tax advisor or the IRS directly to make certain you are on firm ground.

Projected Capital Expenses

Capital expenses will require a unique line or a complete section in your start-up budget; you must keep those expenses separate from your other operating costs. A capital expense is money you plan to spend on things that are going to last longer than one year, are often fairly expensive, and are necessary for the functioning of your organization. It might involve the purchase of computers, a vehicle, or even a building.

Before you can figure out what you will need in the future and what dollar amount to attach to those needs, take stock of what you currently have. Capital expenses will be different for every organization, and to some extent, they will be program-specific.

A direct benefit of the ongoing self-assessments the board members should be undertaking is the ability to identify needs that they believe would help the organization fulfill its mission. Some of those needs will involve capital expenses spread out over many years, which will also form the beginning of these line items in your budget.

Office equipment is a very common capital expense. For budget purposes, keep the equipment separate from the office supplies, such as paper and pens, because the equipment will outlast the supplies.

The reasons to keep a large capital expense separate are numerous:

1. The costs involved may overshadow your general operating expenses, making it appear you are already in the red without having done a thing.
2. It is likely the actual payments for these items will be prorated over many months, if not years. You must be able to show that clearly in your budget, especially if you are projecting the budget out three, five, or seven years.
3. It will be to your advantage to point directly to capital expenses when discussing your funding needs with potential supporters. Many individuals and philanthropic organizations are restricted from directly supporting operations. Help offsetting capital expenses is permitted because it is considered a long-term investment in your organization.

Depreciation

No discussion of capital expenses would be complete without an understanding of depreciation. Factoring depreciation into your projected budget allows for accurate forecasting.

Depreciation is a means of measuring the amount of monetary value something loses from the time your organization purchases it to a set time in your fiscal year. It gives a very accurate picture of the health of the organization. You will use formulas to determine the value of depreciation of anything of value you report on your Form 990, so having these values in your current and projected budget is a good idea.

Calculating Depreciation

Generally, depreciation is calculated by dividing the cost of the asset by its useful life. If a $100,000 item, also called an asset, has a useful life of ten years, then you calculate depreciation by dividing $100,000 by 10 to get $10,000 per year.

Each year the organization must show that $10,000 as an expense of doing business, and these numbers need to appear in your projected budget. These calculations will also be entered on Form 990, which you will complete each year. Adding the total amount of depreciation registered by all active assets gives your organization's total depreciation expense for that year, which is the figure that appears in line 42 of the form.

Adding the total amount of depreciation charged to date against each individual asset since it was first acquired gives the accumulated depreciation shown in line 57b. Dividing line 57c by line 42a gives the accounting age of property, plant, and equipment.

There is a good reason for this level of detail about depreciation in a discussion about projected budgets. First, these numbers should appear in your budget. Second, these numbers will give any prospective funder an accurate—if sometimes unflattering—snapshot of your real financial health.

ESSENTIAL

Put simply, the higher the number representing your accounting age, the older your property; the lower the number, the more up-to-date your investment. The most frequent use of these numbers is to compare one nonprofit against another. It might not seem fair or right, but that is how it works.

If your accounting age shows you are not able to replace worn-out equipment and are postponing the purchase of big-ticket items, it means you need a little extra assistance in that area and should be focusing your fundraising efforts accordingly. On the good side, if you are just starting out and the organization's main assets consist of secondhand office equipment and furniture from the local thrift shop, the accounting age will be very low and will look quite good in comparison to a group that owns a lot of things but is not able to upgrade regularly.

Projected Staffing Expenses

When a nonprofit organization is first formed, everyone may be willing to volunteer their time and expertise because they believe strongly in the mission. However, in terms of developing your budget, you should begin contemplating eventual staffing needs. It may be a year or two before there is movement to compensate personnel, but having a line in your budget to accommodate that possibility will place the group well ahead of the game. Start by looking at the board's assessment of where the group should be in the next few years and pick out instances where it is clear the group may need an "outside" person to assist. The first couple of years you may only need a compensated consultant to help with a board retreat or an accountant to review your books or prepare your Form 990.

A Word about Compensation

One of the common misunderstandings about nonprofits is the notion that no one can be paid. Nothing is further from the truth, but there are a few basic rules that need to be clearly reflected in both the current and projected budget.

First, anyone employed or contracted must do so at an agreed-upon fee for his or her services. A sliding-scale fee is not acceptable or legal, for it would allow that person to benefit personally from the organization. If this situation came up in a for-profit corporation, any type of negotiation between the organization and a potential employee would be acceptable as long as minimum wages were being met. Not so in a nonprofit.

Similarly, if it appears that someone is receiving a fee well above the community standards for a similar position, the organization runs the risk of being penalized for an excess benefit transaction. These fees will be reported on Form 990. Having to deal with excess benefit transactions can lead to increasingly severe penalties, up to and including a revocation of your tax-exempt status.

In-Kind Labor

The time and expertise of your volunteers have real monetary value that your budget needs to reflect. Although no money is changing hands, work is being done. If the people doing that work charged the organization market fees, it would represent a substantial sum.

It is therefore appropriate to assign a monetary value to the tasks and determine the fair value of the donated labor needed. The monetary value of in-kind services should accurately reflect what that person would charge for doing the task. You can determine the real rate by calling a few people who do that work for a living.

Organizational or Administrative Expenses

Working up projections for the general organization, or administrative expenses, is your final step in creating a budget. This is the part of budget development where you focus only on the organization and what it needs to continue to function.

ALERT

Under no circumstances should you allow your administrative expenses to exceed 35 percent of your budget. Most individuals will question any organization if it budgets more than that amount for its administration and not for the services it provides.

Your administrative expenses include funds necessary for general operation; for example, expenses incurred for board meetings and retreats, in-house training sessions, building rental, legal fees, necessary travel, and similar activities.

An Ideal Budget Breakdown

As you begin to factor in budget items related to administration, it is good to strive for an 80–10–10 goal.

- 80 percent of your expenses to your charitable purpose
- 10 percent of your expenses to administration
- 10 percent of your expenses to fundraising

Of course, these are guidelines based on best-case scenarios, but they give you a baseline. Investment funds kept in savings accounts are not part of these percentages. That money is carried on the books as investments. The only administrative expense associated with savings accounts might be a transaction, but otherwise nothing of any consequence.

It's Okay to Be Low

As an organization forms and gets organized, it is normal to rely on volunteer labor and to do as much as possible on the cheap. This kind of planning will help keep your organization expenses low for your first few years because all money will go into programming and outreach.

This is a very good strategy; try to maintain it as long as possible. Funders look favorably on an organization that actually does the work of its mission and does not spend excessive amounts of money on itself.

CHAPTER 11

Bank Accounts

Opening a bank account for yourself or your family is a simple matter, but opening an account for a nonprofit organization or an organization in the preapplication stage is more complicated. This chapter will cover the forms you need to take with you, the many types of accounts banks and credit unions have specifically for nonprofits, and the mechanics of setting up accounts with multiple check-signers and deposit-only accounts for fundraising activities.

Be Prepared

Nothing is more frustrating than finally being ready to open an account and finding that the staff of your neighborhood bank can't help you. Changing banking regulations may require multiple documents to prove that your small, start-up nonprofit is legitimate and that you are authorized to open the account.

ALERT

Be sure to take the original articles, which should be stamped with the state seal, and your original state or city business license. More often now, bank personnel require original documentation from individuals who want to open bank accounts on behalf of businesses.

The days of opening a personal savings account and attaching a DBA (doing business as) to your name are quickly becoming history. If you are prepared and remember to take the required documentation, the process should run smoothly.

Authorized Check-Signers

Be sure to maintain a clear separation of responsibilities among the board officers. Similarly, maintaining a basic system of checks and balances within a small nonprofit is easily handled by determining who will be authorized to conduct bank business on behalf of the organization.

Although there are no hard rules in this area, common practice suggests it is best to limit the check-signers to the board president, the board treasurer, and one other person. That individual may be a trusted volunteer or the lead person required to draw funds in the course of a major project.

The other check-signer can rotate as necessary, and there may be extended periods when no one has that position. When the organization grows enough to have an operations manager or director, that person will customarily become a check-signer simply to facilitate his responsibilities.

Pre-Signed Checks

No one will officially recommend keeping a small number of pre-signed checks, but it is a common practice, especially in small organizations run by volunteers. The purpose, as the term suggests, is to have a few checks that already have one signature and only need the second signature to make the check legal.

FACT

Your home bank, the actual bank building where you opened the account, maintains a file of signature cards. These cards contain all the signatures for every account opened at that bank. Due to recent changes in overall security, a new person must accompany the person already authorized to complete the process. Faxed or e-mailed signatures will not suffice.

If your account only requires one signature, then you are able to use a check immediately. It just isn't possible to predict when an emergency will arise that requires immediate access to the checking account. If one signer is out of town or otherwise unavailable, having that check kept in a safe location known to very few people will make all the difference.

Check Limits

On a similar track, the bank or credit union may be able to establish a maximum amount any one check can draw. The bank can print this number on every check or attach a notice to your account.

ATM Cards

Most banks that offer business accounts will also offer a business ATM card. Use these cards as you use your personal debit cards.

ESSENTIAL

As a group, decide if you are comfortable having only one signature on every check or if you will require two. This is not to question any person's integrity; it's about what is best for the organization as a whole. An alternative is to require one signature for amounts up to a certain level and two signatures above that level. Banks will always work with you on these details if you ask.

As with check-signing, your group must decide who will have the access code and use the ATM card. There are generally built-in limits on withdrawals to lessen the chance of mischief, but be sure to verify this with your bank.

Types of Banks

When you are starting out as a new nonprofit, it is imperative to find the bank that will best suit your needs. Selecting a bank requires a basic understanding of what the various types of banks actually do and why there are different types of banks. Keep in mind that as banking laws change, so too will the services a particular bank might offer.

Commercial Banks

A commercial bank works with businesses. Businesses have unique needs that consumers do not have. For example, some businesses need a commercial bank that can accommodate a large volume of credit card payments and cash deposits. Commercial banks also often function as retail banks, serving individuals along with businesses, and usually provide basic services such as savings and checking accounts, loans for real and capital purchases, lines of credit, letters of credit, payment and transaction processing, and foreign exchange.

Retail Banks

A retail bank works with consumers, otherwise known as retail customers, providing basic banking services to the general public, including checking and savings accounts; certificates of deposit (CDs); safe deposit boxes;

mortgages; auto, boat, and miscellaneous home-improvement loans; and unsecured and revolving loans such as credit cards. Retail banks are often located on urban street corners; you probably use a retail bank for your personal checking account. In addition to helping consumers, retail banks also serve businesses, so they, too, can serve as commercial banks.

Credit Unions

Credit unions are nonprofit organizations owned by the "members" or customers; they traditionally strive for service over profitability. These organizations have the same types of personnel as banks. Upper management consists of a board of directors that makes decisions on credit union operations. This board is composed of elected volunteers who are also credit union members who want a say in the operation of the business.

FACT

A line of credit is a pool of available money that you can borrow. When you get a line of credit, you can draw up to a predetermined limit. This is slightly different than applying for individual loans to meet a specific need; the line of credit is already approved for your organization to use if and when necessary.

Credit unions are required to limit their membership to people who have a common bond. This bond may be geographic, religious, or occupational, but it must exist or the entity risks losing its status as a credit union.

Credit unions typically offer the same products and services as larger banks. However, some will choose not to offer every product and service, because they do not do the same volume of business as larger banks. Banks can afford to have loss leaders, products that get customers in the door but do not bring in much money themselves. Credit unions are more likely to offer only the products and services that a large portion of the membership is likely to use.

Deposits are insured very much like bank deposits, but the two types of institutions are insured by different organizations. The National Credit Union Share Insurance Fund (NCUSIF), financed by the credit unions and not the federal government, handles all deposit insurance in a credit union.

This insurance offers the same level of protection as the more familiar Federal Deposit Insurance Corporation (FDIC), which is financed by the federal government.

Investment Banks

Investment banks help organizations use investment markets. For example, when a company wants to raise money by issuing stocks or bonds, an investment bank helps it through the process. Investment banks also consult on mergers and acquisitions.

They work primarily in the investment markets and do not take customer deposits. However, some large investment banks also serve as commercial banks or retail banks, which is why they are discussed here.

Savings and Loan Associations and Cooperative Banks

Savings and loan associations (S&Ls) were originally established in the nineteenth century to provide a means for factory workers and others of limited financial means to purchase homes. After World War II, the U.S. government helped build the savings and loan industry by insuring deposits on savings accounts. This encouraged people to save their money, despite federally regulated low interest rates.

Those funds were then used to make loans we all know as mortgages; in particular, the thirty-year mortgage allows a homeowner to pay back the loan with a series of low monthly payments over a long period. With the increased popularity of the money market, fewer people were saving in the more traditional manner, meaning there was less money for savings and loans to lend as mortgages.

Currently, S&Ls handle most traditional banking needs, including business transactions. They are for-profit corporations with investors who hope to realize a profit on those investments.

Online Banks

Online banks are banks that are primarily (or exclusively) used on the Internet. They allow the customer more choice and flexibility. Online banks often offer better rates than physical banks. They claim they do not have the overhead and expenses associated with brick-and-mortar banks, which allows them to pass the savings on to you.

These banks offer most of the same services as retail banks. However, keep these points in mind when dealing with online banks:

1. Obtain and retain the physical address and telephone number of the bank in the event there is a problem.
2. Maintain extra care when sending sensitive information. You are now handling more than your personal funds; you are managing funds for the organization.

Types of Accounts

Just as with your family's banking, the most basic accounts for your organization will be a savings and a checking account. There are more options, but it is good to understand these basic accounts first.

Savings Accounts

A bank savings account is designed to hold money to which you do not need immediate access. When contrasted with checking accounts, savings accounts tend to pay slightly higher interest rates.

Savings accounts offer easy access to your cash. In other words, your money is liquid (meaning you can make a withdrawal easily and quickly). However, savings accounts are not as liquid as checking accounts; you can get money from a checking account simply by writing a check. Banks vary with respect to policies for withdrawals, so make certain their policies and your needs are identical before opening the account.

Deposit-Only Accounts

Deposit-only accounts are an excellent way for the public to contribute to your organization. Your bank or credit union will set up an account, usually with a memorable name, and anyone at any time may make a deposit. The contributor will have a record of the deposit for his or her records, and the deposit will go directly into your organization's auxiliary account or into your working account.

Checking Accounts

Checking accounts are similar to savings accounts in that they offer a safe place to keep money you do not need immediately. The bank will issue checks in your organization's name, and you can use them to pay bills.

Unlike personal checking accounts, most financial institutions charge fees associated with check use for corporate accounts (including nonprofits). As you consider all the options, look into the fees you'll be charged to write checks.

Certificates of Deposit

Certificates of deposit (CDs) are debt instruments issued by banks and other financial institutions to encourage individual or organizational investors to put money in their bank. The investor receives a set rate of interest in exchange for lending the bank or credit union money for a predetermined length of time. Maturities on certificates of deposit can range from a few weeks to several years. The interest rate your organization will earn increases in proportion to the amount of time the money is in the CD.

QUESTION

What does maturity mean?
Maturity is the length of time you have agreed to allow the CD to remain in the bank before deciding to withdraw it or renew it. The time period might be six months, one year, three years, or any other time offered by the bank. If you withdraw your funds from the CD before its maturity date, the bank will charge a penalty that affects any interest you have earned.

One of the advantages of a CD is that your organization can calculate the earnings you can expect at the outset when you take out the CD. Certificates of deposit are fully insured by the FDIC and earn slightly more interest than a basic savings or checking account. This makes CDs an easy, safe way to save money in the long term.

But there is a tradeoff. To earn the highest interest rates, you have to opt for longer maturity, which means you lose access to the funds or have to accept a far lower interest rate if you need to cash them out early.

Money Markets

Money markets offer many of the same benefits as CDs with the added features of a checking account. Technically speaking, a money market is more or less a mutual fund that attempts to keep its share price at a constant level of $1. Professional money managers will take the funds you deposit in the money market and invest them in minimal-risk instruments such as Treasury bills, savings bonds, and CDs. Your organization will receive payments from the interest the money market earns.

Investors can open a money market account at most financial institutions. Generally, funds are accessed with checks.

Depositing money in a money market is as easy as depositing cash into a savings or checking account. Cash is immediately available for other investments or other needs.

On the downside, some financial institutions limit the number of checks that can be drawn against the account in any given month. The rate of interest is also directly proportional to the investor's level of deposited assets—not to maturity, as is the case with CDs. The obvious downside is that money markets are disproportionately beneficial to wealthier investors who will receive a higher interest rate.

Establishing Financial Credibility

Unfortunately, there is no simple trick for an organization to establish its financial credibility. Regardless of how you and your organization choose to manage your funds, it is going to be a constant, unrelenting struggle. The sooner you recognize that fact, the sooner you can make plans.

When many people hear the term *start-up*, they wince, thinking immediately of some harebrained scheme that has no chance of success. Some people also have a negative connotation of the term *nonprofit organization,* so start-up nonprofit organizations often find it difficult to establish themselves as credible entities. However, there are a number of basic practices and programs you can adopt at the very beginning that will assist in the process.

Maintaining Confidence in the Community

Meeting all your financial obligations, major or minor, is essential to establishing and maintaining your overall credibility in the community. Much of this responsibility falls to your treasurer or that person's designee. They must make certain checks are in the mail on time and no late fees or overdrafts appear on your bank statements.

FACT

Just as trouble repaying loans or defaulting on bills will affect personal credit, the same thing can happen to your organization. Even though incorporating with the state protects individual board members from being directly liable for actions leading to poor credit for the group, having a poor credit score will severely affect your organization's ability to carry on.

Go Ahead and Brag

When you have good financial news, spread the word. You are going to get your financial footing in due course, and those grant applications are going to bring the results you desire. When they do, it is both natural and perfectly acceptable (unless you've specifically been requested to keep quiet) to tell your membership, the broader community, and especially other grant-makers.

As soon as you receive funds in a competitive cycle, you are going to find increased interest from other funders. It is a curious fact that very few people or funders want to be the first in line. The hardest task is securing that first award.

Get to Know Your Banker

The days of the town banker who knows everyone and is always willing to lend a hand or offer advice are generally gone. However, it is important to establish solid working relationships with people in your local bank or credit union who specialize in nonprofit businesses.

The large retail and commercial banks have people who only work with the nonprofit sector, and a growing number of credit unions are following suit. Nonprofits now represent a huge business sector for banks, and entire departments are dedicated to nonprofit customers.

ESSENTIAL

When you open the accounts, ask for a meeting with a representative of the bank's nonprofit department. If that person does not work at your branch, arrange to meet her, or at least schedule a phone call. Either way, get to know that person as soon as you can.

You'll value the relationship you have with these bankers when you need their assistance to secure a loan or establish a line of credit to improve some part of your operations. Many newer nonprofits simply will not have the financial track record needed for a conventional loan, so they need to know someone in the institution who is familiar with alternative programs or how to navigate the system to get you the funds you need.

Invite Bank Representatives to Your Events

Your financial paperwork will give the people in your bank or credit union most of the information they need. If you are applying for a loan, perhaps for construction or to remodel an existing facility, most of the review process is impersonal.

However, inviting bank employees to visit your site or attend one of your programs will help make them aware of who you are, what you are doing, and why you are doing it. Invite them into your organization as members of the community, not just as bankers. They may be able to refer you to someone in the community who is interested in your mission and may be able to help repair a leaky roof or upgrade your office equipment.

These visits will give everyone involved in the management of your organization an opportunity to chat informally and learn about one another. A personal connection can accomplish far more than a paper application. With an established relationship, the possibilities for increased cooperation will also grow.

Maintain Communication

As your business plan evolves or as you consider major capital expenses, stay in touch with the nonprofit specialists in your bank. They will have valid ideas and suggestions that you may never have considered. Although they sell financial products, they understand the process you are currently going through as well as what you may need in the future. They represent a terrific resource, so use them.

CHAPTER 12

Fundraising

More misconceptions and illusions are associated with fundraising than with any other element of organizing and operating a nonprofit. This chapter will lay it all out. A nonprofit is not a funding magnet; you will probably not have people knocking down your doors wanting to donate vast sums of money. However, with diligent effort, you will find that there are many sources of both cash and in-kind funding.

Commitment from the Entire Organization

To be successful, every member of the organization must share the task of raising the money necessary to operate. Expecting "someone else" to be responsible for maintaining the needed revenue stream while waiting to spend the money is a recipe for trouble.

As your organization matures, you may want to bring onboard a professional fundraiser who is already familiar with your unique environment. Even so, this person will require everyone's assistance to meet the goals you have set.

Committees of the Board

A standing responsibility of every committee established in your by-laws should be to assist in securing funding for any project or other expense item it recommends for the organization. This is especially applicable to programming, building, or similar committees that will be researching and proposing ways the organization can fulfill its mission, usually involving the appropriation of funds.

ESSENTIAL

Consider establishing clearly understood benchmarks for each part of the organization to meet during the course of your yearly fundraising efforts. Present these goals from a positive perspective and make them part of the ongoing board, volunteer, and staff development.

Require your committees to suggest ways to offset the expenses involved in their proposals. This task will help spread the overall fundraising responsibility and provide a true sense of ownership for active committee members. Not only are they going to be proposing action items to the board, but they will also be offering concrete suggestions on how to pay for their proposals.

Community Volunteers

In the early stage of your organization, everyone will need to share some of the responsibility for fundraising. The general orientation given to all new volunteers should include an overview of the finances that allow your organization to function.

They don't need to read and evaluate the projected five-year budget, but they do need to be aware that the organization, while it is a nonprofit, is not isolated from the many challenges in the general economy. All outreach material—newsletters, websites, everything that is designed for general distribution to your volunteers—should include a way for people to get information about contributing as well as make it easy to make a donation on the spot. Your fundraising must become as much a part of your organization as everything else you do.

Ever-Expanding Circles

Well before you formally incorporate and make your application for federal tax-exempt status, there will be a small group of people who form the core of the organization. That group may evolve into your initial board of directors, but even as an informal group of friends and associates, they represent the nucleus of an organization. One step from that core group will be people who attended the initial organizational meeting or others the core group knows personally.

Working outward from that group, there are people who are interested in the group but are not sure what they want to do. The broader community will follow that. As you begin to add your own rings to this group, you will find that people fall into two clear categories.

People Interested in the Organization

Some people are drawn to groups as a social outlet, and their value cannot be underestimated. They often have a knack for working through issues involving process and never-ending bureaucracy, which other people avoid. When you have an issue with the city over parking or noise, these are the people you will be glad you have on your side.

People Interested in the Mission

You will also draw some people who are sincerely interested in your mission but who have no interest in the organizational side of things. These people can share their passion for the work your organization does and inspire others to donate money or time.

The Board and Their Families

Among the first questions you will face from any potential funder will be her need to understand the level of direct financial support already secured from your board of directors. It is an appropriate question, so do not be offended. It is normal for any individual/person or any representatives of other organizations to want to know that before you seek funds to carry on your mission, that you have fully exhausted every area of support in your immediate circle.

FACT

There is a curious belief that all nonprofits and all funders are linked, each waiting for the other to make the first move. Nothing could be further from the truth! Organizations have to ask strangers for money not because they want to, but because they have exhausted all other sources of revenue.

Never be ashamed when asking for money to carry out your mission. There is an entire cottage industry of people who make these requests as well as those who consult with groups to develop comprehensive fundraising campaigns and ultimately make the requests themselves.

Minimum Cash Contributions

You need to determine the actual percentage of the annual operating budget you are going to seek directly from the board (which, by extension, includes family members). Prepare to make this figure known to other funders when they ask. Many organizations require a minimum level of financial support of all sitting board members as a direct means of maintaining their involvement.

The amount of the yearly contribution does not need to be excessive, and it should reflect the actual abilities of the board members to secure funds. However, make it known that you are serious about the need to raise money and are willing to lead by example.

Board Member In-Kind Contributions

If you decide to establish a policy requiring prospective and current board members to be responsible for fundraising during the period they serve on the board, consider making periodic in-kind contributions an option to meet that commitment. There are very likely things of value the organization needs, which an in-kind or other noncash donation of approximate value would satisfy.

Board members could donate office space, legal services, income-producing rental property, and other services.

Direct Appeals to Existing Contacts

From a fundraising perspective, your existing contacts are the most important people in your universe. They will form the base, the core, of all subsequent fundraising activities.

Begin thinking about establishing and maintaining a database designed for nonprofits. One of the best databases in terms of quality and functionality is Kintera, a system developed and maintained by Blackbaud (*www.kintera.com*). At the other end of the spectrum is an excellent program designed and maintained for start-up nonprofits that may not have the money to spend on a Kintera system. It is the Organizers' Database (*www.organizersdb.org*).

Now you must establish a database to track your existing contacts, as well as future contacts that will become your donor base. As simple as it may sound, the only way people will know that you need money is if you tell them. You must maintain a current, accurate list of everyone who needs to know about your work.

Special Perks

Update contacts in your database on everything you are doing so they feel part of the exciting adventure. Consider offering special meetings or tours limited to your donors and supporters. Tours and one-on-one lunches with board members or coordinators are a great way to thank these people for their support and provide the personal attention that is essential to maintaining long-term relationships.

Keeping to a Schedule

Your organization needs to become as much a part of the families of your supporters as are their kids and pets. If you plan to send out holiday notices or solicitations, make it a priority to do so on time. If you intend to have members-only receptions during the year, budget those activities into your yearly plans. Your early supporters will be the base of all your subsequent fundraising activities.

Establish a History

Maintain careful, complete, and accurate records of everything you do, including your meetings and financial transactions, any media coverage, and your public relations material. This level of record keeping is necessary to meet legal requirements and to establish a paper trail. In this context, a paper trail is a verifiable history of your organization for presentation to potential funders.

FACT

Collecting your organizational history will give you as much credibility as possible when approaching a potential funder, so keep that in mind at all times. Operate on the assumption that funders do not know you and are going to be wary of anyone they do not know coming along and asking for money. You must prove your legitimacy, and having a historical record will help you do so.

If your organization is so new that the history is too short to present with any degree of confidence, adjust your narrative slightly to explore the history of the individuals who started the organization and tell their stories. Explain how they came together to form this new organization. Press clippings of their activities will give the reader the needed tangible record of who you are even if the articles don't discuss the organization itself.

Keep a Scrapbook

Sometimes the simplest practices are the most effective. Maintaining a scrapbook of your organization through photographs and media clippings will do more to show who you are than more high-tech methods. The book can be a simple loose-leaf binder filled with material about your founders, your board, and your current activities. It will bring everything into perspective.

Competition for Grants

There are many misconceptions about how the world of grants and philanthropy works; however, the entire process is relatively straightforward. As the number of tax-exempt organizations continues to grow at an amazing rate, many grant-makers have developed formal screening requirements to weed out inappropriate applications. These preliminary screenings occur well before the applications are formally evaluated.

The Common Grant Application

Many regions of the country have a version of a common grant application, which grant-makers and grant-seekers agree to use. Your local grant-writing association, discussed in the next section, will have information particular to your area. The national listing and general information is available on the web at *www.commongrantapplication.com*.

Grant-Writing Associations

Many areas of the country have associations for grant-writers to meet one another, network, and further enhance their profession. These organizations can generally be located through an Internet search or the local telephone book. Consider having anyone directly involved in your development activities join these groups.

Every grant-writing association functions differently, but there will be regular meetings, often luncheons or something similar, where regional grant-makers are invited to share their expertise and perspectives to help their counterparts, the grant-writers, work more effectively. Approach these organizations when your organization is starting up; after all, everyone in the room was, at some point, exactly where you are now.

ESSENTIAL

Grants must be part of your overall fundraising plan but not the complete extent of that plan. The old adage of not placing all your eggs in one basket certainly applies to fundraising.

Public and Private Funding

As your board and consultants develop a fundraising plan, begin breaking down how you would like to spend the money (operations, capital development, staffing, programming, etc.) and where you intend to raise it. You have two clear choices: public financing or private financing.

The IRS has already helped you by mandating that a minimum amount—one third—of your total income must come from public sources. As you sketch out your fundraising plan, begin with that number.

For example, if your overall projected budget is $60,000, you must show that at least $20,000 came from public sources and the remaining $40,000 from private or nonpublic sources. Show hard numbers representing these percentages in the preliminary budget you provide as part of your application for tax exemption and then stick to it in the future. The IRS monitors a new 501(c)(3) organization for five years to make certain it is indeed operating as a public charity and is securing at least the minimum percentage of its operating budget from public sources.

On a basic level, public funding can be broken down as:

• Government funding
• Funding from other public charities
• Other

Government Funding

Government funding can include any level of government, from federal to local, and any agencies within those levels. It can include everything from arts commissions and education departments to public service agencies and municipal humane societies. If the entity receives funds from taxes and has as part of its purpose the requirement to fund activities of nonprofit organizations, it falls under this umbrella. Of course, to learn what government grants are available is a tremendous task; begin by researching agencies with a connection to your particular mission.

Tap into the many listservs and newsletters maintained by the agencies and departments you work with to understand their funding cycles and application deadlines and to get a general feel for what may be available to you as a new nonprofit.

Foundation Funding

Securing funds from other charities is considered public funding when it involves another nonprofit organization whose purpose is to contribute funds to organizations such as yours.

Since the funding organization is operating as a tax-exempt charity and also raised its money, its funds to you are considered public for the purpose of this discussion.

Other Funding Sources

Other public funding might include members of the general public acting as individual contributors, income derived from membership fees, or gross receipts for services directly related to the mission or the tax-exempt function. Box office revenue from public events sponsored by an exempt arts organization is another example of public funding.

Private Funding

Private funding will come primarily from corporate entities and private endowments, particularly at the start-up phase. In return, these contributors will receive good publicity and that ever-important tax deduction. Corporate support often takes the form of advertising (either at your events or in publications), which brings the donor valuable publicity and helps your organization secure much-needed funds.

FACT

You may come across the term *supporting organization,* with the IRS classification of 509(a). A supporting organization is a public charity whose sole charitable purpose is to support another exempt organization—in almost all cases, another public charity. The phrase can cover a wide variety of organizations from endowment funds for universities to entities that provide essential services for hospital systems. It is worth researching these organizations to see if their mandate includes funding nonprofits like yours.

Many larger corporations have a charitable arm, often identified as a foundation, whose purpose is to assist nonprofits in their service area or in the community where their employees live. Identify those corporate-sponsored foundations and begin to develop the relationships you will need when their application cycle comes around.

Development of a Comprehensive Fundraising Campaign

While people tend to cringe at the thought of developing a fundraising plan or campaign, such a plan will prove its value almost immediately. Many organizations manage to survive for a long time without a clear plan, relying solely on random solicitations of friends and supporters for funds. Eventually, however, most organizations realize they need to develop a focused, four-part plan, designed for a month or a year, to give a sense of stability to operations and enhance their overall ability to carry out their mission. Those four parts are the goal: how much money they actually intend to raise; an explanation of exactly why they need that money; a description of how they intend to do it; and finally, a timeline to make it actually come together.

ESSENTIAL

The terms *fundraising plan* and *fundraising campaign* are used to describe the methodology behind how money is to be raised through a focused, deliberate effort. The documents developed to describe either of those routes are as important to the ongoing health of the organization as any of its other core documents. A fundraising campaign is generally an intense effort to meet a specific goal in a set period of time, while a fundraising plan represents a broader view involving an ongoing effort by the organization, parts of which may well be incorporated into a campaign.

The Goal

This discussion is not limited to the operational or capital needs of the organization; at the early stage, these needs may be much closer than they will be in the future as the organization becomes more established. The goal may be directly related to increasing operational capacity, or general outreach, or to increase membership. The goal may be related to hiring a staff person or many staff people, or to repair a wall, fix the plumbing, or put on a new roof—but the goal needs to be the amount of money you, as an organization, intend to raise.

Much of this information may already exist in other documents you have prepared during the life of the organization, so the task now is to bring them into this fundraising plan. Though, if necessary, you may have to create the material from scratch.

If you recently completed the IRS Form 1023 to apply for your nonprofit determination, the projected budget you included in that application will be a good place to start. Be realistic. Looking at your cash on hand and then looking at the amounts you intend to spend over the next few years will give you the difference—or the amount you need to raise.

Why You Need That Money

Once an amount or goal is determined, you need to explain in detail exactly why you need that money. Do not assume the reader will already be familiar with your organization, or that he has read all your assorted publications or meeting minutes. You need to educate the reader about your budget, how the amount/goal fits into that budget, exactly how it will be spent, and the consequences if the goal is not met (if you need to cease, limit, or not expand services). Go deep into the budget lines to explain the need for an IT specialist or an accountant.

ALERT

Developing a complete, comprehensive fundraising plan is beyond the scope of this book; however, many wonderful sources are available on the web as well as in most larger and medium-sized cities. The intention here is to acquaint you with the general requirements any fundraising campaign will need to attain success.

How You Intend to Do It

Identifying how much money you need and how you intend to spend that money is the easy part. Now you need to articulate how you plan to actually raise that money in what is, for too many people, a very tough economy. This is also where you present the very specific detail of exactly what activities you are able to take on, and what totals you expect to bring in from those activities.

Estimate exactly what it will cost to carry out the plan by creating a budget specifically for all the fundraising activities you plan to carry out. There are many ways to raise money! What will be the determining factor is the number of volunteers or compensated staff available to do all the planning and execute the activities.

FACT

A complete fundraising plan is where you will be able immediately to identify the percentage of your overall operating costs being consumed with fundraising activities, and to make certain that percentage never goes above 20 percent. You should maintain a budget solely for all of your fundraising activities, so this information is always available to anyone in the organization or any member of the public.

The Timeline

Even with a clearly understood budget, well-articulated needs, and an excellent explanation of how you plan to carry everything through, projects will not get done if you don't establish a timeline. The timeline is also where you can separate the concept of a focused campaign to fund a particular item from the general fundraising plan, and if appropriate, develop them on unique tracks.

Quite simply, the urgency of the project will also help determine the timeline! If you live in a rainy climate and the roof leaks, you need the money and you need it as quickly as possible. Conversely, if you are operating a music club and want to rotate your artwork, or perhaps you are running a garden society and would like to re-design your newsletter, you can plan on a longer campaign.

A Success Story

Even in the best of economic times, the tasks of developing a comprehensive fundraising plan and making it work are extremely difficult. Even considering this step puts your organization into a very small percentage of nonprofits that realize such a plan is necessary.

This toolkit includes an account of a fundraising success story. It is the case study of Yew Dell Gardens in Crestwood, Kentucky. This nonprofit decided it needed a considerable amount of money to fulfill its mission and then were able to raise the funds. The story is included here as an example of just what a nonprofit can do and to offer some encouragement to groups that are just starting out.

Overlooked Methods

So many new nonprofits are being formed and obtaining their tax-exempt status. That means you'll need considerable effort and creativity to raise the funds your organization will need to carry out its mission. The field of competition will narrow somewhat after you are firmly established and have developed the necessary relationships with grant-makers. However, as the global economy shifts and adjusts, there will always be some competition for limited funds. Too many organizations forget to think creatively in their search for funding streams.

House Parties

House parties have become very popular in the last few years, in large part due to the relative ease of organizing them, low overhead, and good financial returns. Selected individuals who share a common interest are invited to the parties held in private homes.

The program can be simple, but it should include a table with informative literature, a short video presentation, and a brief talk by your board president or another highly respected person whom the attendees know. Follow the program with a formal request for contributions. You can keep overhead costs very low with donated food and drink.

Auctions

Benefit auctions have been catching on as a means to make a considerable amount of money. There is a lot of pre-event work associated with this option. You must verify with your tax advisor how to navigate local or state regulations pertaining to benefit auctions, and be prepared to document the entire event to remain compliant with the IRS. Remember, you may be incurring a tax liability and not all funds may be deductible, so do not hold an auction without doing your homework. There are numerous software applications to assist nonprofit organizations with the bookkeeping associated with benefit auctions.

Benefit Concerts

Benefit concerts will come up in discussion at some point and you need to be prepared. Unless you are working with A-list talent who are donating their fees and all ticket sales, concerts are terrific for outreach but are rarely a sure way to raise funds. If you are still determined, contract with a professional promoter in your region who knows the business. Negotiate a fee and then let that person take the project to its conclusion.

Phone Banks

Although receiving phone call solicitations is annoying, organizations that use phone banks find them very effective. There are a number of large national phone bank operators who work exclusively with nonprofits and are worth investigating if that is a route you want to go.

Using the Internet

If you are not using the Internet as part of your comprehensive fundraising strategy, you are not going to succeed. A strong, vibrant fundraising system that uses the Internet is essential, from direct-deposit programs such as PayPal with a link for donations prominently displayed on your website, to a Facebook page directing people to your site and that link, to additional resources discussed in the following paragraphs.

Utilize Direct-Deposit Systems

In addition to simply accepting donations through any of the direct-deposit systems, consider using them for event ticket sales, or to accept payments for books or recordings you may offer. These systems can also be used as a virtual reception area/gift shop for visitors interested in learning more about your organization.

ESSENTIAL

Most of the online direct-deposit systems require administrative access to your organization's website, and a basic understanding of how to insert a code or a button. If these tasks are beyond your personal knowledge, consider asking a tech-savvy volunteer to help set them up.

Develop One Cohesive Operation

As with general consulting, an entire cottage industry now exists to assist nonprofits with online fundraising. Online fundraising cannot be seen as a side project of the organization. Rather, it must be a central piece of the entire development operation.

Everything—from social media activities, to videos on YouTube, to your direct-deposit button, to the newer crowd-sourcing systems explained later—must be integrated into one cohesive operation intended to drive the Internet visitor to seeing a financial contribution as one way to participate in your mission. Such an approach may seem too direct, but in this fragile economy, it is essential for you to survive in the short term and to plan for the longer term.

Crowd Sourcing

In recent years, another development in online fundraising has been getting considerable attention: crowd sourcing. Among the more prominent examples of crowd sourcing are Kickstarter (*www.kickstarter.com*), DonorsChoose (*www.donorschoose.org*), and Indie GoGo (*www.indiegogo.com*).

FACT

Crowd sourcing, or crowd funding, is a new term for the old idea of presenting a problem to a large group of people and asking them to develop a solution or, in the case of "crowd funding," to become part of a project through the contribution of funds. Add the dynamic of social media and there are suddenly thousands, if not hundreds of thousands, of people aware of and potentially interested in participating.

Although each of their target audiences is different, these three crowd-sourcing options use similar technology. Kickstarter is geared more toward the arts and creative endeavors; DonorsChoose focuses exclusively on the needs of classroom teachers; and Indie GoGo is wide-open. Each site requires an organization to register and present a carefully structured explanation of exactly what it wants to fund, why the mission is important, and how it fits into the site's criteria.

Provide As Many Services Online As Practical

Online ticket sales and the ability to offer/provide services or conduct fundraising auctions online have completely revolutionized the ability of nonprofit groups to generate income. Investigate your options for providing as many services online as is practical. Just make sure that all the items you list online are within your mission statement and are not subject to the UBI tax.

Oh, the Savings You'll See

As a practical matter, no longer having to print paper copies of everything will result in substantial and immediate cash savings. In addition, you'll save money by no longer having to store and insure auction items or books or other items you sell through your website.

A Complete Shopping Experience

The decision to use the website to provide a more complete shopping experience will require extensive modifications to accommodate a shopping cart and all the options that accompany it. You may need to open a special "merchant account" with your bank to enable credit card purchases made through your site to be directly deposited into that account. The costs associated with setting up that system will be recouped quickly, because your audience of potential supporters is now worldwide.

In-Kind Contributions

In-kind contributions are not financial; instead, they are donated time or services that have monetary value. For example:

- A professional athletic trainer donating a few hours a week to run a health class
- The local print shop donating printing for your auction catalog
- A general contractor coming in on his days off to oversee volunteers hanging plasterboard in a basement remodel
- A mechanic offering to keep the organization's vehicles in good condition

Each of these services has real value. However, since no cash changes hands, the contributions are in-kind.

Accounting for In-Kind Contributions

Your organization can and should attach a monetary value to the contribution and include that amount in your budget on the in-kind line in your income section. Determine the current fair-market value of goods or services and use those figures in your budget. For determining salary amounts, use the current salaries the exact service would cost if you had to contract an outside source.

ALERT

Your organization must provide written acknowledgment of the in-kind donation if it is over $250. Furthermore, be sure to conduct a careful accounting of all the details of the contribution, including accurate appraisals to determine the value of items.

Those Contributions May Be Tax Deductible

The incentive for most people to make in-kind contributions is their interest in the mission. Once a dollar amount is attached to that contribution for the purposes of the organization's accounting, however, that amount may be deductible from the contributor's federal income tax. If the organization has a federal tax exemption, the contribution has a deductible value.

CHAPTER 13

Board Development

As you develop the board of directors, you will be imagining the future. Through careful, ongoing work, you will assess your current and potential capacity to carry out your organization's mission. Board development should become part of your ongoing work. This chapter will explore how to evolve from the group that made up the founding board to a working unit that will take you into the future.

Basic Procedure

Board development is a fancy term to describe the need to keep a volunteer board of directors engaged and excited about their organization and everything taking place within it. In an ongoing, practical sense, board development also is a reminder to remain constantly alert for people who might be invited to join the board. Current members will choose to step aside or not seek re-election, and it will be necessary to find a replacement. Additionally, shifting needs and expanding membership may create new seats that need to be filled by individuals with specific talents.

Time to Refer to Your By-Laws

You determined the mechanics of how to add new people to your board when you drafted your by-laws. As you think about the deliberate process of creating a board of directors, circulate copies of those by-laws to everyone, even the current board who may have drafted them. It's a good idea to refresh everyone's memory about the agreed-upon process.

QUESTION

Isn't board development when the board assumes a larger role in fundraising?
Not really. Although fundraising will remain an important responsibility for any member of a nonprofit board, taking a holistic approach to board development by incorporating governance, outreach, and long-range goals into your thinking will make your organization much healthier in the long term.

Many organizations actively look forward to the process of enriching and enhancing their boards because it offers a chance for reflection and fun.

Engaging a Consultant

When considering formal board development, think about including a consultant. He may have limited direct knowledge of the personalities and dynamics of your particular organization, but he will have an expert understanding of how small groups function and will be able to help your board reach its full potential.

Many nonprofit boards are made up of people who have a passion for the mission rather than an acute business sense. This situation gave rise to an industry of consultants who use a combination of education and experience to fill precise holes in nonprofits on a temporary basis. If you find your organization in a situation where professional consulting is necessary, it is a sure sign that the nonprofit is maturing and is able to recognize its needs before problems occur.

FACT

Board-development consultants are generally independent contractors who work for a negotiated hourly or daily fee and can be found through a simple Internet or telephone directory search. If you are located outside an urban area, be prepared to pay for your consultant's transportation and lodging in addition to his professional service fee.

Activating Your Nominating Committee

If your by-laws require the establishment of a formal nominating committee to facilitate the search for new board members, you can start the process with a simple agreement of the board by recorded motion to establish and activate such a committee. The nominating committee should work closely with the board and any outside consultant to establish the board's needs and how best to fill those needs by inviting individuals from the community into your organization as potential board members.

Expanding Your Reach

The founding board members probably knew each other professionally or socially and agreed to pitch in to get the organization running. Their incredible drive and personal commitment has helped the group reach the point where you are free to think well beyond the confines of a start-up and finally prepare to realize their dreams.

Viewing Committees as a Route to the Board

The committees established through language in the by-laws have become far more than a way of spreading the work to fulfill your mission. They are a training ground for potential board members who are already accustomed to the way the organization functions. Inviting community members to become active at the committee level where they can contribute their time and expertise as they learn more about the organization is an excellent way to prepare them for possible board involvement.

Exercise Care When Extending Invitations

Drawing from your committee membership can be an excellent way to develop the board in a way that both complements and enhances the group. However, each individual must also meet the specific needs identified by the board through a careful assessment of the organization's strengths and weaknesses.

ALERT

Founders' syndrome, in which the original founders remain in positions of authority longer than necessary, is a problem that many start-up nonprofits must face and address head-on. By broadening the circle of people with decision-making authority, everyone—including your founders—will be much better off.

Much of your carefully planned outreach will now come into play. As more people learn about the work your organization does, its name will become more recognizable. This increased recognition, in turn, will lead to the identification of more highly qualified people who may meet the specific needs the board identifies as necessary for growth.

Assessing Immediate Needs

As a planned activity, board development provides an ideal opportunity for self-reflection. It is a way to re-engage the broader community, your supporters, and your colleagues and to gain their insight and opinions about the group's overall goals and the people you need to help you realize those goals.

People and Money

The immediate needs of most start-up nonprofits generally fall into two areas: finances and staffing. There never seems to be enough money to get everything done, and everyone already has too much work to do. This is a perfectly normal situation. It is not ideal, but you are not alone. Step back and assess where you as individuals are on a board, where your organization is in relation to your personal needs, and how those elements are affecting your programming and mission. Once you have articulated those elements, you will be well on your way to understanding your current situation.

ESSENTIAL

If the person handling your books and other bank business is feeling overworked and under-appreciated, she needs immediate help. You may need to hire an accountant. You may need to weigh this decision against your desire to remain an all-volunteer group.

Assessing your immediate needs may require your board members to decide if they are happy with how the organization is being received in the community. Record the answers everyone offers. As problems are expressed, find out how these issues might be improved. A discussion of your current needs will lead directly to assessing future needs and developing a plan to address them. This is not a time to be overly deferential or to avoid making judgments based on experiences and observations that may seem harsh.

Every group has its own set of variables, so there is never a perfect time to assess your organization. You should schedule a formal assessment every year. It does not have to be a complicated undertaking, but it should be clearly defined. All board members, your board administrator (if you have one), and senior volunteers or staff should actively participate.

Don't Complicate the Matter

An assessment can be as simple as making lists of what seems to be working and what needs improvement, and encouraging everyone to offer as much detail as they are comfortable with so the entire board can understand the entire situation. Assessments can take place as part of an already scheduled meeting, at a special session, or even by mail. How you choose to do it is not as important as the fact that you are willing to do it.

FACT

The members of your board came to you or were invited to join the board because of their leadership skills and their ability to analyze a situation and arrive at a solution. Now is the time to call upon them to do just that. This is a time to think outside the box.

Assessing Future Needs

The most exciting part of board development is stepping back now and then to take in the broader view. Think about where your current board wants to take the organization and exactly what types of skills and experiences you will need in new board members to help you get there.

Although no list will cover every nonprofit organization in the country, use the following ideas as an example of the backgrounds and professional training that would be an asset to any organization. You will always need to recognize any conflicts of interest that may arise and take appropriate steps to defuse them.

▼ **BOARD OF DIRECTOR DREAM TEAM**

Long-Term Plan	Potential Board Member
Purchasing Property	Real-Estate Agent
Building or Remodeling	General Contractor
Raising Money	Investment Banker
Producing Concerts or Recitals	Promoter or Artist Representative
Increased Involvement in Health Care	Physician, Hospital Administrator, or HMO Representative
Zoning Changes	Lawyer

Long-Term Plan	Potential Board Member
Increased Fundraising	Foundation Program Officer
Media Sponsorship	Columnist or TV Personality

Examine your business plans, budgets, and long-range goals with an eye toward locating the future board members who will help drive the efforts of your organization to reach those goals.

Example of a Conflict of Interest

Let's look at Ms. Jones. She is a highly respected real-estate attorney who is a tremendous resource on the board for her contacts and business relationships in the community. Ms. Jones happens to own a few small rental properties around town, one of which is being considered for the organization's new headquarters. In this situation, Ms. Jones would become the group's landlord and benefit financially if the group decided to rent her building, so she needs to recuse herself. In other words, she must sit out all discussions on this particular topic and she may not vote.

Conflicts of interest will inevitably arise, but the knowledge and experience your board members bring to the organization far outweigh the minor inconveniences such conflicts cause.

The Roles of the Board

This is an excellent time to begin defining roles within your current and ideal board. The tasks of a nonprofit board are generally divided between governing the organization and leading ongoing fundraising efforts.

Board Governance

Governance involves all the actions that set policy, hire staff, oversee the budget, and generally keep the organization humming along. Fundraising efforts might involve governance from the board as well. The board must mandate systems and put budgets in place before the organization can solicit funds. However, actual fundraising is a standalone activity, generally with its own board committee, processes, and personnel.

Board Fundraisers

The need for members of any nonprofit board to assist with fundraising is sometimes the third rail of board development. It's there, everyone knows it's there, everyone can see it—yet the tendency is to avoid it until it becomes unavoidable. While involvement in the governance side of board operations is obviously a responsibility of board membership, fundraising is a bit more daunting for new board members. Once the financial responsibilities and the methods to help with the fundraising are explained, however, most concerns melt away.

Connecting with Other Nonprofits

There are thousands of nonprofit organizations in the United States. Some have become household names, while others are just starting out.

Meet Your Peers

Whatever your mission and purpose for organizing, it is essential to introduce your organization's board to other boards and nonprofits. There is a huge, wonderful community of nonprofit organizers and groups doing good work, and they are generally more than happy to help the boards of other nonprofits. It is no secret that the entire nonprofit sector of our economy becomes stronger and more vibrant when nonprofits form working alliances and collaborate with one another.

By contrast, profit drives the for-profit sector, and competition is a fact of doing business. Among nonprofits, cooperation and mutual support are vital. Connecting with others in similar situations will enhance your networking opportunities, which will lead to additional funding streams and increased capacity. You will soon recognize other organizations as allies—not rivals—in your community. Of course, there is competition for some funding, but as you become more established in your niche, your relationships with funders who are interested in your unique mission will solidify, lessening the sense that you are competing against other organizations.

Researching Other Nonprofits

As you think about expanding your board, check out the boards of other organizations. Learn which board members' terms may be expiring and find out who may have an interest in joining your board. An individual with experience as a nonprofit board member is valuable to your organization, especially if he also meets your stated criteria.

FACT

Many nonprofit organizations offer reciprocal memberships to encourage exchanges of newsletters and other printed material with nonprofits that have similar missions, generally at no cost. Contact nonprofit organizations whose missions align with yours to see if you can arrange mutually beneficial partnerships.

Expand your horizons—don't limit yourself to building relationships only with organizations that have identical or similar missions. The purpose of developing these relationships is to help at the board level, not necessarily with programming or operational issues. The mission of a school for homeless kids may be very different from a school teaching creative dance, but at the board level they share similar needs, perhaps related to capital improvements, zoning, and administrative staffing.

Local Grant-Writing Associations

An excellent opportunity for building these relationships is through regional grant-writing organizations. These groups provide opportunities for development directors and their staffs to meet periodically over luncheons or presentations. Many grant-writing associations also maintain active newsletters and listservs that are open to anyone in the field. These tools help their members stay up-to-date and connected with the larger community of their professional peers.

Smaller start-up nonprofits tend to rely extensively on volunteers who have other responsibilities and may be struggling to get one grant application out the door on time. The professional organizations are made up of people who were (or are) in your exact situation and who will understand what you are going through.

Continuing Education

New board members generally arrive with either a passion for the organization's mission or because of their stature and connections within the community. They should also meet the specific criteria you established for new board members and share a profound interest in the group's mission and the work you are doing. Regardless of the manner used to select individuals to join a nonprofit board, they will arrive at that first meeting as a blank slate.

ESSENTIAL

Before any new board member's first meeting, present her with an informational notebook containing copies of the founding documents, the current by-laws and mission statement, minutes from a few recent meetings, a synopsis of the current budget, and a brief history of the organization to date. Include a copy of your IRS determination letter, if you have it, and a copy of the most recent Form 990.

You will initially need to provide basic education. Board members need to learn about the inner workings of your organization, even if they have experience on other boards or have been involved in other capacities with your organization for years. A carefully chosen board may need to be educated on the details they will be working with, so time spent on bringing everyone up to speed is a positive, long-term investment.

Retreats

Carefully planned and facilitated board retreats provide an opportunity for a crash course about the organization, board member responsibilities, and miscellaneous housekeeping details. During a retreat, encourage members to envision a future for the organization and brainstorm ways to meet goals.

FACT

Contrary to reports in popular media, board retreats do not have to take place in resorts! Most organizations hold retreats in offices or private homes where everyone feels comfortable and can participate productively. You can often hire the same consultant you brought in to help with general board development to facilitate a retreat.

Using Educational Programs Offered by National Organizations

A number of national organizations offer a wide array of classes and seminars designed specifically for nonprofit board members. These programs try to meet the needs of board members at every stage of their personal and organizational development, with offerings that include pending federal legislation affecting tax codes, funding ideas, and learning to work with a group of strangers. Many organizations offer partial scholarships for board members of smaller organizations so they can attend without impacting strained finances.

Reflecting Your Community

A large part of successful nonprofit board development is simply understanding your service area or client base and then committing to reflecting it.

Confronting Discrimination

In the early stages, you crafted articles of incorporation, which included language relating to your commitment to avoid discrimination in any form. As you develop the board of directors and take your organization to its next level, you have an opportunity to put your words into action.

ALERT

Many private funders want to see clear evidence that organizations that have applied for their financial support are indeed practicing non-discrimination and are actively working to make their boards more reflective of the communities in which they operate.

This may be some of the most difficult but necessary work you will do. This aspect of board development requires you to trust yourselves, your mission, and your organization enough to welcome into your decision-making body people whose gender, race, ethnicity, and life experiences closely reflect your neighborhood and general population.

At the core of any successful, respected nonprofit is the belief that it is serving the community and is a part of that community as well. Making a conscious, determined effort to live the words in your founding documents will speak volumes about your intentions to do good work as you move forward.

Diversity Training

Incorporating diversity training into long-range planning helps many organizations gain insight into how they function in their communities. A poorly attended two-hour session on one weekend in the middle of winter is not sufficient to explore the ways in which an organization can interact with others in the community. Instead, the trend is to develop a program to move the group toward becoming a more inclusive organization. When these programs are planned in collaboration with your board, they can be a lot of fun and educational. Contact any of the national organizations to develop plans suited to your organization. Let them know you are a small organization still in the early development stage, but that you are interested in their programs to recognize the strength diversity brings to any organization.

It Will Always Involve Money

As every new board member learns and as every viable nonprofit organization quickly recognizes, a board of directors focuses on community, doing good work, and maintaining the vision. But boards are also about money.

Taking Credit and Responsibility

If your organization is in a financial bind, from either poor decisions or external events, the responsibility for the group's financial health rests with the board of directors. By the same token, if the group is financially stable, pays all its bills, and can focus on its mission, the board gets the credit. The reward for this success is the chance to recommend opportunities for enhanced programming or outreach, which is the ultimate goal of any organization. Board development must always involve an assessment of the ability of prospective board members to raise money through their networks of family, friends, and associates.

The Suggested Donation Option

Some boards stipulate a minimum yearly donation from all board members as one of the criteria for consideration for membership. Although such requirements are usually associated with well-established and well-endowed organizations, it is an avenue to consider as soon as the current board has reached the level of maturity necessary to raise that option. Only the board can address raising the funds necessary for a nonprofit to carry out its mission and maintain access to financial reserves.

CHAPTER 14

A Business Plan

A business plan shows potential funders how you intend to carry out your operational goals. It is also an important element of your Form 1023 to the IRS when you apply for your nonprofit status. There are no mysteries in developing a clear, concise business plan, just hard work. This chapter will try to make it a little easier.

A General Overview

When most people think of a business plan, they think in terms of a plan geared to a for-profit company. There are more similarities than differences when comparing that to a nonprofit business plan, so a for-profit plan is a useful model. Naturally, one of the main underlying factors in developing a for-profit business plan is factoring in a financial return to the investors or owners.

QUESTION

How important is a business plan?
On a scale of 1 to 10, with 1 being a make-work document to keep a volunteer busy and 10 being a document essential to your organization's survival, a business plan easily ranks at a 15. No business plan—no survival.

While there is most likely a huge degree of passion on the part of the owners of a for-profit company, they are involved to make money. The parts of their business plan will have the same headings as yours, but the over-arching purpose will be different. Let's work through the four main parts of any business plan, with the elements you will want to include.

1. A description of the business. This part describes what you want to do and why you want to do it.
2. Marketing. This part details how you plan to let the public know you exist to stimulate revenue.
3. Finances. This part lists the funds available, where those funds came from, and how they will be spent.
4. Management. This part discusses your management team, what you have done, and why anyone should take you seriously.

Consider these sections as you review the raw material your group has collected. Then edit and organize the material in a way that facilitates a systematic assembly of the business plan. You need to begin thinking on a macro level about how to introduce your organization in a way the world can understand.

Contents

The core elements and terminology of a complete for-profit or nonprofit business plan are very similar. There are ingredients that any potential funder will expect to see, and you need to include them.

The Cover Sheet or Executive Summary

Although this will be the first page the reader will see, it should actually be the last page you write. It is a summary of what is to come, so wait until your business plan has been fully developed and you will know exactly what your cover sheet should say. Keep your sentences short and to the point, but explain who you are, what your company or organization intends to do, and how you plan to do it. No potential funders are going to make a decision based on this summary alone. However, they may decide to continue reading based on what you write here.

A Statement of Purpose / Mission Statement

Your mission statement must clearly describe the services you provide to the community and the passion of the individuals involved in your organization.

The Table of Contents

The reader needs to know what he is getting into when he begins to read your plan. The table of contents will provide an immediate guide, which the reader can also use to locate specific data. If you are writing for online distribution, use the table-of-contents function in most word processing programs, which enables a quick jump to specific sections. If you are planning to print a hard copy, be careful to cancel that option so you don't have the hyperlink lines running through your document.

A Description of the Business

Make the description of your business or organization clear and concise —no longer than a paragraph. Many details that might fit in the description will appear in detail elsewhere in the plan.

Marketing

Marketing, particularly when focused on nonprofits, means fully understanding the needs of your clients or community and then managing your organizational response to meet those needs. It is not simply your publicity efforts, although they may play a role in it. Attach any informational brochures or other outreach material you have developed for general reference.

Here is where you mention any use of focus groups to help you evaluate how well the marketing is working or where improvements may be necessary. Be sure to indicate who is conducting the groups and how frequently they will occur. Likewise, identify by name who is directly involved in or leading your marketing strategy

Competition

Regardless of the type of service you are planning to provide, there is a good chance someone else is offering something similar. Be honest in your analysis of that competition and point out exactly how your organization will be different and why that difference deserves to be funded.

Operating Procedures

Here you may want to attach or reference your by-laws. The point of this section is to help the reader fully understand how your organization functions, where the decision-making responsibility is, and what the process is for accountability. If you included clear nondiscriminatory clauses in your by-laws, this is a fine opportunity to share them.

Personnel

Personnel may include your staff and any consultants. List them here with a sentence describing each person's position and qualifications. Resumes or the curriculum vitae of the board members will be included later as supporting documents.

FACT

If you do not have personnel yet but intend to bring staff on as time and finances permit, say it in this section. Honesty is more powerful and refreshing than prose that tries to obscure the obvious.

You want to convey that your organization has good, competent people in positions of responsibility. If your organization is fortunate enough to have the services of someone whose name is known throughout the community, mention it in the narrative.

Supporting Financial Documents

Supporting financial documents are one tier below the general description of who you are and what your organization plans to do. Here you need to provide as much solid documentation as you can to back up the good intentions in the overview.

Breakeven Analysis

This section of the business plan explains what the organization is doing to break even. If you are falling short, outline what is planned in the next fiscal year to correct existing problems.

Three-Year Financial Summary

This summary will be similar to that required when you prepare Form 1023 to apply for a tax exemption, if you are going to file before you have a multiyear history. Any standard grant application requires this kind of summary.

Pro-Forma Cash Flow

If you do not have a three-year financial history, use the pro-forma cash-flow document to project estimated income and expenses that you are confident the organization will have, but you do not as yet have the hard numbers to back up the calculations. *Pro forma* simply means "as if" and is used when you need to discuss funds that do not exist yet, but you are confident that they will.

Balance Sheet

The balance sheet can be a summary of your current fiscal year's budget, or you can attach a more comprehensive document. As with other parts of the plan, be careful not to provide so much information that the reader loses interest.

General Supporting Documents

Supporting documents provide the real-world evidence that what you are saying is real. These documents are essential to show the depth of your organization, giving a clear picture of who you are and what you are doing in the world.

Copies of Licenses and Other Legal Documents

The board secretary should have copies of all documents the organization has compiled since the decision to incorporate. For the purpose of the business plan, you will generally only need the cover sheets, because they have the legal date stamp or other indicator that the particular license or permit is valid. Once you have obtained your federal tax exemption, you will only need to present the determination letter to verify your status. Likewise, include a copy of the latest Form 990 as a matter of principle.

Very few grant-making committees will have the time or inclination to read through pages of documentation. They want to see that your organization has the documents and that they are current, particularly with respect to any financial documentation.

Copy of a Proposed Lease or Purchase Agreement for Building Space

This paper is very important because it shows one of the major expenses your organization already has, one that would obviously affect your ability to function if it were cut. This documentation also points to the current stability of the organization; the fact that the leadership has agreed to a long-term project indicates stability.

Business Insurance

If you are carrying any type of insurance—such as property or vehicle insurance or board insurance—note it here. You are including this information to give the reader as clear a picture of your organization as possible. Carrying an insurance policy is evidence that your organization is responsible and that you are taking necessary precautions and limiting unnecessary risks. A fully exposed organization that does not carry basic insurance will make potential funders nervous, so providing this documentation will help allay those concerns.

Copy of Resumes of All Principals

You should have a one-page resume or curriculum vitae (CV) from each of your board members or, at the very least, from your current officers and any staff with direct responsibility or oversight for the organization's finances. Although your group is incorporated and that incorporation entails the legal separation between the individuals and the corporate entity, your business plan is still going to be reviewed by real people.

ESSENTIAL

A well-designed one-page resume for each of your current board members will show the community exactly who is running the organization and make your project much more likely to receive the support you need. Include a small photograph of each person to help readers connect faces to your organization.

It is essential that your readers feel comfortable enough with the people who represent your organization to make a financial contribution. Although there will be opportunities for in-person meetings, everyone involved at this stage will base their decisions on the paperwork on the table, and that paperwork must show your organization in its finest light and prove that the people running it have the experience to make everything work.

Copies of Letters of Intent

These copies may be necessary if you want to show that your organization is a viable business with outstanding financial obligations. Letters of intent identify the amount of money you are requesting and fully document the need for those funds. The ability to provide the actual letters of intent from the businesses you are working with and who will ultimately receive the requested funds shows the full and comprehensive nature of your business plan.

Loan Applications

Include any pending loan applications in this section. Although they are financial documents, loan applications are not money you currently have to work with but rather funds you hope to receive. The purpose of including them here is to present as much about your business as possible.

The information can be as complete or abbreviated as you are comfortable with, but potential funders need to know the financial health of your organization and be aware of your current loan application(s).

Capital Equipment List

A start-up nonprofit probably won't have anything beyond basic office equipment, but even that has value. The depreciation on this equipment will appear in your budget, so including it here will show that entire document is complete.

Nonprofit Business Plan Overview

Throughout this guide, there have been numerous references to the differences between a nonprofit and a for-profit organization. Nowhere will that difference become more immediately apparent than when your organization develops its business plans. All business plans change over time to account for shifts in internal or external situations. This change is to be expected; in fact, you would be remiss if you did not adjust parts of the plan, or indeed the entire document, should circumstances require it. Think of your business plan as a fluid work-in-progress, and be willing to make adjustments.

The biggest difference, of course, is how you handle any money above the amount that is necessary to operate the organization. Many of the terms used in a for-profit business plan need to be adjusted to accommodate the unique situation of a nonprofit. These subtle edits are necessary to appreciate the differences between for-profit and nonprofit business plans and the terminology used for each.

Customers Become Clients

This is a subtle but essential change in terminology. You are crafting a business plan whose focus is on returning funds to the organization to further its mission rather than returning profits to investors or increasing the profit margin.

Investors Become Funders

The idea of investing in a project or an organization comes with an expectation that there will be some form of benefit to the investor in exchange for the money. In a for-profit business, that benefit may take any number of forms, from appointments to high offices to a thank-you payment at the end of the year. However, any of those benefits are illegal in a nonprofit organization because no one is allowed to use the work of the organization for personal gain.

Any perception of personal gain can jeopardize your tax-exempt status and all the work you have put into developing the organization. Instead, people who give money to your organization must be seen as funders who contribute because they feel strongly enough about the merits of the organization's mission to be willing to write a check. The only direct benefit to those funders will be their ability to deduct that contribution from their tax liability; they can expect nothing else from the nonprofit they helped fund.

Products Become Programs or Services

It is entirely appropriate for a for-profit business to create, produce, and sell a product—something of value that can be touched or experienced. Product lines in a for-profit business can be adjusted with very few legal restrictions. The owners are legally free to modify product lines without any explanation. Naturally, there are market limitations and cash-flow issues, but on a basic level, it is unlikely that the IRS will question a decision to change or drastically modify a product line.

A nonprofit is limited to providing a service that falls within the broad interpretation of its mission. Its tax-exempt status depends entirely on its ability to carry out its stated mission without straying from it.

A Profit and Loss Statement Becomes a Statement of Financial Activities

Profit and loss statements simply do not appear in the financial documents of a nonprofit, but you do need to show the financial health of the organization. If you are already familiar with the way a for-profit business works, you may want to think in terms of profit and loss, but it is more accurate to begin to see the whole of the financial situation.

A statement of financial activities is a basic document that measures an organization's finances during a specified time. The function of a financial statement is to total all sources of revenue and subtract all expenses related to the revenue.

Having a financial statement prepared on a regular schedule enables the organization to quickly get a sense of its financial health. If the statement points to a problem each month, you will be able to address it before the problem becomes a crisis. Likewise, if the numbers are consistently good, you are definitely doing something right!

CHAPTER 15

A Mission Statement

In one or two paragraphs, your mission statement explains the core elements of your organization: its purpose, its target population, and what it does. Every nonprofit organization needs a mission statement. The statement may evolve slightly over time as the organization adjusts and active personnel change, but the mission statement will remain the guiding document.

The Soul of the Organization

Any organization, yours included, remains a group of individuals who agree to work together for a common purpose. When you peel away all the legal documents and budgets and rules, you will still have what you started with: a group of firmly committed individuals.

The actual people will change over time. However, those changes will be moderated to some degree by the systems you establish in your by-laws on filling new seats or replacing board members to ensure that the board is made up of people who continue to share the basic beliefs of the founders.

ESSENTIAL

Ask potential board members to explain their philosophies as they relate to your mission statement. The board is responsible for maintaining the standards set by the statement, so new board members need to be in full agreement.

To understand the soul of the organization requires understanding the people who attend the meetings, write the press releases, make the phone calls to volunteers, and consistently raise the money necessary to operate. You must explore and understand your soul and the souls of those directly involved in the creation of the organization.

Time for Research

Developing a clear, concise mission statement is difficult, especially when you are working with smart, passionate people who want the very best for the organization. Mission statements are not the depository for the wishes and desires of every person involved in the group; rather, they are a place to distill those ideas to their essence. They need to be presented clearly, concisely, and in a manner that internal or external audiences can easily understand.

Look at the mission statements of other organizations. Try to understand how the work they do lines up with their mission statement.

The Statement Can Always Evolve

Sometimes a group simply gets stuck or finds it is unable to agree on the precise wording. Sometimes, as your organization grows, your mission may shift, or the way you view the work may adjust. This is completely natural.

FACT

Many nonprofit organizations have their mission statements on their websites, often in their "about us" sections. This section of a site may also include information about the organization's history and founding principles. Locate and compare at least a dozen mission statements. You'll look at them differently now that you can understand the tremendous work that went into each one.

If the mission statement is no longer accurate, or the wording you settled on a few months ago is simply not correct, review it and make the needed changes. The adjustments must go through your board of directors, who will very likely have their own input and who need to agree to the changes.

Vision

It's important to define your vision so that people who have never heard of your organization understand what you are doing and are inspired to join your effort. Some people are uncomfortable discussing their vision because it may involve deeper feelings that are distinct from the actual operations of your organization. Vision may touch on the underlying beliefs of why you are doing the work you are doing. Faith-based nonprofits often weave their core vision into their ongoing work, whereas secular groups may have to start from the beginning to understand and be comfortable articulating the ultimate purpose of their work.

Fascinating, Not Funny

Over the past few years, there have been a lot of jokes (including one from a former U.S. president, commenting about the "vision thing") illustrating the problem of explaining and defining the visions of organizations and even countries. Most of the jokes start because the idea of analyzing a group's core beliefs can be uncomfortable until those involved attain a level of trust that encourages real communication.

ESSENTIAL

Do not get too caught up trying to overanalyze the vision of the group. If a simple phrase covers it, accept it and move on. Remember that these are the tools an organization needs, not the actual work.

It is not easy to explain your passion for stray animals, forests, the performing arts, or any of the countless other missions the nonprofit community takes on. However, explain it you must. Articulate it in such a way that the many intended audiences—members, funders, and the general public—will also understand and share that passion.

Introduce Yourself to the World

The "world" is the general population; it includes your neighbors, the media, and people who have learned of your existence and are curious enough to look a little further.

Most of these people will never actually read the mission statement; they don't need to read it. The way your organization functions and the work it does will speak for itself. The mission statement anchors the organization; the organization's purpose stems from the principles it lays out.

Play to Your Audience

Always remember the audience you are trying to reach. Over time, the members of your core group will understand one another through working and discussion. The mission statement is not the place to talk to yourselves, as fun and as easy as that may be.

You are preparing a document that will be read by people you do not know and may never meet. Do not waste time developing wording that impresses your group. You need to remain focused on the external audience and how they will read and interpret your words.

Do More Research

Just as it is helpful to review other mission statements to understand how they read and how they are put together, it is also wise to look at the grant applications of potential donors. This research allows you to see exactly what they are seeking and what they want to see in the mission statements of the groups they choose to fund.

Private foundations may choose not to reveal the groups and organizations they fund, but government agencies and public charities do. You will find more than enough examples to review.

The purpose of this research is not to copy or emulate the wording of another organization. You are trying to understand how a more mature, successful group communicates the essence of its purpose through its mission statement.

QUESTION

What is meant by the key documents?
The key documents that are easily obtainable consist of the organization's annual report, which may include its mission/vision statement, or its 501(c)(3) application, which is public record. Obtaining them is simply a matter of calling or e-mailing the group and asking for a copy of their documents.

Introduce Yourself to the Funding Community

A great deal of the organizational work involves money—planning how you are going to raise it (development), raising it (fundraising), tracking it (accounting), and then doing it all over again, year in and year out.

Funders are not some sort of organized group waiting to pass judgment on you and your organization. They are individuals in your community who happen to be in a position financially to assist organizations they endorse. There are a number of general things you as a new nonprofit can do to place your organization in the best possible light when you decide to approach these individuals or businesses for support. Rarely is anyone so taken with your personal presentation that they open their checkbook and beg you to take their money.

ALERT

When considering how your statement will be read by those in the philanthropic community, keep in mind that funders look at hundreds—if not thousands—of requests for money every year, so be brief. They need to see something in these documents that catches their attention and imagination.

Potential donors will need time to review material about your organization to become comfortable that your work clearly lines up with their philosophies or interests. This is why your mission statement is so important.

The mission statement will be the document most funders need to give them a picture of your group that goes beyond budgets and a business plan. They will get to know what makes you tick, what drives the group to take on a task or a project, or why your group is putting everything it has on the line with no expectation of financial reward.

Guiding Principles

If you are ready to develop a mission statement, you are already well ahead of most groups that are still struggling with the basic elements necessary to organize as a nonprofit. Having reached this point, articulating your group's guiding principles should not be that difficult. Nevertheless, the final document must state them clearly.

Stating the Obvious

Your guiding principles may be similar to the basic rules all children learn: to respect other people, to work toward the enhancement of a community or a way of life, and not to engage in mean or violent activities. Although these principles may be second nature to your group, until and unless you state them, no one outside your group is going to realize how you are thinking and how serious and committed you are.

FACT

You may want to restate portions of your founding documents, the by-laws, or other materials you have already developed to introduce yourself to the world. If your group is satisfied with the wording, move on.

The fact that your organization believes in principles that go far beyond its actual tasks will show the community and the many audiences who might read your mission statement that you are willing to state the beliefs that guide everything in the organization.

Exercises to Use

Fortunately, there are a number of exercises to help groups develop their mission statements. The general ideas and theoretical background are necessary for everyone involved in crafting a mission statement, but you also need to do the work. The exercises can take place during board retreats, or they can be part of your regularly scheduled meetings. In addition to helping the organization develop a much-needed document, the exercises can be a lot of fun, so approach them in that spirit.

The Sticky Dot Exercise

This exercise requires the following:

- Butcher paper
- One person to act as the writer
- A package of colored sticky dots with equal numbers of three colors: green, yellow, red

In this exercise, the butcher paper is hung on an easel in the front of the room and the writer stands beside the easel. Encourage everyone in the room to call out what they think the real mission of the organization is (or should be!).

There is no right or wrong suggestion. Ideas can be expected or outlandish; they all need to be written on the butcher paper as clearly as possible in *big letters*. Remember, there is no criticism, even if a suggestion sounds ridiculous.

ALERT

Consider inviting an outside facilitator who is familiar with nonprofit boards to assist in whatever exercises you decide to use. An outsider will not have emotional ties to the group and will be able to lead the exercises in an unbiased manner.

This exercise has a secondary benefit of providing much-needed humor and opportunities for camaraderie. Some of the suggestions may be silly, but they will often be an understood silliness that allows everyone participating to have a laugh and bond just a little bit more.

After a predetermined time, the writer calls for final suggestions and closes this part of the exercise. It is a good time to take a break and encourage everyone to walk around and look at the suggestions. See which ones make the most sense or reflect each individual's ideas about the organization's true mission.

Now, distribute the sticky dots. Everyone should have an equal assortment of colors. Place the green dots by ideas that individuals think are appropriate. Place the yellow dots near ideas that are neutral, and the red dots next to suggestions that individuals cannot support. It does not matter who put what colored dot by which suggestion.

At the close of this part of the exercise, the colored sticky dots will clearly tell which elements the group thinks are important enough to include in the mission statement. These suggestions or statements will give the group a clearer understanding of their mission and will find their way into the mission statement.

The Round-Robin Table Exercise

An individual who is not directly involved in the organization but who is familiar with developing nonprofit mission statements is the best facilitator for this exercise. Attendees are placed into small groups, ideally at small tables that allow them to sit and have room to write.

Each group compiles a list of what they think the organization represents, information that accurately describes the work of the group. After a set period, a representative from each table visits the other tables to glean ideas from those groups and take them back to his or her group. Allow plenty of time for the representatives of the different tables to understand the ideas as they are stated as well as any impressions or nuances.

The original tables or groups then incorporate their original list of important elements with the other groups' ideas. The purpose of this exercise is to bring out as many ideas as possible in a nonthreatening environment.

FACT

Moving around the room and interacting with different people is the secret to these exercises, which are merely different ways to express similar ideas. One table's discussions may have taken a completely different direction, which will add to the richness of the final document.

After this portion of the exercise, each group reads its final results. With the help of the facilitator, the ideas are merged into a list of elements. This list can be used to draft a rough document, which is then edited and prepared for the board of directors for eventual adoption. Then it will become part of the group's constantly evolving record.

CHAPTER 16

Publicity and Outreach

Organizations need to reach out to the general community to publicize the wonderful work they do. This kind of publicity can result in increased membership, new fundraising opportunities, and name recognition. Be sure to document your publicity and outreach efforts as part of the 1023 application to the IRS.

Websites

Your organization must have a website. A website is not an option; it is a necessity, so take it seriously. The Internet is without question one of the finest tools in any organizer's toolbox, but it must be developed and actually used to be effective.

If your personal experience with the Internet has been primarily as an end user with an e-mail account or as a casual web surfer, you need a brief overview of how websites are born. Then you will be able to use and share this basic understanding in developing your organization's site.

ALERT

Do not allow development of a website to dominate your life or take undue amounts of time in your meetings. Think of the website as another part of your overall operations. It is unquestionably an exciting part seen by millions of people, but it must represent who you are, not "be" who you are.

Your website can serve many purposes, from providing general outreach to boosting fundraising to facilitating internal communications. What you actually want and need, plus what your group is able to pay for, will determine its design.

Selecting a Webmaster

At some point, your organization may have a fully functioning information technology department, but in the beginning, you need to identify and contract with someone who will be able to put together and maintain a website for you. That person is a webmaster.

Your webmaster must obviously understand the technical aspects of the task, but most important, she must be able and willing to listen to your wants and needs. You do not want someone who speaks in streams of jargon and expects you to agree.

Since the webmaster will need information relating to both web content and features from the committees as well as the board, having a clear line of communication is essential. Therefore, she should be in regular communication with one board member or a liaison designated by the board. In time, you may incorporate web development into a standing committee, such as publicity or outreach, but when you are trying to get all the essential elements in place, it's fine to have the web functioning ad hoc.

FACT

Relying on the friend of a friend to handle all the necessary details involved in developing your website is often a recipe for trouble. Contract with a professional web developer to handle this project so you can be assured that it is done correctly and on time, and with all the features your organization needs.

The Basic Tasks

Website creation and development is complex and requires a competent professional. As the end user, there are a few things you should do to speed up the process. First, select and register a domain name with any of the main registration companies such as *www.mydomain.com* or *www.godaddy.com*.

Your domain is your address on the Internet. It must be unique (not already taken), easy to remember, and accurately reflect who you are. Your organization name may still be available, in which case you are set. If it's not, be creative. One way or the other, it must happen. Once you have a domain name, you must select a web-hosting service.

These services can be free or there may be a monthly charge. First, identify the service you want to use and the amount of money you want to spend, but hold off on doing anything until you have selected a person to put your website together. Next, you must select the software you want to use to author the website. This program helps you put together the actual content that is uploaded to the server. One of the favorite web-development software programs in the nonprofit community is Drupal (*www.drupal.org*), an open-source software (there's no charge) designed for the end user (you!) to be able to add to or change content after learning the ins and outs. As with much of the open-source software, the expenses for the end user begin to accumulate during setup and continue with ongoing maintenance and consulting fees. Ask your webmaster exactly what costs you can expect over the course of your contract. Work those projected costs into your yearly budget so there are no surprises.

Selecting Content

The type of content you are able to put on the website will be determined to some degree by the program you selected to build the site and your webmaster's ability to adjust that program to meet your specific requests and needs. Possible elements to put on your site include the following:

- An opening/home page introducing your organization
- A blog that is updated on a regular schedule
- The ability to make immediate donations
- Links to your committees and board members
- Reciprocal links to organizations and businesses in the community that support your efforts

Newsletters

Even in this age of instant communication, do not underestimate the importance and value of a well-produced newsletter. Newsletters can and should be put on websites, but design yours for printing and distribution throughout the community.

Whereas a website requires a person to find you, newsletters are mailed directly to your supporters. Newsletters are distributed throughout the community. They are a proactive means of reaching a new audience wherever they might be. A newsletter can be as simple as a one-page sheet copied on an as-needed basis or as elaborate as a multiple-page tabloid that resembles a newspaper more than a traditional newsletter.

FACT

A printed newsletter will not only be read by the addressee; he or she will share it with family, visitors, and business associates. A newsletter is "current" for the duration of the month/quarter on the cover. People will continue to share and circulate it throughout that time.

Desktop Publishing

Now is the time to become familiar with the range of desktop-publishing options available. Some of the software is free, but high-end programs that cost thousands of dollars are also available. Some form of desktop publishing may have come with your word-processing program, so look at what you already have before buying anything. Keep in mind you are not publishing a piece of art destined for an art gallery; you are publishing a newsletter for your organization.

Most desktop-publishing programs, even those that are part of the major word processors, include templates for newsletters. Open them up and play with them. Try out the styles and the options until you settle on one that pleases you or your newsletter committee. Do not try to get the entire organization to agree on this element.

Distribution

A newsletter is worthless if you do not have a means in place to distribute it. Put your newsletter onto your website as soon as it is complete. Printed hard copies should be mailed to or made available to the following:

- Contributors, members, and interested community members
- Local cafés, community centers, theaters, or other locations appropriate to your organization
- Organizations doing similar work in other parts of the country

Content

The content of your newsletter will depend on your specific mission and activities. People expect to see:

- A monthly calendar of scheduled events
- A directory of the key people in the organization and a synopsis of their responsibilities
- A membership form that can be cut out and mailed if you are a membership organization
- A message from the board president or others who are helping grow the organization

Space is used up quickly; once you have settled on a template, the problem will be what not to print.

Press Coverage

Learning to work with your local and regional media is an important part of becoming a viable organization. The media—whether print, broadcast, or Internet-based—can reach far more people in a shorter time than any organization, regardless of its size, can hope to do. To be as effective as possible in your interaction with the media, and in turn gain as much coverage as you can, try looking at the world from the perspective of the working press and help them do their job.

The Value of a Designated Media Person

Your organization may find it helpful to select one person to develop contacts and build needed relationships with your local media. Regardless of where you are located, there are numerous media organizations, from free weekly newspapers to the regional television outlets to AM and FM radio stations. Each outlet has staff dedicated to covering local activities. Your media person needs to meet that individual.

Send this person any press releases or general advisories about things your group is doing, as well as personal invitations to attend your board meetings, tour your facility, or attend one of your events. You want to build a relationship, so when the media have a question, they will know exactly whom to contact. Likewise, when you have something you think is newsworthy, you will have the right person already in your directory.

FACT

A newsletter will more than likely contain the beginnings of a press release. When you announce something your group is doing in the newsletter, use the same words, condensed to one page, and turn it into a press release.

Press Release Template

Making a press release template and storing it on the organization's computer will make the task of generating press releases easy, quick, and efficient. The template is only one page and sent on letterhead. You can literally list Who, What, Where, When, and Why, and fill them in. Do a "save as" for the event or topic of the release and send it to every media outlet in your region. Before long, the media organizations will recognize your press releases and begin giving you necessary coverage.

Fairs and Community Festivals

Community festivals are a terrific opportunity to get out, meet people, and let everyone know what you are doing. People are already in a good mood, so it is easy to engage complete strangers in conversation. There are a few ways to approach local festivals, but the first task is to obtain a comprehensive list of every event in your region, including dates, locations, and contacts.

Every state and most counties operate tourist or visitor information offices. As part of their services, they offer calendars of events for their service areas. Those listings will include every conceivable type of public gathering, many of which might be perfect for your organization to attend. Many festivals make special allowances for nonprofit organizations to have a booth or table at a reduced cost or at no cost, with the stipulation that it is for informational purposes only. This is an excellent opportunity to get your material into the hands of many people in your community, add names to your mailing list, publicize upcoming events, and conduct outreach.

Booths at Street or Craft Fairs

It is well worth your time to contact the overall coordinators and ask about the process for participating as a nonprofit organization. You may need to comply with certain requirements to receive the reduced rate. If you are only interested in promoting your organization and do not plan to sell anything, a booth at a fair is a wonderful method of outreach, and it's also a lot of fun. You can usually make your newsletter available, invite people to join your mailing list, and generally get the word out to a lot of people in a very short time.

Be open to sharing a booth with other nonprofits, if space is at a premium. Many long-running craft fairs throughout the country started as and continue to be fundraisers for the sponsoring organization, so the event coordinators know what it's like to be in your position and often have a soft spot for the efforts of the start-up nonprofit.

Sponsor a Stage or Area

Many street fairs have outdoor stages where local performers can entertain the crowds throughout the event. If your budget allows, consider sponsoring a stage or helping to underwrite some cost associated with it. In return, your organization will be included in any event publicity, which helps establish your group as a member of the community.

Mailing Lists

Maintaining an accurate, up-to-date mailing list is essential. In the beginning, your mailing list will be made up of people who were active in the initial formation of the organization. Slowly, that list will grow to include people who have helped in one way or another, including financially. In time, you will find it beneficial to open your general mailing list to anyone who expresses even the slightest interest in what you are doing, and the collection of names will become a high priority. Of course, there is no point in collecting names simply for the sake of growing the list. The mailing list has a number of very definite purposes.

Mailing Lists Are the Beginning of Your Fundraising Drive

The greatest fundraising letter in the world will not do much good if you do not have places for it to go. Mailing lists are considered money in the bank for many organizations. These lists contain people who came to you; they are already supporters.

Keeping your mailing list on a simple spreadsheet organizes information about when people joined the list, what types of contacts have been made, and what, if any, contributions have been made. Obviously, as your organization matures, your fundraising campaigns will become more sophisticated and you will want to consider very precise queries, but in the beginning, you need to collect and carefully maintain your core supporters.

Mailing Lists Are Currency

It is highly unethical to sell or trade a mailing list. However, you can offer to include information from like-minded groups in your mailing. In exchange, those groups should include information from you in their mailings. This is a perfectly acceptable way for your information to reach the mailing lists of like-minded organizations while keeping each group's list private. Establishing clear criteria for accepting this type of cross-promotion is a function of the board of directors. You will find it necessary to turn down most inquiries you receive, but it can be a good way to broaden your coverage, build alliances with other organizations, and ultimately help the nonprofits in your area.

Public Access Television

Public access television has been around for decades, yet it remains a mystery to many organizations. If a cable television provider serves your region, you have a public access television channel. It might be the channel that carries your city or county council meetings or high school athletics.

Congress established the rules for putting a program on a public access station, and they continue to exist as a free speech platform for local citizens to use. Your local cable provider will have specific details on how to submit a program. Many parts of the country offer two options: a scheduled slot that occurs every month or week, or a completely random slot that usually ensures your program will make it in, but not at a designated time. From a production standpoint, there is no difference.

As an organization, you will be responsible for all the production and editing. Many communities have organizations to assist with public access production, which includes training people to operate cameras and use current editing software.

The Scheduled Program

As a nonprofit, you may be able to secure a regular slot in the public access schedule. If this is an option, do it. Generally speaking, if the program is geared to all audiences (no profanity), and there is space in the schedule, you will have an equal chance of securing a slot as any other organization or individual.

Committing your organization to a regular production is a huge step, and one you do not want to take on until you have enough support. If there is interest in using this wonderful community resource, talk with your local cable provider and other programmers to get their opinions on how effective their programs have been.

Random or Drop-Off Programming

Most public access channels allow program material to be dropped off at established times for broadcast when there is nothing else scheduled. Such material must be in a "plug and play" format. This requires the station engineer to start the program you dropped off at the business office and then walk away from it, allowing it to run. Do not expect any production assistance with this option. If there is a mistake on the disk you deliver to the station, that mistake will go out to all the cable subscribers. This is an option if you lack the production ability to put together a regularly scheduled program.

CHAPTER 17

Staff

Staff can include volunteers, individuals contracted to fulfill a particular responsibility, part-time workers, or full-time employees. Although there are a few rules that are unique to operating in a nonprofit environment, the most important rule to remember is that without the people to do the work, the organization's mission will never be accomplished. Developing a clear set of job descriptions serves several purposes. When someone is hired for a position, a job description lets him know exactly what his responsibilities are and what is expected of him. Job descriptions also remind the board what areas are being handled by staff so they can remain focused on the larger issues affecting the organization.

Office of the Executive Director

The executive director in a nonprofit maintains complete oversight of all operational components and is responsible for all other paid or volunteer staff. The board of directors hires the executive director and she remains responsible to them. Her main task, with the cooperation and assistance of her staff, is turning the board's policy directives into actual programs. The executive director is one of the main people to speak for the organization in the community, so she must have a full and complete understanding of every possible element.

Executive Director Job Description

The job description for an executive director, while obviously addressing details specific to your organization, has a number of common points. These points will give any applicant a clear sense of the responsibilities of the position and will also remind the board of the job functions. Here is a guide to use in building your description. Make sure you include the following essential duties:

- Responsible for overall operations, asset protection, and marketing/ public relations
- Oversees all accounting functions, including those necessary for auditing, budgeting, financial analysis, capital asset and property management, and payroll in accordance with generally accepted accounting principles
- Handles or delegates all aspects of human resource management, including but not limited to hiring and termination, developing position descriptions, setting compensation, and applying board-approved employee policies and benefits in accordance with federal and state requirements
- Interacts with other personnel and organizations, such as local, county, or state governments, business associations, trade and professional associations, and others
- Assists in the development of current and long-term organizational goals and objectives as well as policies and procedures for operations

- Establishes plans to achieve the goals set by the board of directors and implements policies, subject to approval by the board

Administrative Assistant

An administrative assistant works closely with the executive director. This position will become a necessity when your organization reaches a level of maturity that requires hiring an individual who is able to provide support to the director, other professional staff, and the board of directors. A professional in his own right, the administrative assistant will be the first face and voice of the organization that many donors, prospective donors, and members of the general public will encounter.

Here are general points you may want to include in the job description. Your group will have its own specific needs that will build from these tasks:

- Provides executive-level support as required by the executive director and other professional staff
- Prepares agendas and any material needed for general organization meetings, records the minutes of the meetings, and transcribes and distributes the minutes in a timely manner
- Processes organization correspondence—both hard copy and e-mail
- Assists with Internet research on current and prospective donors, entering collected data into the database and creating unique donor profiles
- Staffs events and receptions

Board Liaison

A board liaison is the contact between the members of the board and the staff, both paid and volunteer. Individually and as a group, the board has a tremendous amount of time and resources (possibly including money) invested in the organization, and the members will want to be involved directly in day-to-day activities. Boards bring in executive directors to handle these operations, but they still want that hands-on feeling.

For this position, communication strengths are essential. The liaison must keep all lines of communication flowing smoothly so that everyone feels as if they are on top of what is happening, even if they are not directly involved in a particular issue.

In collaboration with the administrative assistant, the board liaison also helps prepare all necessary materials for the board members prior to their meetings and assists the committees on an as-needed basis. The liaison performs a variety of high-level administrative tasks that are quite different from an administrative assistant. The administrative assistant helps with the organization's overall operations, whereas the board liaison focuses on the board of directors and keeping lines of communication open.

The board liaison is also responsible for developing board retreats and any other special meetings involving board development. Working in a unique zone between staff, volunteers, and the board, the liaison has the freedom to develop longer-range thinking that will help the board do its work. This person has the ability to draw the best ideas and talent from any part of the organization to assist in the task.

The Development Director

The development director is responsible for creating and then implementing the overall fundraising plan for the organization. This position involves a lot more than applying for grants, though grant-writing is often an important part of the job. The development director is one of the few positions that do not require daily interaction with other staff members, making it ideal for telecommuting. Files and hard copies of applications should be kept in a central office, but the actual work can be done anywhere there is a computer with access to the Internet.

There is going to be confusion, particularly among the board members, about the differences between fundraising and development. The board's role is to assist with fundraising and ask for money based on a development plan drawn up by the development director.

More than any other position in the organization, the development director must be completely comfortable talking to strangers, colleagues, other organizations, and business groups about the organization and its development efforts. In light of the global economic crisis, many of the usual rules and methods for nonprofit development are being revised, so development directors must to be able to adjust and adapt.

Nonprofit development has become a highly sought-after position, with people learning the intricacies for many years before taking on the full responsibilities. It is also a position with tremendous responsibilities. If general operating funds are in jeopardy, the development director may have to find new funding sources. The position involves the following:

- Plans and administers all fundraising programs and activities
- Oversees the development department, ensuring staffs and systems operate smoothly and within budget
- Administers annual membership of the organization, including membership drives and solicitations
- Develops and coordinates all capital campaigns for building, expansion, and other programs
- Produces and provides regular detailed accountability reports on finances and fundraising operations
- Offers creative and active leadership for the organization at large
- Spearheads efforts to identify and obtain individual, corporate, and foundation contributions
- Produces proposals, sponsorship invitations, and requests for grants for procuring funds for organizational efforts and causes
- Oversees preparation and production of all promotional mailings, printed pieces, and web communications related to fundraising
- Solicits and cultivates strategic donors
- Devises and executes annual fundraising plans, special events, and programs
- Directs appreciation mailings for all donors
- Serves as a fundraising liaison with the organization's board of directors
- Oversees special events such as auctions and house parties

Volunteers and the Volunteer Coordinator

Volunteers are the lifeblood of every nonprofit organization. Without people who are willing and able to give freely of their time and expertise because they believe in the mission of the group, the vast majority of nonprofits would either cease to exist or be so limited in their ability to fulfill their mission that they might as well close their doors.

ESSENTIAL

Always remember that volunteers are helping because they want to do so; they will leave if they feel their work is unappreciated or if the environment is no longer comfortable. Volunteers should feel comfortable approaching the volunteer coordinator with concerns, and the volunteer coordinator should make it a priority to keep the lines of communication open.

In the beginning, as you are getting the group up and functioning, everyone will be volunteering their time. In time, as the group begins to mature and revenue increases, you may be able to compensate people in the lead roles. Until then, volunteers will be responsible for running a large part of the organization.

Volunteer Coordinator

A volunteer coordinator needs to be the classic "people person" who honestly enjoys working with all types of people and understands your organization and its mission. She is often a member of the public's first point of contact when he calls or drops by offering to help, so an immediate feeling of welcoming and support will go a long way in recruitment and retention of your volunteer base.

In the early, formative stages, the volunteer coordinator's first responsibility will be to get people registered and entered into your general database. The registration form should include questions about the person's particular interests or skills. Then the volunteer coordinator must match those skill sets with the needs of the group. To allow for scheduling, she must communicate regularly with everyone involved in operations to determine what the need for volunteers will be on any given day.

The core tasks of any volunteer coordinator will include:

- Continually seeking new sources for volunteer recruitment
- Preparing material describing volunteer responsibilities
- Interviewing, selecting, and placing qualified individuals in the organization
- Planning and implementing volunteer training programs
- Keeping accurate records of volunteer service time
- Keeping volunteers motivated and enthusiastic

Volunteer Recognition

The key to keeping the best volunteers actively engaged in the organization is always to thank them and recognize their contributions for what they are—essential. Having a party to stuff and mail a few thousand envelopes may seem boring, but when everyone remembers why those envelopes are going out—to bring in more people to make the organization grow—the value of their time becomes clear.

Organize special events from time to time. They do not need to be elaborate, but they must take place. Establishing the bond between the organization and its volunteers is one of the benefits of the nonprofit sector, and it is too often overlooked.

About Special Events

Getting involved in existing events or starting one on your own is one of the best ways to let your community know what you are doing and why you are doing it and to encourage others to join you. As a nonprofit organization, you may qualify for reduced fees to participate in existing events, so make sure to tell the event coordinators a little bit about your group. Don't be shy!

Producing any type of event on your own is going to require a lot of work, so take a good look at your current capacity before committing the group to something that you may not have people to see through.

Here are a few examples of special events you may want to consider:

- **Craft/street fairs**. They usually have an area set aside for nonprofit groups.
- **Special events at your local mall or shopping center**. Ask for the mall's Calendar of Events and see what is appropriate for you.
- **Business organizations' meet and greets**. Usually held monthly, these events will always welcome new organizations as guests until you are able to join.
- **Open houses**. Throw open your doors and invite the neighborhood in for beverages and conversation.
- **Film nights**. Feature a movie associated with your mission.
- **Cosponsorship of events produced by other organizations**. This is a means of keeping your name visible and a way to be seen working with more established organizations.

ESSENTIAL

Many organizations have a complete volunteer application on their websites, allowing people to fill in and e-mail it directly to the volunteer coordinator. This saves steps and eliminates the delay between an individual thinking about volunteering and actually doing it.

Volunteer Recruitment

Maintaining a good, strong volunteer pool is not always easy. People come and go. You will lose some of the best people and need to find replacements with similar skills. The organization's website and newsletter are among the most useful tools to find new volunteers.

Preparing notices for submission to the newsletter will keep the need for volunteers on people's minds and will return good results. If you are having trouble getting good volunteers from your existing membership, ask the local service organizations. Many of these organizations try to place their members into volunteer positions in local nonprofits as a way of contributing to the community. Likewise, many larger businesses have in-house programs to help their employees locate volunteer opportunities. These options generally bring out highly skilled, motivated individuals who will be delighted at the opportunity to work with your group.

The Accountant

The staff accountant or bookkeeper is responsible for day-to-day financial operations. This person will be in regular communication with the executive director and the treasurer, keeping everyone current on the financial health of the group. Much of the responsibility for accounting in a nonprofit is identical to that in any business; the main differences lie in the state and federal reporting requirements. With a solid background and understanding of accounting principles, that switch is rarely a problem.

ALERT

If your organization can only compensate one person, hire an accountant or bookkeeper. As your organization grows, having the financial records in perfect order is going to be more important than anything else you will do.

Accounting software such as QuickBooks is pretty much the de facto norm, making financial data and record keeping uniform throughout many businesses. Your accountant/bookkeeper will handle most of the day-to-day business with your bank, from deposits to payroll. Depending on your organization and the amount of cash involved, he or she will also handle receipts and be responsible for entering and reconciling accounts.

While no list of responsibilities is complete or satisfies every need of every organization, here are some qualities to look for when searching for an accountant to work with your organization:

- Is comfortable using math to solve problems
- Understands economic and accounting principles and practices
- Communicates information and ideas in such a way so others will understand
- Realizes that others in the organization may have limited understanding of what an accountant does

- Has a working knowledge of accounting software and is able to generate reports and run detailed queries
- Has a sense of humor, as it is necessary
- Possesses a general understanding of what a nonprofit organization is (other than the yearly filing of Form 990 (the federal financial document), there are no differences between the accounting needs of a for-profit and nonprofit organization)

Program/Project Coordinators

Coordinators who handle specific projects your organization decides to undertake can be a huge staffing issue. In the early stages of your nonprofit, the core of your group and your trusted volunteers will coordinate projects.

As you continue to grow, however, the workload may simply be too large, and it may become necessary to hire someone to coordinate a particular project or event. Although coordinators can be board members who organize committees for the sole purpose of moving a project forward, sometimes it is easier to outsource the task and make it an official job position.

The responsibilities assumed by the ideal project coordinator will depend on the actual project. It will be necessary to have a core knowledge base relevant to the project before anything else can be considered. If you are establishing an inner-city dental clinic, you will be seeking someone far different than a coordinator for bird-watching field trips as part of an avian society. However, there are some general elements that will apply across the spectrum.

A project coordinator should:

- Have a basic familiarity with budgeting principles and grant writing
- Possess skills in Microsoft Word, Excel, and Power Point (or the Open Office equivalents)
- Have excellent organizational and communication skills (verbal and written)
- Be self-motivated and able to work with minimal supervision
- Understand and have experience working in resource-scarce environments

- Be flexible with working hours
- Have a good sense of humor and make people smile

Compensation

Brand-new nonprofits are rarely in a position to pay anyone right away. If this sounds familiar, don't worry.

In time, the workload and associated time commitments will stretch your volunteer base to its limit. Before you reach that limit, you must think about compensation for a few people and put those figures into your budget.

As in the for-profit sector, you are going to get what you pay for, with an added bonus. People who are already drawn to your organization and its mission may negotiate with your hiring committee and ultimately your board to make their employment a win-win situation. There are two important details that everyone involved in the hiring process must understand, regardless of the position and the compensation package: (1) the salary you offer must be a fixed amount, and (2) your pay structure must be in line with the community—in other words, no excessive compensation.

Agreeing to a Fee

The fee must be a fixed number, not a changeable figure based on "how well we do this year." Tying pay to the organization's performance gives the impression that the employee is personally benefiting from the organization, which is not permitted under IRS law. Such an arrangement would potentially jeopardize your nonprofit status. Although this kind of pay structure is perfectly acceptable in the for-profit world, it is not allowed in a nonprofit. You need to agree on a set fee and factor that into your overall operating budget.

The Big No-No: Excessive Compensation

A report of your organization's paying excessive compensation is not the type of publicity you want to see on your local television news program. Remember, the public is supporting your nonprofit, either by contributions or because your organization does not pay income tax.

ALERT

You can lose your tax-exempt status if it is determined that your organization is paying excessive compensation. If there is any concern, contact your tax advisor.

There are no hard-and-fast rules to determine what constitutes excessive, which makes it a complex topic. Percentages can be endlessly debated, but if your pay structure clearly exceeds a comparable position in the community, you may be close to crossing the line. You need to understand what compensation norms are in your area and use them as your guide.

CHAPTER 18

Finally! The 1023

After long months of hard work and planning, countless meetings, conferences, and more meetings, you are finally ready. It is time to fill out IRS Form 1023, the actual application that allows you to be recognized as a nonprofit organization by the federal government. It is not an easy application, so this chapter will cover each of the main parts of the application in detail. In addition to the application form, the packet must include a number of supporting documents and materials. This chapter will also cover the most common types of support material.

The Anatomy of Form 1023

Form 1023 is made up of eleven parts (I–XI) that you must fill out with the supplementary information requested.

FORM 1023 PARTS

- Part I. Identification of Applicant: This part is self-explanatory. It asks for basic information about your nonprofit; fill in the organization's name, mailing address, Employer Identification Number, and other relevant information.
- Part II. Organizational Structure: Identify how your organization is set up (corporation, limited liability company, unincorporated association, or trust) and provide supporting documents.
- Part III. Required Provisions in Your Organizing Document: When you wrote the articles of incorporation, you included two specific clauses to comply with IRS requirements. You will need to refer to those clauses that (1) define the purpose of your nonprofit, and (2) outline what happens to excess funds (those remaining after all the bills are paid) when the organization closes.
- Part IV. Narrative Description of Your Activities: Write a description of your organization's activities.
- Part V. Compensation and Other Financial Arrangements with Your Officers, Directors, Trustees, Employees, and Independent Contractors: If you are paying anyone for services directly related to the operation of your organization, identify them here and give details of their compensation.
- Part VI. Your Members and Other Individuals and Organizations That Receive Benefits from You: This part contains a series of three yes or no questions.
- Part VII. Your History: There are two yes or no questions in this part.
- Part VIII. Your Specific Activities: This series of questions asks you to go into detail about how your nonprofit operates.
- Part IX. Financial Data: This chart asks you to outline your finances for the current tax year and the three previous years. If your nonprofit was formed within that time frame, you must make good-faith estimates regarding your future budget. New rules allow a new organization that may not have a financial history to include its current budget,

and two projected "accounting periods" (understood to be years) as evidence that it fully intends to be a public charity rather than a private foundation. In plain English, the IRS is now willing to accept your word that you plan to follow the rules with respect to where your operating funds will be coming from, rather than having to show past evidence that is simply impossible for a new organization.

- Part X. Public Charity Status: This part defines your nonprofit as a private foundation or a public charity.
- Part XI. User Fee Information: This section determines your fee for submitting Form 1023.

In addition, there are eight schedules. You will only have to complete the one(s) that apply to your nonprofit.

SCHEDULES
- Schedule A. Churches
- Schedule B. Schools, Colleges, and Universities
- Schedule C. Hospitals and Medical Research Organizations
- Schedule D. Section 509(a)(3) Supporting Organizations
- Schedule E. Organizations Not Filing Form 1023 Within 27 Months of Formation
- Schedule F. Homes for the Elderly or Handicapped and Low-Income Housing
- Schedule G. Successors to Other Organizations
- Schedule H. Organizations Providing Scholarships, Fellowships, Educational Loans, or Other Educational Grants to Individuals and Private Foundations Requesting Advance Approval of Individual Grant Procedures

Form 1023 is lengthy, but most of it is self-explanatory. The sections that need more explanation will be explored in this chapter.

The First Challenge: Part IV, the Narrative

The first three parts of Form 1023 are straightforward and self-explanatory. If you have been working through each element of establishing your organization, you will be in a good position to complete this form.

The first challenge for every group applying for tax exemption is Part IV, the narrative. The narrative does not need to be lengthy, but it does need to cover a number of essential points and avoid a few common mistakes. Begin with a few short paragraphs explaining what your organization is and what it does. Let the reader know in the first or second sentence that the group was formed "for exclusively charitable and educational purposes."

Offer a brief history of the organization, focusing on activities that clearly point to the requirements of a 501(c)(3) organization. If you are applying as an educational organization, identify activities that support that application. Only discuss projects that are actually taking place or are planned.

ESSENTIAL

Under no circumstances can you discuss projects that are merely speculative and that have no concrete planning or identification in your budget. Ideas that came out of a brainstorming session might be terrific, but do not include them until they are part of your real plans and you can provide documentation supporting them.

You can quote portions of the IRS code in your narrative and then explain precisely how your organization complies not only with the spirit of the law but also with the precise language. The audience for this narrative is the IRS. The personnel who read this want you to succeed, but they must be certain that your organization complies with every element of a precise law.

Avoid any mention of restricted activities. Your entire focus must be to show how your organization adheres to the narrow definitions in the Internal Revenue Service code. Also, avoid any suggestion of lobbying. If your organization's mission is to offer after-school tutoring to inner-city kids, stay with that discussion; do not drift into any suggestion about proposed changes in the federal or state budget that may affect your program. The narrative is the time to detail how you will follow the exact language of the law. It is not a time to convince anyone of anything except your understanding of the IRS application. Although individual members of your organization may be directly involved in lobbying one side or the other, you, as an organization, must stay clear of any such activities. You certainly do not want to bring them up here. Similarly, do not suggest that your work will help the members of your organization.

The organization must help the community. Your members are a part of the community, but the focus cannot be on them. If you put in language to the effect that the membership is going to be a primary beneficiary of the group's work, you probably won't qualify for tax exemption.

A nonprofit organization may not participate to any substantial extent in business activity unrelated to its purpose and mission. As you describe your business activities, show how those activities directly relate to your purpose and exist only to support your charitable goals.

Refer to Attachments

Every activity or program you identify in the narrative must have some form of supporting documentation. Each time you refer to an event, consider what resources you can use as supporting attachments. If you have a schedule of ongoing events, include a copy of your monthly calendar. If you have press clippings, include copies. If you maintain a monthly newsletter detailing current and planned activities, send a representative sample as part of your narrative.

Explain clearly what your organization is doing, provide documentary evidence of your activities, and show precisely how your program complies with the letter of the IRS code. By showing why and how you will follow any reasonable interpretation of that code, you make the case for why you should qualify for tax-exempt status.

Financial Data

The budget you include with your application will assist the IRS in further understanding any details you discussed in the narrative. It is also easy to verify that you are not crossing any lines with respect to excessive compensation. If your group claims to be operating as a public charity, your budget clearly indicates how much of your income is from public sources.

Preparing a budget for inclusion in your 1023 application will not be a huge problem if you have developed your organization's budget from the beginning. No particular format is required, so use whatever system you have set up and include it as an attachment to the application.

If you have been in existence for a short time and do not yet have a multiple-year budget, expand upon what you do have to show how you plan to operate in five years. The main point is to show that you expect continued and increased funding from public sources and that your budget corresponds to the narrative.

ALERT

The budget you submit can be a general overview budget. It does not need to be fully itemized. You need to show that you are a charitable organization and that the money you bring in is used for the exempt purpose.

There is a sample budget in this toolkit that you can follow as you create your own. There is no prescribed format, but standard spreadsheet programs are perfectly adequate. The IRS is interested in determining whether you have followed the instructions and are making your case for exemption.

User Fee Information

One of the first questions most organizations ask when they consider making an application for federal tax exemption is "How much does it cost?" The user fee, or the money the IRS charges to accept and review your application, is completely separate from any fee you negotiate with a tax consultant or lawyer in the preparation of the application.

The user fee is due with the application. If the fee is not included, the application will not be reviewed. The fee is nonrefundable; if your application is rejected or you receive a determination other than what you wanted, the fee will not be returned. There are actually two possible fees, depending on what your gross receipts are or what you project them to be over the next four years.

- If your organization's gross receipts will be $10,000 or more, your user fee will be $750.

- If your organization's gross receipts are under $10,000, your user fee will be $300.

These amounts were current as of the publication date of this guide, but they may change. The IRS will cross-reference your revenue projections with your user fee to make sure you paid the correct amount.

The Advance Ruling Process

In the course of your research and talking to other people who have made successful applications for tax-exempt status, you have probably heard the term *advance ruling*. This process allowed a new organization that lacked years of documentation to obtain a favorable determination and then have five years to show that it was a publicly supported organization. At the end of those five years, the organization had to file another form showing that it met the standards and should be granted a final determination.

As of 2008, the rules changed for the better. The advance ruling process was eliminated. You still need to plan for and show in your budget that your organization is indeed a public charity. If your organization is relatively new, and thus has not been receiving public funds for several years, you need to show in your narrative and in your budget that you can reasonably expect to be publicly supported. You must meet that one-third threshold before the IRS will accept that you are a public charity.

The IRS will now accept that you are a public charity based on the documentation you provide. You must meet the established one-third threshold for five years. With your sixth taxable year, you must file your yearly Form 990, showing you meet the public support test.

Assembling Supplementary Materials

There are no rules on exactly what supplementary materials you should assemble. You must include the formally required elements, but any supplementary information can be included or excluded at your discretion. Keep in mind that you have one chance to introduce your organization to an IRS agent who has never heard of you or your group. In the course of that introduction, you must clearly document the fact that your organization understands the language governing a nonprofit organization.

The agent will be familiar with Form 1023. It details your financial history and is, to some degree, presented on good faith by all parties involved. The supplemental materials should drive home the fact that you are a viable organization with media coverage, regular recorded meetings, classes open to the public, an engaged and supportive membership base, and a community already aware of and committed to supporting you in a number of ways.

The reason you want to have a clear media strategy and cultivate good contacts in the local press is to increase your media coverage because you can use samples of that coverage to document your activities to the IRS. These early budgets and program samples can help show that you are a viable group, actively doing what you say you are doing.

There is also no definitive rule on how much assembled material to include with your application. Any activity that you reference in your narrative or any line item in your budget that has a real, tangible result will help your case.

Outside Review

Completing a 1023 application is difficult. There are many reasons that this is one of the more complicated government forms, not the least of which is the IRS's interest in making absolutely certain that any organization applying for tax exemption meets all the requirements and understands the responsibilities of a nonprofit organization. Because this form is so difficult—particularly if you tackled the application yourself—it is strongly suggested that you ask an expert to review all the materials before you submit them.

FACT

Be prepared. It is possible that after a review of your application the consultant will advise you to make an application for a 501(c)(4) determination, rather than the 501(c)(3) if it appears that your chance of a successful determination is low. This is not necessarily a bad thing; it will still secure your nonprofit status, leaving open the option for a future change.

Review by a Tax Professional

Most nonprofit tax consultants will, for a fee, review your completed application and make any suggestions they feel will increase the likelihood of a favorable determination. Be exceptionally careful that the tax person is familiar with nonprofit tax law and Form 1023 in particular.

There are many, many areas within the federal tax law, and no tax advisor is going to be knowledgeable about each of them. Just as with medicine and law, tax advisors have special areas of expertise. Take the time to locate a professional who understands nonprofit application requirements, or you will waste your time and money.

Review by a Tax Lawyer

Any competent lawyer whose area of specialty includes nonprofit organizations can help you through the entire process, from filing incorporation documents to drafting by-laws to completing Form 1023. Your lawyer will know what the IRS expects to see, and she can make sure you have all the materials you need. Expect to work closely with her. She may know the tax code, but she also needs to know everything about your organization—who your organization serves, where you expect funding to come from, how you will use the funds, and countless other details. The more she knows about your organization, the fewer questions the IRS will have about your application and the more smoothly the application process will go.

The Application Packet

The application packet must include everything the IRS expects to see. Each item should be clearly marked with the organization's name, mailing address, and Employer Identification Number. Do not send loose clippings or half-completed forms. The following is the basic list of what you need to include. Use it as a reference or as a checklist. Not all of these forms will be required for every organization; they are included here for reference purposes only.

- An envelope containing the check for the user fee. Make your check out to "United States Treasury" for either $300 or $750.

- The two-page Form 1023 Checklist, found at the end of Form 1023. You need to tell the IRS which Form 1023 schedules you are filing as well as where to find your organization's purpose and dissolution clauses.
- Form 2848, Power of Attorney. If your organization is represented by a tax professional, this form identifies him and states your relationship.
- Form 8821, Tax Information Authorization. Fill out this form if you want the IRS to discuss your application with a third party. Most groups will never file this form, so you probably do not have to worry about it.
- Expedite Request. If you are asking the IRS to expedite review of your application, you can submit this request in the form of a letter. Ask an outside expert to review this letter to ensure it meets your needs and those of the IRS.
- Form 1023
- Articles of Organization. If you are incorporated, this should be the articles of incorporation. Otherwise, submit your constitution, articles of association, or other governing document. By-laws alone are not enough. Articles of incorporation should clearly show that they have been filed with the proper state authority. The IRS usually asks for two signatures on the governing instrument of an unincorporated association.
- By-laws. These should be signed and dated.
- Form 5768. Fill out this form if the organization has decided to make expenditures to influence legislation under section 501(h) of the Internal Revenue Code. This is an area most start-up nonprofits should avoid, but it is included in the checklist in case you need it.
- Actual financial data, including income statement(s) and a recent balance sheet, if the organization has had any financial activity.
- A two-year projected budget, showing both expected sources of income and anticipated expenses. Sometimes the IRS asks for a projected budget even when the applicant can provide a full year of actual financial data.

Here are a few other items to include in your packet:

- Printed materials describing the history of the organization, its activities, and its plans for the future (e.g., brochures, pamphlets, descriptive literature, published materials)
- Sample copies of your organization's newsletter if you publish one
- Any materials prepared for members, membership application forms, promotional materials, sample membership certificates or identification cards, sample copies of member-only publications, and so on
- Copies of newspaper clippings, transcripts of interviews, and so on
- Any documentation you have regarding grant monies (i.e., grant applications, grant contracts, or correspondence between your organization and the grantor organization)
- A schedule of events, showing where and when your organization has held informational or other events during the last twelve months; include approximate attendance figures
- If you have a scholarship or grant program, a description of how potential applicants will hear about your program
- Letters between your organization and potential members or board members, letters of appreciation from groups where you have made presentations or otherwise helped out, or even letters from public officials commenting on your efforts
- Advertisements, copies of contracts, rental agreements, leases, and loan agreements involving your organization
- Copies of federal, state, or local legislation, if any, regarding the creation or continued existence of your organization
- Resumes of board members and/or key employees
- Independent appraisals of assets the group is renting or purchasing

The Determination Letter

After submitting the application, you can expect a letter from the IRS in about eight weeks acknowledging the receipt of your application. Usually the letter will ask you for additional information. This is entirely normal and is not a cause for alarm. If you had a tax professional prepare your application, she can help you with this stage. If you have not had anyone review your application, this is a good time to reconsider that decision. If there are questions, carefully prepare a written response.

If there are ten or fewer questions, you are probably in very good shape and you can expect approval of your application without additional hassle. If, on the other hand, there are fifteen or more questions, there may be problems with your application. Regardless, answer all questions truthfully and in detail and submit the answers to the IRS within the deadlines stated in the letter.

The letter will give you the name and telephone number of your contact person at the IRS. Call this person and find out exactly what he wants to know. Contact people can often be very helpful, and the information they give you can help you focus your response to the letter.

If It Is Not on Paper, It Does Not Exist

Any telephone conversations you have with your IRS contact person are informational only. The only answers to the written questions that matter are your written responses. Both your organization and the IRS are establishing a paper trail, which allows everyone involved to reference what happened before so there are no misunderstandings.

Remember, the IRS is not trying to stall the process or otherwise complicate matters. They do, however, need to be absolutely certain that you have met all the required benchmarks if they are going to issue a favorable determination.

The Determination Letter

In due course, the IRS will send you either a favorable or an unfavorable determination letter. If it is unfavorable for a 501(c)(3) determination, some applicants are offered a favorable determination for a 501(c)(4) organization. If it is favorable, you have every right to celebrate. Save this letter. It is very important. Not only does it give you critical information about compliance with the IRS, but your potential funding sources will usually ask you for a copy. Make copies of the determination letter and keep the original in a safe place. Over the life of the organization, you may send out copies of that letter dozens—if not hundreds—of times, so make certain you never lose the original.

A Denied Application

There will be situations when the IRS determines that your organization does not qualify for a 501(c)(3) determination, and grants you a 501(c)(4) status as an alternative. They may also deny you, without presenting an alternative.

One common problem is that supporting documents are not strong enough. You may believe you qualified as an educational organization, for example, but the material or your narrative didn't support that claim.

If you are not satisfied with the decision, you have the right to appeal within thirty days of the decision. The appeal needs to be initiated by a letter to the IRS Appeals Office detailing the reasons you feel the decision was not accurate and requesting a conference. The address to send the letter will be on the denial letter you received from the IRS.

If the appeal is not made within the thirty-day window from the time the denial was issued, the decision will be considered final. Likewise, if the decision on appeal is not favorable, you will have exhausted your options.

If you plan to appeal the decision, consult an attorney familiar with the IRS appeal process. The stakes are too high and the possible details so numerous that it is best to seek such consultation.

CHAPTER 19

Board Liability Insurance

Although the issue of personal and organizational liability is likely to be on every board member's mind, it should not dissuade anyone from serving on the board of directors. This chapter will cut through some of the common misconceptions about the board and its members' liabilities, as well as present insurance options designed specifically to address these concerns.

Overview

Not long ago, most small nonprofit organizations gave little thought to insurance. They believed that because they were nonprofit, owned little of real value, and were doing good work, they were essentially immune from the messy lawsuits that abound in the for-profit corporate world.

For some groups, this remains a fine way to operate, especially in the start-up phase. But as an organization grows, purchases property, and brings in outside people as contractors or formal employees, that approach may have to change.

One reason informal groups decide to incorporate is to give the individuals involved—owners in a for-profit or board members in a nonprofit—some degree of personal protection from liability. Unfortunately, this does not protect the board as an entity from lawsuits that might be filed over any number of issues, completely apart from financial or fiduciary responsibilities.

Board members can still be exposed to lawsuits. A board member can be named as a defendant if a lawyer decides to name anyone and everyone involved with the organization. Such an action can and will wreak havoc on the organization if you are not prepared.

As soon as your organization feels it is necessary, purchase director and officer insurance (D&O insurance). One way that a nonprofit can protect its directors and staff is via the indemnification provision in its by-laws. Although such indemnification is allowed to some extent by all states, it may not be available if the organization simply cannot sustain the losses.

"Good Faith"

Lawyers often use the term *good faith* to describe how board members must act at all times in order to avoid lawsuits related to their duties on the board. In general, as long as each board member individually meets her fiduciary responsibilities as well as she can (acting in good faith), lawsuits against individual board members for the handling of board affairs can be minimized. The board must also, as a group, understand its duty to act in good faith and operate responsibly to minimize the threat of lawsuit.

In addition, you must maintain transparency in all financial dealings. People involved in the organization at any level should be able to see and understand exactly what you are doing and why you take the actions you choose.

Common sense should be an underlying requirement in all of your planning and in all of your actions. Many of the legal problems that engulf nonprofit organizations result from forgetting to use common sense when working through a problem.

Reducing Risk

Try to minimize risk to the organization and its board members by creating operating policies that clearly forbid questionable activities. These policies must be taken seriously.

It is impossible to guarantee that no one will ever bring suit against the group, but deliberate risk management is essential. The law does not require that your organization always make perfect decisions, but it does require that the group follow appropriate guidelines for making decisions. This is why you must have a clear set of by-laws to govern how all decisions will be made.

Your organization should clearly state how a group member should conduct himself while representing the group. A high priority for every nonprofit must be to recruit and retain effective board leaders who accept their responsibility to do a conscientious job. Board members must do their utmost to uphold the overall health of the organization and minimize the potential for lawsuits.

The board should establish and diligently follow rules and procedures governing its operations. The minutes of the board meetings should demonstrate that the board consistently exercises due diligence and seriously considers the consequences of important actions in advance. These minutes and other important organizational documents should be readily available for periodic reviews and updates.

To reduce the risk of lawsuit, and as a matter of personal financial security, each board member must do the following:

- Ensure that the organization is operating within 503(c)(3) guidelines
- Accept the board's legal responsibility to protect the group's assets
- Confirm all major contracts with formally recorded board authorization
- Attend board meetings and recognize that repeated absences may be interpreted as indicating a lack of serious dedication to the obligations of the position
- Require a thorough debate on controversial or complicated issues
- Exercise sound judgment even when relying on the accuracy and integrity of others (including areas of special competence)
- Avoid any conflict of interest or appearance of conflict of interest

If a board member is connected in any way with a business transaction with a friend's group, the board must be prepared to demonstrate clearly that fairness was maintained.

Never assume that actions are acceptable simply because the group agreed to them. Likewise, do not rely on the president of the board to know what is appropriate and what is not. As an individual member, you must be satisfied with each action. It's that important.

Insurance for Employment Issues

The overwhelming majority of lawsuits filed against nonprofit organizations involve issues related to employment. The specific issue may involve discrimination in the hiring or termination process, harassment, payment issues, or another area. More often than not, lawsuits are brought by people who feel they had no other recourse or had exhausted all other avenues to resolve the problem.

People who work in nonprofit organizations often develop a special bond with the organization, its mission, and their coworkers. This bond makes legal action different from what might occur in a for-profit company. However, a lawsuit is still a lawsuit. If all attempts at mediation fail, you will have to go to court, where someone will win and someone will lose. Director and officer insurance is essential to protect your board in these situations.

Director and Officer (D&O) Insurance

Although the fact that your organization is incorporated with the state protects your board from the financial liability of the organization, it does not protect them from legal actions that might by brought against them. For that protection, you need to carry D&O insurance for every board member.

FACT

Employee insurance is intended to protect the organization from legal actions that may or may not have merit. Purchasing insurance does not infer that you would treat an employee with anything less than respect. It is no different from auto insurance. People buy it, but they never intend to drive carelessly.

D&O insurance protects nonprofit organizations when claims arise from allegations that nonbodily damage resulted from policy decisions made by the board of directors or from actions by the board and volunteers based on those policies. These damages are considered to be the result of wrongful, intentional acts rather than mere negligence. About 90 percent of D&O suits against nonprofit organizations are employment related. These lawsuits include wrongful termination, sexual harassment, and age, sex, or race discrimination. Most of the remaining 10 percent of D&O suits deal with allegations that the board of directors committed a breach of their fiduciary duty to appropriately use and protect the organization's assets and resources. All organizations, regardless of whether they have employees, must carefully consider their exposure to this particular risk. The accusations may be directed against the entire group or against individual members of the group and may come from donors, concerned citizens, or government officials.

Employee Insurance

Some organizations choose to purchase another level of protection specifically designed to address negligence on the part of the organization. These policies have many names, but they are often bundled with the D&O insurance policies and are intended to protect board members against lawsuits brought by current or former employees.

A very important consideration that your insurance carrier can more fully explain involves the limitations of most policies that address employee lawsuits. A general liability or D&O policy protects the organization as long as there was coverage when the alleged incident took place, even if the policy was later discontinued for whatever reason. However, policies that protect against employee lawsuits must have been in effect when the incident took place, and they must still be in effect when the lawsuit is filed.

This is particularly relevant in overtime pay lawsuits and certain types of harassment, where the employee has many years to file a legal case. The insurance must be retained or the organization will be fully exposed with no possible way to collect if it is determined that they are indeed at fault and are required to pay.

Maintaining an open-door policy throughout the organization and keeping your financial affairs as transparent as possible will go a long way toward eliminating many of the risks that insurance policies are designed to handle. By and large, people involved in nonprofit organizations are not itching for a legal fight. However, they also represent a highly educated part of the population who know and understand their legal rights and will not tolerate any perceived abuse of those rights.

Still there is absolutely nothing you can do to protect your nonprofit from someone who is intent on bringing a lawsuit against you or the organization if their sole purpose is to disrupt your operations. This is why D&O insurance is a good idea.

Insurance for General Liability with Real Property

The moment your organization owns or leases anything of real value (such as property, structures, or even a vehicle), you need to seriously consider obtaining insurance. General liability insurance provides protection from claims arising from bodily or property damage considered to result from simple negligence. Every group is at risk of such claims. For example, a volunteer's actions could injure or damage another person or someone's personal property. A person could be hurt or experience property damage while attending an event on your property. The injured party might claim your organization or an individual was negligent or reckless. Liability insurance will pay for legal defense and any financial judgment incurred. To protect assets that belong to the group, such as office equipment and merchandise inventory, you may need to buy personal property or physical damage insurance coverage.

Maintaining a Sense of Perspective

Any discussion about insurance will inevitably drift to every possible worst-case scenario. We live in a highly litigious culture where it seems people will sue anyone at any time for any perceived slight. However, as a start-up nonprofit, you need to differentiate between the risks you may truly face and the risks that do not apply to your situation.

Until you have employees or own property, you may be able to satisfy your coverage with basic D&O insurance. No one will to try to sue an organization that has nothing to lose.

Insurance for Specific Situations

Depending on the type of services or programs you offer, you may want to investigate other categories of insurance. Many venues that regularly rent their facilities to community organizations will require the renter to carry public-assembly or mass-gathering insurance. Cities may require a similar type of policy if you are planning to use a public park or public facility for your event.

ALERT

Since the attacks of September 11, 2001, many mass-gathering or public-assembly insurance policies have had an optional terrorism rider. Currently, no venues actually require this additional coverage; it is only an option. You and your organization need to decide if the cost of the premium is justified.

If your organization is planning to hold events on public property such as a city park or street, meet and get to know the people in your city's or county's risk management office. These people are responsible for protecting the city from any liability, and they are the ones who will require you to carry insurance policies. More often than not, the fact that you are a nonprofit has little bearing on their concerns, but it will be important when you take out a policy with an insurance carrier.

If you are planning any type of festival that will have booths and food, require each vendor to carry insurance and name your organization as the insured party. You can present this when you go through the permitting process to hold your event.

ALERT

Ask your insurance agent if you can purchase a multi-event insurance policy. If you produce a number of public events each year, this policy will enable your group to have a lower premium and you won't need to worry about having the necessary coverage each time you have an event.

These policies protect your organization as well as any municipal jurisdiction from damages that may result if someone gets hurt during the event and decides to seek a legal remedy. These policies are usually written to cover up to $5 million per incident. This may sound like an incredible amount of money, but most city risk-management departments will require it.

Volunteer Accident Insurance

The Volunteer Protection Act of 1997 provides that a volunteer meeting certain criteria shall not be liable for damage resulting from "simple negligence" while performing authorized volunteer activities for a 501(c)(3) organization. The definition of a volunteer as an "individual performing services without receipt of compensation (other than reasonable expense reimbursement) or any other thing of value in lieu of compensation in excess of $500 per year" also includes directors and officers.

Although the Volunteer Protection Act protects volunteers from being held liable for damage caused by their acts of "simple negligence," it does not protect against liability for damage caused by "gross negligence." The exact line of demarcation between "simple negligence" and "gross negligence" is difficult to determine, both practically and legally. Other aspects of the act's provisions, including the concept of "authorized" activities and "things of value in lieu of compensation," are also somewhat open to interpretation. In addition, the act does not actually prohibit lawsuits against volunteers. It was primarily intended to protect the assets of directors, officers, and volunteers by making the nonprofit sponsor the one held accountable for damage resulting from a volunteer's simple negligence.

CHAPTER 20

Operations Staff and the Board of Directors

As your organization matures the roles of the board and those of operations staff will probably conflict. This is normal as individuals settle into their particular areas of interest or are drawn to participate without understanding the larger picture. Through careful guidance and a commitment to working together, you can avert potential problems and resolve the issues that arise.

An Age-Old Conflict

The people who are drawn to the operations side of any organization are invariably slightly different than those who are drawn to the policy-making side. It may be the water they drink or the genes they were born with, but there is a distinct difference that needs to be recognized and acknowledged for the health of the organization.

Some of the conflict surfaces because the board is made up of volunteers who may only attend a few meetings a month yet feel the need to stay involved in day-to-day operations. It is a natural desire to want to shepherd and nurture an organization they feel strongly about, and it needs to be respected. However, board members also need to trust the people who are responsible for the daily running of the organization.

The operations staff may have a better view of how policies impact the community the organization exists to serve, and they may be frustrated by their inability to make changes they know are needed. This is why establishing firm lines of communication and developing mutual respect between the board of directors and the operations staff is crucial.

ALERT

To further complicate matters, your membership and possibly the general public will want to enter the conversation on any number of issues, inevitably coming down on one side or the other. Your task is to welcome that input and direct it in such a way that it alleviates, instead of contributes to, any tension.

There are, of course, very real legal responsibilities that come along with being a board member. Those responsibilities need to be woven into any understanding of how the board and staff work together and interact.

Walk in the Other Person's Shoes

Although most staff people will find any possible reason to avoid attending a board meeting if they are not required to, extend the invitation broadly or to specific people now and then. People who say they don't like meetings may actually be saying that they don't understand what is going on and they feel out of place.

Assure them that they don't have to participate; they can simply observe and get a feel for the dynamics of the board of directors. If they have questions, encourage them to ask them after the meeting. At the meeting, simply introduce the guests in the room and let the meeting progress as usual.

ESSENTIAL

Remember, there may be a future board member or someone with leadership potential among the volunteers and staff. Although some initial awkwardness may be felt as roles become blurred, a fantastic element of nonprofits is how quickly people can adapt when the organization requires it.

Strongly encourage board members to spend time with the volunteers or staff, helping in a hands-on way with the real work of the organization. For many, this is already a normal part of how your group functions. If not, this will help the board understand the frustrations and worries as well as experience the complete joy in work they might otherwise only see through the monthly financial reports.

Seek Out Counsel and Advice

Along a similar vein, it may be beneficial for board members to be available for informal conversations with staff and volunteers who may be having trouble or simply need a little help. The board members made it onto your board because they brought clearly identifiable talents or resources to the organization. Although most of their time may be committed to board functions, your organization can only benefit if they are also of direct assistance to the larger group. This is not an invitation to meddle or micromanage; instead, it is an opportunity to offer wisdom and knowledge with the luxury of being one step removed from the ongoing work.

Back to Those Committees

Working, active, and engaged committees that grow out of the board of directors are often the hidden treasure of nonprofit organizations. Creating a supportive committee structure that encourages board members and community members to assume governance responsibilities provides an outlet for creative ideas and helps funnel those ideas into productive actions without cluttering up already full workloads. Many of the stresses that come from having either a detached board or too many people involved in making operational decisions can be alleviated by making certain the committees are up and running.

Defining Board Oversight

The board must remain focused on the big-picture issues that affect the organization. This oversight function involves ongoing communications with major donors and others in the community who feel comfortable only when they are dealing directly with a board member.

ALERT

Be sure to have at least one board member work with your lead operations person on basic items such as developing agendas for board meetings. This involvement ensures that no one feels left out and directly encourages full participation. This simple act may eliminate communication problems well before they arise.

It is also good for individual board members to know that one of the most important contributions they can make to the organization is to maintain their strong connections within the broader community.

There is a fine line between being a board member with an eye on the big picture and a board member who thinks she is in charge and adopts an attitude or presence that simply annoys the volunteers. Board members who find themselves on the wrong side of that fine line can inadvertently cause serious problems, even in well-established organizations. Avoiding or fixing this predicament takes time and effort. Staff and board members must develop a mutually respectful relationship. They must recognize one another's strengths and build an atmosphere of trust.

Far too many organizations have fallen victim to internal conflicts that can only be described as turf battles. These conflicts can be avoided when everyone understands how they fit into the overall organization, are comfortable with it, and have the necessary level of trust with everyone else involved.

Not Another Great Idea

As your organization grows, you may have to deal with one or more board members who continually offer terrific ideas without any means of carrying them out. This situation is distracting to the board and frustrating for the staff, and there is rarely a mechanism to deal with it. These people mean well; in fact, they firmly believe that their input is fulfilling the oversight role they took on when they joined the board. The board liaison or the board president in collaboration with staff will need to redirect these great ideas into real work plans that have a solid chance of success.

Financial Responsibility

To a large degree, the financial responsibility for the organization will be a shared responsibility. Even so, you need clearly defined roles to avoid conflict. Particularly in the start-up phase, the board president, the treasurer, and the person who is overseeing day-to-day operations need to collaborate to develop the budget. An executive director, if you have one, must be directly involved with the board members to provide the real-world guidance they may need.

For the budget to work, everyone must understand that a fine line exists between cooperation and micromanaging. It is time to choose the best people for the tasks. The monthly board meeting is the traditional time to discuss the financial health of the organization. If you are using standard accounting software, monthly financial statements are a simple matter to produce, but there is no guidance on interpretation.

A Staff Member Presenting Financial Information

Many organizations have a staff person present financial updates to the board, either in a narrative form or with copies of the financial documentation produced using accounting software such as QuickBooks.

This reporting method is not without problems. It can go right over the heads of board members who may not have been following the operations as closely as staff does. It also places an artificial barrier between the board and the staff person who presents the information precisely when all barriers need to be removed so honest assessments can take place. The monthly reporting needs to be as free from potential conflict as possible.

ESSENTIAL

Regardless of who actually presents the financial information, consider setting up a formal one-day class for your board on reading and understanding financial data. Far too few boards of directors understand modern accounting or learned how to read a profit and loss statement, but pride or embarrassment keeps them from speaking up.

A Board Member Presenting Financial Information

An excellent alternative to having a staff person present the financial report to the board is to have the treasurer open the conversation by presenting the report. This option offers a completely level playing field to discuss your finances because a peer makes the presentation.

Of course, the treasurer needs to be conversant with the details of the budget and must know how to read a spreadsheet to lead the discussion. Discuss who should present the "financials" with the board and ideally with any staff directly involved in preparing the monthly reports. This strategy enables you to reach a decision that meets everyone's needs.

Programming

Programming covers everything the public sees, such as the services your group provides, the classes you run, or the lecture series you present. It is your public face in the community; it defines who you are. Programming should follow the broad, general outlines developed by the board but executed by the staff in their operations capacity. Programming and budget will forever go hand in hand, so you can never consider one without looking at the other.

The Multiyear Programming Plan

A multiyear plan that outlines your programming goals will give your members and the community a clear sense of your plans and intentions. The plan does not need to be complex, but it should identify fully achievable goals in one-, three-, and five-year sections. The plan does need to be coordinated with sources of projected and realistically expected funding, such as membership dues, fees for service or grants, or other sources. Do not list projects that have a limited chance of being funded, but rather put down your realistic expectations that have a planned funding stream in place.

Use of Planned Series Programs

Developing your long-range programming around any number of "series" is one way to expand a small start-up program plan into a multiyear cycle. For example, if a class is held three times a year, draw up a prospective schedule that stretches three to five years into the future. Selecting approximate dates and times for the classes shows the planned continuity of your programming. This becomes very important when talking with potential funders, and it is also a good way to keep your board interested and your staff motivated.

A Board Liaison

Bringing on a board liaison may be among the best personnel decisions your organization will ever make. It makes little difference if that person is compensated or volunteers her time. The ability to funnel ideas and process through one central point has saved many start-up nonprofits from an early demise. The liaison's immediate task is essentially clerical. She must obtain and update the contact information for the board and everyone involved in your group's operations. Much of the role will be to facilitate ongoing, open communication, so having all necessary contact information is important.

The liaison should also be involved in building the agenda for your monthly board meetings, which will require access to the operational documents and materials in process. Likewise, the board needs to become comfortable addressing operational inquiries to the liaison, as well as raising financial questions so they can be folded into any discussions that are to take place. When practical, the board liaison should attend meetings of the board's standing committees, not as a board member or staff member but as a liaison, working equally with all the groups that make up the organization.

An Open-Door Policy

An open-door policy can help maintain a positive, upbeat feeling throughout the organization. People have different roles and responsibilities, but to maintain a smoothly running organization, the lines of communication must be as open and free-flowing as possible. An open-door policy is the operational equivalent of maintaining transparency.

When people know that nothing is being kept from them, they will remember why they chose to work together to form or join the organization. They will be less likely to get bogged down in petty disagreements. If you choose, include the policy in the by-laws. The only possible limitations will occur when dealing with the following issues:

1. Pending legal issues. If your organization is involved in any type of legal action, do not broadcast the information.
2. Personnel issues. Any discussion of salaries, professional reviews, or issues surrounding a termination is confidential.
3. Real-estate transactions. Until a deal is final, any number of things can upset ongoing negotiations.

CHAPTER 21

Personnel Issues

Working for a nonprofit organization is a wonderful experience, but it's very different from working for a for-profit company. There are special rules, mostly with respect to compensation, and a unique sense of shared purpose and shared mission rarely found in other sectors. Since the overall environment is different, the ways in which that environment is managed are also different.

A Unique Sense of Ownership

There is just something about working for a nonprofit. Whether or not pay is involved, nonprofits seem to attract a wonderful group of people. These are individuals who could generally involve themselves in the for-profit sector in a heartbeat, but decide to apply themselves to organizations that all too often struggle financially and seem, at least to the casual observer, to be lurching from one crisis to the next.

People are drawn to nonprofits because they believe more deeply in the mission of the organization than in a desire to gain great wealth. Even so, employment in these groups is by no means entirely altruistic. Positions with nonprofits are real jobs with real responsibilities. The difference is that taking the profit motive out of the daily picture makes it possible to devote yourself to the actual work beyond the bottom line.

Working in the nonprofit sector has become a unique employment, as though different skills are required than in a for-profit company. Nothing could be further from the truth, but the phenomenon remains.

There is also a real sense of ownership unlike anything you'll encounter in a for-profit business. Working at a nonprofit often becomes much more than just another job. The mission—the core of the organization—is the driving force in all aspects of the organization. It affects all who work or volunteer their time.

From Clients to Staff

In the for-profit world, it's rare that a customer will actually buy a company. However, there is a fascinating phenomenon in nonprofits in which clients become staff or volunteers. A person who brings lost animals to a shelter may wind up volunteering a few hours a month behind the desk, or the parent of a kid in a nonprofit summer camp may become an instructor in that very same camp.

Because of the special relationships nonprofits can establish in a community, the traditional lines between service beneficiary and service provider blur. Unless there are clear conflicts of interest, which normally won't be an issue unless the roles involve board membership, there is no problem with people taking on different roles within the organization.

Conflict of interest is a very real problem precisely because people feel comfortable moving from position to position within the organization. Be sure to have a policy in place that addresses this issue. You can use the sample policy presented in this toolkit as a model. When these issues arise, your board of directors will need to resolve them.

Pride from the Community

There is a very deep sense of pride that comes from working—either for pay or as a volunteer—for most nonprofit organizations. People love to share the achievements they have been involved in—for example, the opening of a community garden, working in a small art school, or protecting an ancient forest from development. This sense of pride is infectious. As outsiders learn about an organization's mission and the good work it does, they want to be a part of it as well. The people at the core of your organization need to understand the passion and excitement your mission inspires and to value and seek ideas from those you have moved.

The Personnel Committee

Many organizations form a personnel committee to handle the human resource issues that may arise. Although this is a committee of the board, its membership can include anyone the board chooses. Unlike other committees, personnel meetings are rarely open. Deliberations are not reported in the general board minutes but in confidential reports to the board.

There are many reasons for confidentiality when dealing with personnel issues. First, you always must respect the feelings and reputation of an employee who may be having a difficult time with issues that are unrelated to the organization but that are nonetheless affecting performance. In addition, if the personnel committee also acts as a hiring committee, it is inappropriate to divulge names of people you chose to not hire. These people may be involved in your community, and announcing that they were not hired would cause, at the least, embarrassment and, at the worst, serious harm to their reputation.

The second and perhaps most important reason to maintain confidentiality is the threat of lawsuits. Employee-related lawsuits represent the greatest need for board and officer insurance. Like it or not, people often pursue legal action even when calm negotiation or binding arbitration would have resolved the problem.

ALERT

If your personnel committee sets any type of formal interview process, it must adhere to a legal framework that includes such factors as maintaining the uniformity of its questions (every candidate is asked the same questions). Never ask inappropriate questions that would reveal a candidate's age, religion, sexual orientation, or nonwork-impacting handicap. It may be wise to review proposed questions and interview methods with an attorney.

The threat of legal actions goes both ways. Volunteers or paid employees can and do bring legal actions for any number of reasons, but organizations do the same thing. So plan strategies to avoid potential litigation. Maintaining strict confidentiality is an excellent start.

Employee Policies

Before it can make any hiring decisions, the personnel committee usually must draft and submit an employee manual for approval by the full board of directors. There are many examples to draw from to establish a basic manual. Other nonprofits will be more than willing to share their employee manuals with you. Before going into the specifics, include a welcoming page from the director or board president. A new volunteer or paid employee will be nervous in the beginning, and reading a friendly note from the people at the very core of the organization will ease the transition into the group.

The first major section of the handbook contains employee policies. These policies inform employees and volunteers what you expect of them. Cover details such as schedules, use of the computer, and confidentiality issues regarding the organization's records. It is also the best place to spell out the general expectations the organization has for everyone, volunteer or paid staff. This may include the mission statement or other documents that explain why the organization exists.

The handbook is also the place for general housekeeping details such as hours of operation, recognized holidays, and basic procedures. If compensated personnel are involved, include details about pay and deductions.

Employee Grievances and Reviews

Establish a personnel committee to provide an arena to arbitrate problems that will inevitably arise among people who work together. A committee consisting of people representing many parts of the organization often encourages an increased level of openness not possible in traditional employee/employer meetings. Minor grievances can be resolved painlessly as soon as people are comfortable and begin to talk. Situations that are either very serious or very complicated will require outside help or mediation to resolve. For most situations in small nonprofit organizations just starting out, few problems will accelerate to a level that requires such intervention.

ESSENTIAL

Schedule formal written reviews of paid employees and valued volunteers at least once a year. The reviews are an excellent way to offer support to the people actually carrying out the organization's mission. Stress the positive contributions people make to the organization.

Weekly or even monthly staff meetings for everyone involved in operations are essential. Having the opportunity to talk with and listen to one another often resolves potentially problematic situations long before they escalate. Remember that your volunteers are every bit as important as any paid staff and should be included in meetings or other communications. The reliance on volunteers is a two-way street; they give you their time and expertise, and you must give them respect and gratitude for their hard work.

A Code of Conduct

The code of conduct in a nonprofit must reflect and represent the very best of who you are. As a publicly supported entity, your inner workings are mostly exposed. How you decide to articulate acceptable (and, conversely, unacceptable) behavior by everyone involved in the organization speaks volumes about who you are.

FACT

The code of conduct represents how the volunteers and staff are to interact with each other, but consider including how you as an organization expect visitors, patrons, or others in the community to act when working with you. It is leading by example.

Post the code of conduct in a public place where it is visible to anyone in your organization as well as to members of the general public. It is a reminder of what types of behavior are acceptable and what types of behavior are simply not tolerated. Over time, some parts of the code of conduct simply may not work, may seem out of touch, or may need to be changed. Bring up the code and invite input at staff meetings, committee meetings, or even larger organizational meetings. If changes are necessary, propose to the board that adjustments be made.

Contractor or Employee

At some point, your organization will need outside help for tasks that are well beyond the capabilities of the volunteer pool. You will have to decide whether to employ people or hire them as independent contractors. There are advantages and disadvantages to either option, and there are also ethical questions you may have to consider. Businesses in the for-profit sector also face these questions, but the difference lies in how and why you make these decisions.

Staff as Independent Contractors

An independent contractor is essentially a private business of one person. By signing a legally binding contract, he agrees to provide a specific service to your organization for a set fee.

You have probably already hired independent contractors and never thought about them as such. The electrician who rewired the office and the webmaster who maintains your website are examples of independent contractors. They agreed to perform a service, you paid them, and that was the end of the story. The individuals may have been employed by a company—perhaps an Internet service provider or an electrical service company—but in their working relationship with your organization, they were contractors.

This situation is far different from contracting with someone to handle a task on an ongoing basis. The advantage of such an arrangement for the contractor is the relative freedom it offers. He is only committed to a set period or to complete a specific task.

QUESTION

What does "exempt employee" mean?
An exempt employee usually refers to a salaried employee, or someone who does not work by the hour and therefore is not eligible for overtime pay. There are other requirements to be considered exempt. Speak to a lawyer who has a background in employment law if you have any questions about how your employees should be classified.

The contractor rarely receives benefits such as health insurance, is often responsible for his own taxes, and is not eligible for unemployment compensation. This arrangement can be a major disadvantage for the contractor, but it can be an advantage for the organization that hires him. For this reason, it is a potential source of conflict. Many nonprofits need to address the moral dilemma of securing the long-term services of an independent contractor for these very reasons.

Staff as Employees

The other option is to hire an individual as an employee following a process identical to that used by for-profit companies. As an employer, the organization becomes responsible for payroll withholdings for taxes and social security and can offer health insurance, if that is an option. Federal and state labor laws immediately cover the new employee; these laws exist as a baseline for issues ranging from minimum wages to required hours to holidays.

A negotiated contract can outline all the particulars and responsibilities of both the employee and the organization. Hiring employees inevitably means more complex bookkeeping, so anticipate needing a competent, professional bookkeeper.

Collective Bargaining

By definition, collective bargaining is the good-faith process between an employer or management and a trade union representing the employees. It is the process for negotiating wages, responsibilities, working hours, working conditions, and other details that affect what the employees do and how the interaction between the employees and the organization moves forward.

Collective bargaining is the fundamental principle on which the trade union system is based. On the surface, collective bargaining in the context of a nonprofit is not particularly different from any other labor negotiations. But dig a little deeper, and things can be very different.

The Right to Organize

American labor law makes very few distinctions between for-profit and nonprofit businesses. When most labor laws were written, the nonprofit sector was so small that it was of little consequence. Only in the past twenty-five years have nonprofits grown large enough to warrant organizing. The rights of a worker—any worker—are basic to our economy.

A number of national organizations that represent many classifications of workers are actively organizing individuals in the nonprofit sector. This has generally been a positive trend for the employees and, ultimately, for the organizations in which they work.

Confrontation

Many for-profit businesses were founded and continue to thrive in a highly competitive environment where intense negotiations and indeed confrontations may be necessary. Prevailing in such an environment is part of doing business. But many people who are drawn to nonprofits feel differently.

ESSENTIAL

Employees and organizations can derive excellent benefits from developing good relationships with the unions. There may be opportunities to join large health care pools or to voice opinions on community issues. As a 501(c)(3), you cannot directly lobby for legislation; however, many unions are able to do so, which benefits everyone who supports your particular cause or issue.

Unions deal with for-profit and nonprofit businesses differently in terms of how the negotiating parties view each other and how they arrive at a fair and equitable contract. Many employees have a deep emotional bond with the mission of the organization and naturally seek consensus over confrontation, so the idea of a labor-bargaining session can be upsetting.

A number of forward-thinking unions are recognizing the differences between nonprofit workplaces and companies in the for-profit sector. They are learning to work for the good of both the workers and the organization, seeking that proverbial win-win outcome.

CHAPTER 22

Changing from a For-Profit Organization to a Nonprofit

For one reason or another, you may find that your for-profit organization is better suited to be a nonprofit. The modification can take place, but it is not easy. The change will require a thorough understanding of what a nonprofit organization is, as well as the ability to explain why your organization should now become nonprofit.

Where You Are Right Now

Any change to your basic structure that moves your current for-profit business into the nonprofit sector will require intense analysis. The core reasons that prompt the change must go far beyond your current cash flow or profit and loss statement. If that is your primary motivation, stop right now. However, the relationship your business has with the community you serve may lend itself to a nonprofit status. You may receive a certain level of public support and your business may have an honest focus that lines up with the IRS requirements for nonprofit status.

Learn All You Can

If you are considering transforming a for-profit business into a nonprofit organization, there is a good chance you have heard the term *nonprofit* but have never had any reason to learn exactly what is involved in starting and running one. Gather as much information on the topic as you can find. Talk to people who are involved in running nonprofits in similar fields, read books, and research websites, including the IRS site.

ESSENTIAL

If you currently have investors, tell them about your plans as soon as they come together. One of the overriding rules of any nonprofit is that no one may personally benefit from the organization. Unfortunately, this is exactly what an investor does; her relationship with a for-profit entity is based upon a financial return on her investment.

It's *All* about the Money

Previous chapters have dealt with the financial elements involved in starting and operating a nonprofit organization. Once a group has incorporated and is working, the focus shifts to income sources, the stream of income, and the importance of spending money on projects and operations that are in alignment with the mission and the nonprofit regulations. For anyone considering a conversion from for-profit to nonprofit, the sources of income are crucial.

The decision will rest on where your funding comes from (the charitable question), and you must be absolutely certain that all expenditures are in absolute compliance with the rules governing nonprofits. Unlike a start-up nonprofit, a for-profit business already has income sources and expenditures, which may not align with the rules governing nonprofits.

No Deception

If you are considering changing from a for-profit to a nonprofit to avoid any corporate income-tax responsibilities, stop immediately. You are on a dangerous path. You are hardly the first person to come up with such an idea, and your intentions will become very clear to any IRS personnel who review your application.

If you try to falsify your financial documents to meet standards you believe will prove your case, you will dig yourself deeper into a legal hole. When your charade is exposed (as it surely will be), it will cast a long shadow over the entire nonprofit community that has been living and working by the rules all along. It is hard enough to maintain the cash flow necessary for nonprofit organizations to do their essential work without having to answer for people who are trying to scam the system.

Financial Trouble Is Financial Trouble

If your business is struggling financially, becoming a nonprofit is not going to change very much. A for-profit organization operates very much the way a nonprofit does, except that no individual may benefit financially from the work of the organization. If your supplies are costing too much, your expected fees for service are not meeting projections, or you are having trouble making payroll, becoming a nonprofit is not going to help you. If your business plan and projections are not working, adjust them to current economic realities instead of scrapping them with an eye toward reorganizing the entire company.

ALERT

Consider working up a simple side-by-side analysis of your current for-profit business and a proposed nonprofit. Look at the numbers and consider the public or community support you think would be available. Determine whether you would be able to maintain viability and meet the requirements to be a public charity.

From For-Profit to Nonprofit: A True Success Story

A small, for-profit restaurant/coffee shop, the Riverview Café, operated for many years. Over the past dozen years it had had a handful of different owners, each drawn not so much by their desire to make vast sums of money but because of the status the Riverview had in the community. The last owner kept terrible books, so bad that upon sale of the business, the entire incorporation process had to start from scratch. The customers never knew the difference. The place never made any real money, but it did manage to stay open, pay the counterperson, and keep a good supply of fresh food in the kitchen.

The Riverview hosted a weekly open mic/jam session and made the space available on weekends for small concerts, either self-produced or presented by outsiders who paid a percentage of the door receipts to the café. Most people assumed that the café was a nonprofit, run by the core of musicians who frequented the business, even though it was not.

The decision was made to form a nonprofit organization, and have all the assets of the commercial business transferred to the nonprofit, which would then be operated by a board of directors who could (and did) hire the former owner to manage the property. This was possible since the decision was made well before the twenty-seven months (discussed later) from the sale/reincorporation had run out. The business name remained the same, although the legal ownership name reflected the change.

Because the sale of food by a nonprofit would have been unfair competition to neighboring for-profit businesses and was outside the stated nonprofit purpose of providing an arts/educational venue, a percentage of the café was determined to be nonexempt and taxes continued to be paid on that portion of the income.

The arrangement passed all the requirements set forth by the IRS, and the new organization received its nonprofit determination well within the usual response window and with only a few clarifications requested by the IRS. Remember that converting a for-profit to a nonprofit can and does occur, but it also requires a tremendous amount of work and very likely the involvement of a creative tax lawyer.

The Twenty-Seven-Month Rule

If you have not been in business for twenty-seven months, you may have a chance of switching from a for-profit to a nonprofit. From the viewpoint of the IRS, you are simply a business paying your corporate taxes like anyone else.

ALERT

This is the time to consult with your general tax advisor and a lawyer who is well versed in current IRS law. You are going into some of the most complicated areas in nonprofit law. A general guide is no substitute for professional advice geared specifically to your situation.

The first question, provided you are indeed within the window, is what you indicated when you incorporated with the state. Remember, all your documentation regarding incorporation is a state issue, not federal. You will most likely need to file extensive articles of amendments, essentially reforming your organization to comply with the nonprofit standards as opposed to the for-profit ones you originally created.

Either you or your attorney needs to make an initial inquiry to your state secretary of state or the office where you filed your original articles of incorporation to determine the process you need to follow to make the switch at the state level. Get the names of each person you speak with, and prepare a follow-up note to reiterate the issues discussed.

Be certain that everything you do is in writing. Telephone calls are fine for general questions, but they are worthless in establishing a paper trail.

Inside the Twenty-Seven-Month Window

If you are within the twenty-seven-month window, you must still check with the office in your state where you filed the articles of incorporation and make the necessary changes to your core corporate documents. You may have to file articles of amendment, but you will probably also have to explain in detail how and why the original circumstances have changed and why your organization is now seeking incorporation as a nonprofit. It may be possible that you simply made a mistake in filing the initial articles of incorporation, which can be rectified with a letter of explanation and amended articles.

Twenty-Seven Months and Beyond

If, on the other hand, you incorporated as a traditional for-profit business, have been operating as a for-profit business for twenty-seven months or longer, and now decide you are really a nonprofit charitable organization, you will face an uphill struggle. It is highly unlikely your group will be able to gain a favorable decision, and it may be time to seek an alternative route to gaining nonprofit status.

Rethinking Business Plans and Terminology

To change from a for-profit to a nonprofit is more complicated than filling out a few forms. It may require adjusting how your entire organization views itself and its place in the community. You will have to re-examine a number of the core assumptions that very likely motivated you when you started your for-profit business. One of the largest sticking points may be your interest (or your investors' interest) in making money.

You must also completely rethink what you do and why you are doing it. With any contemplation of the transition to nonprofit status, you need to reconsider why you are even in existence. The IRS is very clear on the basic criteria that any organization must meet before it obtains a favorable nonprofit determination. Those criteria do not suddenly change to accommodate someone who is interested in turning a for-profit business into a nonprofit—in fact, you can expect a narrow interpretation of the rules and more pointed questions or a need for clarification.

Identification of the Operational Changes

You will have to identify the internal changes you adopted to qualify as a nonprofit. Simply deciding you are a nonprofit is not enough. Your entire organization must meet the criteria for a nonprofit, including how you are organized and whether anyone owns shares or stock or, in any way, expects to see a return on some sort of investment in the organization. These elements will immediately disqualify your group from attaining nonprofit status.

Identification of the Revenue Changes

You must show clearly that your base of financial support is the public and that you should be granted nonprofit status. This is not going to be easy. The entire premise of a functioning for-profit business is exactly the opposite of a nonprofit.

Using our Riverview Café as a further example, its revenue was derived from the sale of tangible goods (namely, coffee and food). The profits generated went to the owner. There was a significant level of public support from patrons paying to see performers, but it was not the primary income for the business.

As a nonprofit, it became essential to show that the public support for the concerts, educational workshops, and musical instrument lessons were responsible for keeping that portion of the facility, designated as a nonprofit organization, functioning. It was also essential to show, through budgets and bank statements, that the profit from that portion of the facility (which was the nonprofit) was returned to the organization, never to any individual.

Forming a Nonprofit Within Your Current Operation

One option that has been implemented successfully is to form a new nonprofit within your existing for-profit business. The purpose of this new organization would be to carry out the elements of your overall mission that fall within the parameters of the IRS tax-exempt regulations, even as you operate the for-profit business. Although it is certainly not a guarantee of success, this model has been followed by a number of organizations around the country that did indeed receive their IRS determination letters.

There are obviously many issues to be addressed. You'll need to explain how one space can be used by two different entities and who takes financial responsibility for the many items delivered to the businesses and possibly shared in the normal course of doing business.

A slight modification of this option is to form a parallel 501(c)(3). The new nonprofit could be financially supported, at least initially, by its for-profit parent. This particular model allows current investors to remain fully involved. Although they will no longer be seeing a financial reward, they may become contributors to the new nonprofit. As such, they will be able to deduct all or part of that contribution (depending on the particulars) from their personal income tax liability.

The parallel organization cannot be a carbon copy of the existing for-profit business. It must be organized as a self-sustaining nonprofit, following all the rules and requirements of any other 501(c)(3).

Starting from Scratch

Consider starting from scratch if you are contemplating a change after you have been incorporated longer than twenty-seven months or if you have other complicating factors that make the change to a nonprofit simply too difficult or impossible. The huge advantage of starting another organization is that you will already have the contacts, the infrastructure, and possibly the staff. You and your organization will also have the most valuable commodity to bring to the table: real-world experience in running a business and working with people.

What's in a Name?

If the decision is to start over, you may have to change the name of the organization so it is not the same as the former business or adjust it so that it is recognizable but clearly different. This is no time to be overly clever. Think of yourselves as completely reorganizing, which may unfortunately mean a name change if you have well-established name recognition in the community.

Change Happens

Businesses and organizations change their names and, at times, endure entire makeovers. Sometimes the transformation is due to marketing plans or changes in leadership, or perhaps to define more accurately the organization's place in the community.

Many start-up nonprofits would love to have the level of experience an incorporated business uses every day. This is definitely a strength that needs to be recognized and utilized as you move forward with a complete reorganization of your for-profit business.

In reality, apart from those directly involved in the governance of an organization and those who have been financial contributors, no one really pays attention to these details. The community the organization serves and the general population might notice a name change, but with good publicity you may be able to mark the name change without changing the public perception of your organization.

Far more complicated than a name change will be the need to fundamentally change the organizational/corporate structure of a for-profit business to comply with both the letter and spirit of the IRS code as it pertains to nonprofit organizations. A board of directors will become the governing body, which can mean that the former owner or manager will no longer have the final word on operational decisions. Rather than having a revenue stream based on the sale of goods and services, revenue will now show public support in any of the forms discussed elsewhere in this book.

Finally, you will need to eliminate the entire concept of expecting a return on investments made to a business. People will forever be encouraged to make contributions and donations to the organization, but they can never do so expecting to see a financial return as with an investment in a for-profit company.

A Successful Fundraising Campaign: A Case Study, Yew Dell Gardens, Crestwood, Kentucky

Everyone understands the need for nonprofit organizations to raise money, either for general operating expenses or capital improvements, or both. All too often, the ambitious plans of an organization run up against the incredibly difficult task of actually raising the money to carry them out. What follows is the real success story of a small nonprofit organization, Yew Dell Gardens (*www.yewdell.org*), located near Louisville, Kentucky.

The Story of Yew Dell Gardens

This small nonprofit understood that in order to realize the dream of its founder and current board of directors, it needed to raise a considerable amount of money. Rather than attempt such a major fundraising task alone (something the board did not feel qualified to handle in-house), the group decided to seek an outside consulting firm to provide assistance. This is a decision that many nonprofits choose to make, but it is one that must be taken with great care. It is difficult for a group that has worked so hard to bring a dream to this point to engage an outside organization that has no connection to the nonprofit's mission. The information presented here will give you and the nonprofit you are working with the encouragement and confidence to move forward with your fundraising efforts.

A Unique Site

Yew Dell Gardens is a unique botanical garden and arboretum developed by the late Theodore Klein, a prominent nurseryman and plant expert, on thirty-three acres near LaGrange, Kentucky, northeast of Louisville. Following Mr. Klein's death in 1998, a group of culturally minded community leaders in the Greater Louisville area organized themselves as the Friends of Yew Dell, to save the gardens from redevelopment and preserve them for public enjoyment.

Early in 2001, the Oldham County Historical Society engaged Goettler Associates to conduct a planning/feasibility study. The study tested a $4.8 million program to purchase and renovate the existing properties; develop additional facilities, exhibits, and programs; and establish an endowment.

Based on the results, the firm recommended a phased development program. In Phase I, $1 million or more would be raised to purchase the property, sustain operations, and prepare a site plan and business plan. Phase II would seek an additional $2.5 million to develop the property into a major cultural attraction.

Over the succeeding four months, Goettler Associates provided periodic consulting services to assist the Friends in preparing for the Phase I campaign. During this period, the consultants prepared the cases for the support and campaign plan. They identified prospects for major gifts and initiated a leadership awareness program to introduce them to the project.

From this foundation, the development of the gardens has steadily gained momentum. In the summer of 2003, Yew Dell Gardens, now separately incorporated, received grants of $500,000 from the James Graham Brown Foundation and $75,000 from the Gheens Foundation. In the same year, the nonprofit hired a full-time director, and the Garden Conservancy (a national organization dedicated to the preservation of historic gardens) completed a stabilization plan.

To date, more than $3.5 million has been raised. Considerable restorations and renovations have been completed, and public tours are now offered. The group hired a full-time development and marketing officer and launched a membership program.

Educate the Public Before Asking for Money

The project did not take place in a vacuum. Before bringing an outside consultant into the project, the organization had expertly educated the public and its supporters to the need it was facing.

What follows is an example of the promotional material developed to introduce Yew Dell Garden to the public well in advance of the actual campaign to raise funds. Even though a well-established organization developed the material, it still provides an excellent example of what your organization can aspire to with respect to public outreach and education. This level of sophisticated outreach will be necessary regardless of any decision by your board either to engage outside consultants or to develop your fundraising campaign on your own.

The Yew Dell Gardens

"The Friends of Yew Dell" is a Committee of the Oldham County Historical Society. The mission of Yew Dell Gardens is to continue the legacy of Theodore Klein; to encourage exploration of its arboretum, theme gardens, and extraordinary architectural setting; and to provide opportunities for education, enrichment, and enjoyment.

Preliminary Statement of Objectives

Theodore Klein, an internationally known and respected nurseryman and plant expert, devoted much of his life to horticulture. As a businessman, Klein succeeded in providing varieties and quantities of plants required by leading residential and commercial developers. As a visionary, Klein's interest went far beyond the day-to-day business of managing nursery stock. His beautiful horticultural creation—the Yew Dell Gardens, located in Crestwood, Kentucky—stands today as his unique legacy to our community.

"The Friends of Yew Dell" (a committee of the Oldham County Historical Society) have developed a plan to preserve the property as a legacy for the enrichment and enjoyment of future generations. To do so, the committee is considering a capital fundraising program to raise the $4,825,000 required to purchase the thirty-three-acre estate, renovate the handsome Klein home and miniature medieval castle and outbuildings, and provide for the first three years of operation. With community support, we will preserve an endangered and charming green space in Oldham County.

Yew Dell Gardens: A Legacy and a Vision

Theodore Klein acquired over a thousand rare and unusual specimen trees and shrubs during fifty years at his "Yew Dell Farms." After his retirement, Klein devoted himself wholeheartedly to collecting trees. His arboretum represents an outstanding private collection. The ongoing inventory of trees and shrubs in the arboretum indicates the presence of over 1,137 individual specimens. This includes 114 different genera, 240 species, and 528 cultivars and selections. Some of these cultivars are plants that Klein selected, propagated, named, and introduced to the nursery trade.

Klein built a charming limestone home with a slate roof and a miniature stone castle, complete with turrets, stained glass windows, and stone carvings. The property also includes barns, a stone smokehouse, greenhouses, and a log cabin. Most of the extensive woodwork in the house was made by Mr. Klein, who was an accomplished carpenter. He was a fine craftsman, and taught himself to forge iron and to carve stone. In his garden,

Klein created many "rooms," among them a walled rose garden, a sunken garden, a secret garden, a pleached alley of hollies, and an evergreen serpentine garden.

William Noble, director of Preservation Projects of the Garden Conservancy (a national organization dedicated to preserving exceptional American gardens for the public's education and enjoyment), observes: "As with other gardens of the arts and crafts style, Yew Dell's beauty and diversity of nature is celebrated and the hand of man has crafted a house and garden that is in harmony with nature."

It is the intention of the Friends of Yew Dell to restore and enhance Theodore Klein's homestead. The vision for the garden is:

- To preserve and renovate the existing buildings, arboretum, and gardens
- To provide space to welcome and accommodate visitors, oversee ongoing maintenance, and further develop the property
- To establish educational programs for visitors of all ages including primary and secondary schools, and post-secondary institutions
- To develop and implement interpretive exhibits, guided tours, lectures, special events, a gift shop, and a retreat center for community outreach
- To offer a broad training program for volunteers, docents, and interns

To accomplish these objectives, the committee is planning a capital campaign to raise $4,825,000 from donors throughout our region. The anticipated costs are:

Initial purchase of the 33-acre Yew Dell Farm, Home, and Gardens	$1,000,000
Renovation of the main home, miniature castle, gardens, and arboretum, and for site development	$2,500,000
Operating costs for the first three years	$325,000
Endowment	$1,000,000
Total	$4,825,000

Yew Dell Gardens will offer a quiet space for contemplation, as well as study and visual enjoyment. Visitors will enter into an oasis of beauty and grace—amidst an external setting of rapidly expanding suburban development.

A Well-Rounded Community Asset

The Louisville area is a region of substantial growth. In Oldham County, the population has increased almost 40 percent since 1990. County leaders face the difficult challenge of addressing the demands of a growing population and urban development, while still preserving the rural aspects that have contributed to Oldham County's popularity as a place to live and raise a family.

Yew Dell offers the community tremendous potential as a horticultural, educational, cultural, and economic asset. Oldham County is well regarded for its excellent schools and overall quality of life, which has attracted new residents to the area. As an educational resource, researchers at the University of Kentucky have an expressed interest in partnering with Yew Dell in research, plant identification studies, and field trips. Property that can be committed for long-term horticultural research is in short supply. Yew Dell will also become a prized asset for area schools as well as other horticultural organizations.

Our region offers excellent cultural and sports attractions that have proved vital to the regional economy. They also make a bold statement about our entrepreneurial spirit as well as our expectations for future achievements. However, there are few public gardens.

It is not necessary for an attraction to be huge in size in order to occupy an important place among a metropolitan society's cultural gems. It is the diversity in cultural amenities that reveals the true extent of a community's vision. Yew Dell Gardens as envisioned will add a new dimension to Louisville's regional standing as a business, tourist, and cultural destination.

Mary Anne Thornton, president of Botanica, Inc., observes the necessity for an asset such as Yew Dell: "It has long been felt by the gardening community in the metropolitan Louisville area that there is a dire need for more public gardens here that would enhance the quality of life for all."

With the support of interested civic, corporate, and philanthropic leaders and friends, we can preserve a living legacy and add a new and beautiful feature to our cultural offerings.

[Thank you to Goettler Associates of Columbus, Ohio (*www.goettler.com*) for use of this narrative and detailed information.]

APPENDIX B

Sample Documents

Sample Articles of Incorporation

XYZ Nonprofit
Articles of Incorporation

The undersigned, for the purpose of forming a corporation under the nonprofit laws of the State of Washington (RCW 24.03), hereby adopts the following Articles of Incorporation:

Article I
The name of the corporation shall be XYZ Nonprofit.

Article II
The term of existence shall be perpetual.

Article III
The purposes for which the corporation is organized are as follows:

XYZ Nonprofit has been organized to support groups and individuals creating social, economic, and cultural transformation toward long-term sustainability through the production of an annual festival and other activities.

XYZ Nonprofit may therefore seek, apply for, and receive donations, grants, loans, and other funding from individuals, organizations, corporations, government agencies, and others to support and conduct, in any manner, any lawful activities in furtherance of these charitable, scientific, and educational purposes.

Notwithstanding any other provision of these by-laws, XYZ Nonprofit shall not carry on any other activities not permitted to be carried on by: (a) a corporation exempt from federal income tax under Section 501(c)(3) of the Internal Revenue Code of 1954 (or the corresponding provision of any future United States Internal Revenue Law); (b) a corporation, contributions to which are deductible under Section 170(c)(2) of the Internal Revenue Code of 1954 (or the corresponding provision of any future United States Internal Revenue Law); or (c) a corporation under the Washington Nonprofit Corporation Act (RCW 24.03).

Article IV

The name of the Registered Agent of the corporation is _____. The street address of the Registered Office and Registered Agent is _____.

The mailing address for the Registered Agent is _____.

Article V

There shall be five directors serving as the initial Board of Directors. Their names and addresses are as follows:

Article VI

In the event of the dissolution of the Corporation, the net assets are to be distributed as follows: to organizations of similar purposes, as determined by the Board of Directors, which have established tax-exempt status under section 501(c)(3) of the Internal Revenue Code of 1954 (or the corresponding provision of any future United States Internal Revenue Law).

Article VII

The name and address of each incorporator is as follows:

In witness whereof, each incorporator has affixed his/her signature on this ____th day of _____.

Sample By-Laws

XYZ Nonprofit
By-Laws (Date)

ARTICLE 1—PURPOSES

ARTICLE 2—MEMBERSHIP

ARTICLE 3—DIRECTORS
3.1 General Powers
3.2 Number & Qualifications
3.3 Election & Term of Office

ARTICLE 4—OFFICERS
4.1 Number & Qualifications
4.2 Election & Term of Office
4.3 President
4.4 Vice-President
4.5 Secretary
4.6 Treasurer

ARTICLE 5—COMMITTEES
5.1 Executive Committee
5.2 Other Committees

ARTICLE 6—PROCEDURE
6.1 Meetings
6.2 Notice
6.3 Quorum
6.4 Procedure
6.5 Resignation
6.6 Removal
6.7 Vacancies

ARTICLE 7—ADMINISTRATION
7.1 Fiscal Year
7.2 Books & Records
7.3 Contracts
7.4 Loans
7.5 Checks & Drafts
7.6 Deposits

ARTICLE 8—MISCELLANEOUS
8.1 Offices
8.2 Indemnification
8.3 Amendment
8.4 Dissolution

ARTICLE 1—PURPOSES

XYZ Nonprofit has been organized to support groups and individuals in creating social, economic, and cultural transformation toward long-term sustainability through the production of an annual festival and other activities.

XYZ Nonprofit may therefore seek, apply for, and receive donations, grants, loans, and other funding from individuals, organizations, corporations, government agencies, and others to support and conduct, in any manner, any lawful activities in furtherance of these charitable, scientific, and educational purposes.

Notwithstanding any other provision of these by-laws, the Corporation shall not carry on any other activities not permitted to be carried on by: (a) a corporation exempt from federal income tax under Section 501(c)(3) of the Internal Revenue Code of 1954 (or the corresponding provision of any future United States Internal Revenue Law); (b) a corporation, contributions to which are deductible under Section 170(c)(2) of the Internal Revenue Code of 1954 (or the corresponding provision of any future United States Internal Revenue Law); or (c) a corporation under the Washington Nonprofit Corporation Act (RCW 24.03).

ARTICLE 2—MEMBERSHIP

The Corporation shall have no members.

ARTICLE 3—DIRECTORS

3.1　General Powers

The management and control of the affairs of the Corporation shall be vested in its Board of Directors. Directors shall not be employees of the Corporation, nor otherwise be compensated for their duties except for out-of-pocket expenses as determined by the Board.

3.2　Number & Qualifications

The Board shall consist of not less than five (5) or more than fifteen (15) Directors, the specific number to be set by resolution of the Board. Directors must be at least eighteen (18) years of age. Directors shall be sought who have experience or working interest in areas such as finance, real estate, human resources, event management, and/or possess a specific skill necessary to chair and oversee the Community Committees of the Corporation, and work with Community Committee members to arrive at agreed-upon proposals for presentation to the full Board. This Corporation is committed to a policy of fair representation on the Board of Directors, which does not discriminate on the basis of race, physical handicap, gender, ancestry, religion, or sexual orientation.

3.3 Election & Term of Office

The initial Directors named in the Articles of Incorporation shall serve until the first annual meeting. At the first annual meeting, one-third of Directors shall be elected to one-year terms, one-third to two-year terms, and the remaining Directors to three-year terms. At subsequent annual meetings, Directors shall be elected to three-year terms. The term of office for newly elected Directors shall commence at the succeeding Board meeting. Each Director shall hold office until he or she resigns or is removed or is otherwise disqualified to serve, or until his or her successor shall be elected and qualified, whichever occurs first.

ARTICLE 4—OFFICERS

4.1 Number & Qualifications

The officers shall be President, Vice President, Secretary, Treasurer, and such other Officers and assistant Officers as may be determined by the Board. The same person, except the offices of President and Secretary, may hold any two or more offices.

4.2 Election & Term of Office

The Board at the annual meeting shall elect Officers each year. Each Officer shall hold office until he or she resigns or is removed or is otherwise disqualified to serve, or until his or her successor shall be elected and qualified, whichever occurs first.

4.3 President

The President shall be the principal executive of the Corporation responsible for carrying out the directions and resolutions of the Board. He or she shall preside at all meetings of the Board and Executive Committee. Upon resolution of the Board, and not otherwise, he or she may sign with the Secretary, Treasurer, or any other proper Officer authorized by the Board any deeds, mortgages, bonds, contracts, or other instruments (including acceptances of donations, conveyances, or contributions), except in cases where the signing and executing thereof is expressly delegated by these by-laws to some other Officer or agent of the Corporation, or is required by law to be otherwise signed and executed. The President shall in general perform all duties incident to the office of President and such other duties as may be assigned by the Board from time to time.

4.4 Vice President

In the absence of the President, or in the event of his or her inability or refusal to act, the Vice President shall perform the duties of the President and when so acting shall have all the powers, and be subject to, the restrictions placed on the President. The Vice President shall in general perform all duties incident to the office of Vice President and such other duties as may be assigned by the President or the Board from time to time.

4.5 Secretary

The Secretary shall: (a) keep the minutes of the meetings of the Board; (b) see that all notices are duly given in accordance with the provisions of these by-laws or as required by law; and (c) in general perform all duties incident to the office of Secretary and such other duties as may be assigned by the President or the Board from time to time.

4.6 Treasurer

If required by the Board, the Treasurer shall give a bond, at the expense of the Corporation, for faithful discharge of his or her duties in such sum and with such sureties as determined by the Board. The Treasurer shall: (a) have custody of and be responsible for all funds and securities of the Corporation; (b) receive contributions to the Corporation and receive and give receipts for moneys due and payable to the Corporation from any source whatsoever, and deposit all such moneys in the name of the Corporation into such banks, credit unions, trust companies, or depositors as selected by the Board in accordance with the provisions of these by-laws; and (c) in general perform all duties incident to the office of Treasurer and such other duties as may be assigned by the President or the Board from time to time.

ARTICLE 5—COMMITTEES

5.1 Executive Committee

The Executive Committee shall consist of all Officers of the Corporation. The Committee shall have the power to act on behalf of the Corporation subject to final ratification of its acts by the Board. Any Officer may call a meeting of the Executive Committee.

5.2 Other Committees

The Board may establish and empower such standing Community Committees and ad hoc committees as it deems necessary, and may solicit and approve participation by members of the general public. A Director shall chair every committee. Committee chairs shall perform all duties incident to their office as determined by the President or Board. Committee decisions must be approved by the Board prior to enactment.

<u>ARTICLE 6—PROCEDURE</u>
6.1 Meetings
The annual meeting of the Board shall be held during the winter months for the purpose of electing Directors and transacting such business as may properly come before the meeting. Regular meetings of the Board shall be at least quarterly on a date and time established by the Board. Special meetings of the Board may be called by or at the request of the President, any two Directors, or a majority of paid staff of the corporation. No business shall be transacted at a special meeting except that mentioned in the notice. All meetings shall be held at the principal office of the Corporation or at such other place within the State of Washington designated by the Board or persons entitled to call a meeting. Attendance at meetings of the Board may, in special situations, be by telephonic or electronic means.

6.2 Notice
Unless otherwise stated in these by-laws, notice of all meetings shall be given to the appropriate Directors and committee members not less than ten (10) days prior to the date of the meeting, by or at the direction of the President, Secretary, or committee chair calling the meeting. Notice for all meetings concerning the removal of a Director or Officer, amendment to these by-laws, or dissolution of the Corporation, shall be given to the appropriate Directors or committee members not less than fifteen (15) days prior to the date of the meeting, by or at the direction of the President, Secretary, or committee chair calling the meeting. Any notice required under the provisions of these by-laws or as otherwise required by law shall be given in person or by mail. If mailed, such notice shall be deemed delivered when deposited in the United States mail addressed as it appears in the records of the Corporation, with postage thereon prepaid.

6.3 Quorum
A majority of members shall constitute a quorum for the purposes of conducting business at any meeting of the Board or any committee designated and appointed by the Board. A quorum once attained shall continue until adjournment despite the voluntary withdrawal of enough members to leave less than a quorum.

6.4   Procedure

All meetings shall be conducted according to a standard parliamentary procedure. The Board shall seek to make decisions through the consensus. If consensus cannot be reached in a reasonable period of time, the President may table the decision until the next meeting or ask that a decision be made by the affirmative vote of not less than seventy-five percent (75%) of those present and eligible to vote. Each Board or committee member shall be entitled to one vote. Members not present may vote by written proxy submitted before or at the meeting. Unless otherwise provided for in these by-laws, the act of those present in person or by proxy at a meeting at which a quorum has been attained shall be the act of the body so meeting. Except upon motion properly passed to conduct an executive session, all meetings of the Board shall be open to the public. Executive sessions may exclude anyone not designated in the motion for executive session, but shall be only for personnel matters, property acquisition, and communication with legal counsel.

6.5   Resignation

Any Director, Officer, or committee member may resign at any time by delivering written notice to the President, Secretary, or appropriate committee chair at the registered office of the Corporation, or by giving oral or written notice at any meeting. Such resignation shall take effect at the time specified therein, or if the time is not specified, upon delivery thereof.

6.6   Removal

The Board may remove any Director, Officer, or committee member if they have knowingly violated the rules and policies of the Corporation or carried out activities without Board authorization that have legal or financial consequences for the Corporation. Such termination may take place at any Board meeting. If removal of a Director is proposed, all Directors shall be notified of the meeting and the cause for the proposed termination.

6.7   Vacancies

A vacancy on the Board or any committee, or in any office, may be filled by approval of the Board for the duration of the unexpired term. If the number of Directors in office is less than the minimum required by these by-laws, a vacancy may be filled by approval of a majority of the Directors then in office or by a sole remaining Director.

ARTICLE 7—ADMINISTRATION

7.1   Fiscal Year

The fiscal year shall be the calendar year or such other period as determined by the Board.

7.2   Books & Records

The Corporation shall keep correct and complete books and records of accounts, minutes of the meetings of the Board and committees having any authority of the Board, and, at its registered office, the names and addresses of the Directors and Officers. All books and records shall be open for public inspection for any proper purpose at any reasonable time.

7.3   Contracts

The Board may authorize any Officer or agent of the Corporation to enter into any contract or to execute and deliver any instruments on behalf of the Corporation.

7.4   Loans

No loans shall be contracted on behalf of the Corporation and no evidences of indebtedness issued in its name unless so determined by the Board. No loans shall be made to any Director.

7.5   Checks & Drafts

All checks, drafts, or other orders for the payment of money or other evidences of indebtedness issued on behalf of the Corporation shall be signed by such Officer or agent of the Corporation in such a manner as determined by the Board.

7.6   Deposits

All funds of the Corporation not otherwise employed shall be deposited to the credit of the Corporation in such banks, trust companies, or other depositories as determined by the Board.

ARTICLE 8—MISCELLANEOUS

8.1   Offices

The principal office of the Corporation shall be located in ABC County of the State of Washington. The Corporation may also have offices at such other places within the State of Washington as its business and activities may require and as the Board may, from time to time, designate.

8.2   Indemnification

The Corporation may indemnify to the fullest extent permitted by Washington State law any person who was or is a party to or who is threatened to be made a party to any threatened, pending, or completed action, suit, or proceeding, whether civil, criminal, administrative, or investigative, by reason of the fact that the person is or was a director, officer, employee, or agent of the Corporation against expenses (including attorneys' fees), judgments, fines, penalties, damages, and any amounts paid in settlement actually or reasonably incurred by him or her in connection with the action, suit, or proceeding. In addition, the Corporation may pay for or reimburse the reasonable expenses of a Director, Officer, employee, or agent of the Corporation who is a party to a proceeding to the extent and under the circumstances permitted by Washington State law.

8.3   Amendment

These by-laws may be amended by a two-thirds vote of the Directors at any meeting of the Board provided all Directors have been notified of this purpose, and that as amended the by-laws shall not contain any provision that permits the Corporation to carry on activities not permitted by a corporation exempt from federal income tax under Section 501(c)(3) of the Internal Revenue Code or the corresponding provision of any future federal tax code, or by a corporation incorporated under the Washington Nonprofit Corporation Act (RCW 24.03).

8.4   Dissolution

The Corporation may voluntarily dissolve and cease to operate upon the affirmative vote of not less than seventy-five percent (75%) of the Directors at any meeting of the Board, provided all Directors have been notified of this purpose. Upon dissolution, any net assets of the Corporation shall be distributed in accordance with the provisions of the Articles of Incorporation.

ADOPTION OF BY-LAWS

XYZ Nonprofit Board of Directors on _____ adopted the forgoing by-laws.

_____
Secretary

Sample Budget

XYZ Nonprofit Community Theater Operations Budget OPERATIONS BUDGET OVERVIEW Fiscal Year 2012				
Earned Revenue		**Expenses**		**Net**
Concerts	48,500	Concerts	43,860	4,640
Films	93,600	Films	93,000	600
Arts in Education	15,950	Arts in Education (balance with $15K in grants earmarked for Arts in Education)	17,060	(1,110)
Rentals	130,500	Rentals	99,800	30,700
Concessions	37,200	Concessions	16,020	21,180
Ticketing Fees	34,400	Ticket Handling	24,990	9,410
		Marketing	21,200	(21,200)
Total Earned Revenue	**$360,150**	**Total Earned Expenses**	**$315,930**	**$44,220**
Unearned Revenue				
Memberships	46,800	Membership & Donor Marketing	3,100	43,700
City Funding	10,400		10,400	
County Funding	2,500		2,500	
State Funding	2,000		2,000	
Individual & Business Sponsorships	12,700		12,700	
Monthly Program Guide Sponsors	9,000		9,000	
Earmarked Education Grants	15,000		15,000	
Concert & Film Sponsors	2,500		2,500	
Event Sponsors	22,500		22,500	
Fundraising Events	92,100	Fundraising Events	48,200	43,900
		Payroll	149,990	(149,990)
Interest	24	Bank Loan	-	24
		Overhead Other Than Payroll	40,932	(40,932)
Total Unearned Revenue	**$215,524**	**Total Unearned Expenses**	**$242,222**	**$(26,698)**
TOTAL REVENUE	**$575,674**	**TOTAL EXPENSES**	**$558,152**	
			TOTAL INCOME	**$17,522**

Sample Mission Statements

For a Community Theater

To entertain, inform, and inspire our diverse community through cinema, live performance, and educational programs while preserving the historic XYZ Theater.

For an Arts Festival

The purpose of the ABC Fair shall be to educate and inform the public about choices in personal and community lifestyle through the promotion and preservation of the work of individual craftspersons, artists, artisans, musicians, and performers; displays in a traditional fair setting; psycho-spiritual rejuvenation; and the creation of a public forum encouraging the exchange and discussion of ideas about alternative community organization and the use of economic resources and appropriate technology.

For a Music Support Organization

The purpose of ABC Music is to support acoustic music in the Northwest by fostering a community that nurtures musical growth, creativity, and the appreciation of acoustic music.

For a Community Garden

The mission of Central Community Garden is to enhance the quality of urban life and strengthen community bonds by creating and sustaining an organic garden in Sand Point Magnuson Park that will foster environmental stewardship, horticultural education, rejuvenation, and recreation.

Sample Job Description: Executive Director

Executive Director Position Description

XYZ Nonprofit

Under the direction of the Board of Directors, the Executive Director is responsible for overall management and operation of the XYZ Nonprofit and protection of the organization's financial assets while ensuring compliance with Board directives and applicable grantor, federal, and state requirements.

Essential Duties and Responsibilities

The Executive Director is responsible for overall operations, asset protection, and marketing/public relations for XYZ Nonprofit, a 501(c)(3) nonprofit private research and education corporation. The incumbent also:

- Oversees all accounting functions including those necessary for auditing, budgeting, financial analysis, capital asset and property management, and payroll in accordance with generally accepted accounting principles
- Handles all aspects of human resource management for up to ### employees, including but not limited to hiring and termination, developing position descriptions, setting compensation, working with employees
- Interacts with other personnel and organizations, such as the city, state, and other public and private entities
- Is responsible for grants and contracts management including negotiating research agreement terms that reflect the needs of XYZ Nonprofit
- Assists in the development of current and long-term organizational goals and objectives as well as policies and procedures for XYZ Nonprofit operations; establishes plans to achieve goals set by the Board of Directors; and implements policies, subject to approval by the Board of Directors
- Analyzes and evaluates vendor services, particularly for insurance, employee benefits, and management of XYZ Nonprofit funds, to determine programs and providers that best meet the needs of XYZ Nonprofit and makes recommendations to the Board, as appropriate; negotiates services, terms, and premiums and executes contracts with benefit plan providers, supply and service vendors, auditors, and consultants; manages payroll and benefits programs

Education and/or Experience

No specific education required. However, the Executive Director must possess the above-mentioned skills, knowledge, and qualities, which may result from formal education or at least three years' experience in business, nonprofit operational and financial management, or related areas.

Physical Demands

While performing the duties of this job, the Executive Director is regularly required to sit, stand, walk, speak, and hear. The position requires extensive computer use so the employee must have sufficient hand dexterity to use a computer keyboard and be capable of reading a computer screen. The employee must occasionally lift and/or move up to 20 pounds. Reasonable accommodations may be made to enable otherwise qualified individuals with disabilities to perform the essential functions.

Travel

The Executive Director must be able to travel to attend conferences, training, and other events as required to acquire and maintain proficiency in fulfilling the responsibilities of the position.

Work Environment

The work environment is a small, busy office located in <City>. The noise level in the work environment is usually low to moderate. Reasonable accommodations in the work environment may be made to enable individuals with disabilities to perform the essential functions.

Sample Job Description: Administrative Assistant

Foundation Administrative Assistant Job Description

XYZ Foundation

The XYZ Foundation Administrative Assistant is an energetic, amicable, and highly organized individual who provides key support to the Foundation Director, Foundation professional staff, and the Foundation Executive Committee. The Foundation Administrative Assistant will work independently and with multiple Foundation team and committee members. She or he is a professional in her or his own right, and will be the first face and voice of the Foundation that many donors and prospective donors will encounter. This individual will receive training and will have the opportunity to learn about endowment fund development and the world of philanthropy.

DUTIES AND RESPONSIBILITIES
- Provide executive-level support as required by the XYZ Director
- Schedule meetings and events
- Send out notices for meeting
- Mail out invitations for events
- Prepare agendas
- Prepare any material needed for meetings or events
- Record the minutes of meetings
- Transcribe and distribute minutes in a timely manner
- Prepare reports and statistical reports, as required by professionals
- Post meeting follow-up as required
- Plan staff events
- Recruit assistance from other Foundation administrative assistants, as needed
- Process Foundation correspondence
- Perform Internet research on current and prospective donors
- Enter data into the database
- Create donor profiles
- Maintain files, database, calendars, and hard-copy files
- Record the assignment of donors and prospects into the database
- Maintain accurate records of contacts in the database

- Serve as a liaison between professional staff, other departments, donors, and prospective donors
- Provide logistical support for projects and special events
- Perform other duties as assigned

QUALIFICATIONS
- Advanced written and spoken (English) communication and administrative skills; excellent telephone manner
- Computer literacy including MS Office products: Word, Excel, Outlook, Power Point; experience with mail-merges and with customer or donor databases
- Exceptional time-management, planning, and administrative skills
- Ability to organize and prioritize workload
- High level of diplomacy, sound judgment, and discretion when dealing with donors, volunteers, and community professionals
- Combined four years of full-time work experience and/or higher education
- High degree of energy, self-motivation, and flexibility

Sample Job Description: Board Liaison

Board Liaison Job Description

XYZ Nonprofit

The Board Liaison performs a variety of high-level administrative tasks, which may include budget preparation, travel arrangements and meeting logistics, scheduling, and reporting and tracking information for senior management. He or she provides direct support to high-level Directors and may support other senior managers, including frequent interaction with all members within the organization, as well as customers, vendors, and business relations. The liaison makes interpretations and recommendations as appropriate. His or her duties are highly confidential and require comprehensive knowledge of XYZ Nonprofit's policies, procedures, and operations. These responsibilities require discretion, judgment, tact, and poise. The incumbent has considerable latitude and flexibility in carrying out assigned tasks.

COMMUNICATIONS AND INTERPERSONAL CONTACTS
- Formulate and clearly communicate ideas to others, providing a variety of information to staff and others to assist workflow throughout the organization
- Work and communicate with a diverse group of people, including the Board of Directors, donors, volunteers, the public, and other staff
- Demonstrate professional, positive, and approachable attitude/demeanor and discretion
- Demonstrate sensitivity in handling confidential information
- Coordinate multiple diverse projects with several variables, set realistic deadlines, and manage timelines
- Adapt or modify processes in response to changing circumstances
- Interpret guidelines and analyze factual information
- Resolve routine and complex problems independently, with minimal consultation with supervisor
- Demonstrate common sense, flexibility, and teamwork with the strong ability to exercise independent judgment

SUPERVISION/FINANCIAL OVERSIGHT

- May supervise administrative staff and/or volunteers, interns, and temporary staff
- Financial responsibilities include budgeting for multiple business units
- May serve as delegated financial authority in a variety of areas, such as arranging for large meetings and committing funds related to such meetings and approving expense reports

Sample Document Retention and Destruction Policy

The document retention and destruction policy of the <XYZ Nonprofit> identifies the record retention responsibilities of staff, volunteers, members of the Board of Directors, and outsiders for maintaining and documenting the storage and destruction of the organization's documents and records.

1. Rules

The organization's staff, volunteers, Board of Directors, and outsiders (i.e., independent contractors through agreements with them) are required to honor these rules:

Paper or electronic documents indicated under the terms for retention following will be transferred and maintained by the legal or administrative staff or their equivalents.

All other paper documents will be destroyed after three years.

All other electronic documents will be deleted from all individual computers, databases, networks, and backup storage after one year.

No paper or electronic documents will be destroyed or deleted if pertinent to any ongoing or anticipated government investigation or proceeding or private litigation.

2. Terms for Retention

RETAIN PERMANENTLY

- Governance records: Charter and amendments, by-laws, other organization documents, governing board and board committee minutes
- Tax records: filed federal tax returns/reports and supporting records, tax-exemption determination letter and related correspondence, files related to tax audits
- Intellectual property records: copyright and trademark registrations and samples of protected works
- Financial records: audited financial statements, attorney contingent liability letters

RETAIN FOR TEN YEARS

- Pension and benefit records: Pension (ERISA) plan participant/beneficiary records, actuarial reports, related correspondence with government agencies, and supporting records
- Government relations records: state and federal lobbying and political contribution reports and supporting records

RETAIN FOR THREE YEARS

- Employee/employment records: Employee names, addresses, social security numbers, dates of birth, resume/application materials, job descriptions, dates of hire and termination/separation, evaluations, compensation information, promotions, transfers, disciplinary matters, time/payroll records, leave/comp time, engagement and discharge correspondence, documentation of basis for independent contractor status
- Lease, insurance, and contract/license records: software license agreements, vendor, hotel and service agreements, independent contractor agreements, employment agreements, consultant agreements, and all other agreements

RETAIN FOR ONE YEAR

- All other electronic records, documents, and files

3. Exceptions

Exceptions to these rules and terms for retention may be granted only by the organization's chief staff executive or the President of the Board.

ADOPTED:

Sample Conflict of Interest Policy

This conflict of interest policy of the <XYZ Nonprofit>

1. Defines conflicts of interest
2. Identifies classes of individuals within the organization covered by this policy
3. Facilitates disclosure of information that may help identify conflicts of interest
4. Specifies procedures to be followed in managing conflicts of interest

1. Definition of Conflicts of Interest

A conflict of interest arises when a person in a position of authority over the organization may benefit financially from a decision he or she could make in that capacity, including indirect benefits such as to family members or businesses with which the person is closely associated. This policy is focused upon material financial interest of, or benefit to, such persons.

2. Individuals Covered

Persons covered by this policy are the organization's officers, directors, chief employed executive, and chief employed finance executive.

3. Facilitation of Disclosure

Persons covered by this policy will annually disclose or update, in writing, to the President of the Board of Directors any interests that could give rise to conflicts of interest, such as a list of family members, substantial business or investment holdings, and other transactions or affiliations with businesses and other organizations or those of family members.

4. Procedures to Manage Conflicts

For each interest disclosed to the President of the Board of Directors, the President will determine whether to (a) take no action, (b) assure full disclosure to the Board of Directors and other individuals covered by this policy, (c) ask the person to recuse from participation in related discussions or decisions within the organization, or (d) ask the person to resign from his or her position in the organization or, if the person refuses to resign, become subject to possible removal in accordance with the organization's removal procedures. The organization's chief employed executive and chief employed finance executive will monitor proposed or ongoing transactions for conflicts of interest and disclose them to the President of the Board of Directors in order to deal with potential or actual conflicts, whether discovered before or after the transaction has occurred.

ADOPTED:

Sample Joint Venture Policy

The joint venture policy of the <XYZ Nonprofit> requires that the organization evaluate its participation in joint venture arrangements under federal tax law and take steps to safeguard the organization's exempt status with respect to such arrangements. It applies to any joint ownership or contractual arrangement through which there is an agreement to jointly undertake a specific business enterprise, investment, or exempt-purpose activity as further defined in this policy.

1. Joint Ventures or Similar Arrangements with Taxable Entities

For purposes of this policy, a joint venture or similar arrangement means any joint ownership or contractual arrangement through which there is an agreement to jointly undertake a specific business enterprise, investment, or exempt-purpose activity without regard to (a) whether the organization controls the venture or arrangement, (b) the legal structure of the venture or arrangement, or (c) whether the venture or arrangement is taxed as a partnership or as an association or corporation for federal income tax purposes. A venture or arrangement is disregarded if it meets both of the following conditions:

- That 95 percent or more of the ventures' income for its tax year ending within the organization's tax year is excluded from unrelated business income taxation, including but not limited to dividends, interest and annuities, royalties, rent from real property and incidental related personal property except to the extent of debt-financing, and gains or losses from the sale of property.
- The primary purpose of the organization's contribution to, or investment or participation in, the venture or arrangement is the production of income or appreciation of property.

2. Safeguards to Ensure Exempt-Status Protection

The organization will negotiate in its transactions and arrangements with other members of the venture or arrangement such terms and safeguards adequate to ensure that the organization's exempt status is protected, and take steps to safeguard the organization's exempt status with respect to the venture or arrangement.

Examples of safeguards include:

- Control over the venture or arrangement sufficient to ensure that it furthers the exempt purpose of the organization
- Requirements that the venture or arrangement gives priority to exempt purposes over maximizing profits for the other participants
- That the venture or arrangement does not engage in activities that would jeopardize the organization's exemption
- That all contracts entered into with the organization are on terms that are arm's length or more favorable to the organization

ADOPTED:

Tribal Nonprofit Organizations

In 1982, the U.S. Congress passed the Indian Tribal Governmental Tax Status Act, which was made part of the Internal Revenue Service and recognized as Section 7871 of the IRS Code. Section 7871 treats tribal governments as state governments for a variety of tax purposes. One of these purposes is to allow tribal governments (and their political subdivisions) to receive tax-deductible donations as do nontribal 501(c)(3) organizations.

As more federally recognized tribes continued to open business ventures employing thousands of individuals and generating millions of dollars into local economies, Congress decided to include basic information that will assist tribes with their planning should they decide to utilize Section 7871 of the IRS Code.

The information included in this appendix is used with the kind permission of the First Nations Development Institute. Individuals working with tribes or organizations in some way affiliated with federally recognized tribal governments and interested in forming a nonprofit organization on reservations may contact the First Nations Development Institute for further information and assistance. For more information on this topic, see their website: *www.firstnations.org*.

Section 7871 Defined

Generally, foundations and public charities fall under Section 501(c)(3) of the Internal Revenue Code. For tribal governments, however, the Indian Tribal Governmental Tax Status Act of 1982 is recognized as an appropriate legal, political, and economic means for Indian nations to establish, regulate, and control philanthropic activities within their communities. This act, codified as the Internal Revenue Code (IRC), §7871, treats tribal governments as state governments, allowing tribal governments, their political subdivisions, or any tribal governmental fund, to receive tax-deductible contributions.

Establishing tax-exempt tribal governmental organizations under IRC §7871 allows tribes to maintain a greater degree of sovereignty than they would under the more customary 501(c)(3) designation. Even the U.S. Supreme Court has held that Indian nations possess a status higher than states. Thus, the more traditional 501(c)(3) designation subjects Indian nations (and their political subdivisions) to the oversight of the offices of state attorney generals, where jurisdiction over "expressly public and charitable purposes" is generally housed.

Section 7871 of the IRS Code offers many of the same tax benefits for donors as 501(c)(3) nonprofits, for practical tax purposes, meaning: All donations to a 7871 tribe or organization are tax deductible, and foundations can make grants to such organizations. The 7871 organizations establish their own accountability to their donors. The code specifically conditions deductibility on the gift's being "for exclusively public purposes."

Advantages of Establishing a 7871

The advantages of establishing a tribal nonprofit using Section 7871 are very much under discussion, with all points of view equally valid. Every tribe will have unique relationships with their respective state government, or multiple governments in situations where tribal government boundaries cross state lines.

The issue of tribal sovereignty does play a major role, as do basic economics and the needs of the tribe or its affiliated organizations (i.e., tribe-associated foundations) to secure funding from the corporate and private foundation community. Some tribal nonprofits have decided to forgo the 7871 option, have gone the more traditional route through the state, or are approaching funders as a government entity that may already be recognized as "nonprofit."

Defining and maintaining the unique intergovernmental relationships is generally a responsibility of the tribal attorney, who will need to be in constant, ongoing communication through any process if the 7871 option is being considered.

Effects of 7871 on Potential Donors

The 7871 option is encouraged to help potential donors understand what might otherwise appear to be a terribly confusing relationship between the tribes and the state or federal government. The effect of using this section is to make the entire process of donating funds to a tribal nonprofit as easy and as seamless as making a contribution to any other nonprofit in the country.

A great deal of confusion still exists with respect to how tribes and the local, state, and federal government bodies interact in their official "government to government" capacity. The 7871 option essentially cuts through a lot of that confusion to help donors understand that their contributions are treated just as they are with other nonprofits, with the full understanding and endorsement of the Internal Revenue Service.

Reporting and Accountability

Reporting requirements are not imposed by the federal government. IRS Section 7871 assumes that tribes, their political subdivisions, and tribal colleges will provide fiscal accountability for charitable contributions, as they manage all finances. However, it is important to donors that their contributions are documented and that fiscal procedures are transparent. It is required practice for 501(c)(3) organizations to acknowledge each donation in writing, to report fiscal activities by submitting reports to the state and federal governments (i.e., 990 Forms), and to forbid any substantial part (i.e., greater than 5 percent) of the organization's budget to contribute to lobbying activities (or any portion whatsoever to political contributions). Because donors are familiar with these requirements, they may be worth considering when creating a tribal restricted fund.

Tribal Options Other Than 7871

There is no rule or other requirement that a tribe make use of the 7871 option. It is designed as a tool for tribes or their affiliated organizations to use if, in their opinion, it would help with their overall operations and fundraising. If a tribe wants its nonprofit entity to incorporate with the state, there is no reason they should not do so. Each tribe will need to assess the associated issues of tribal sovereignty before using the 7871 section.

One of the main ideas of this section is to make it easier for nontribal contributors to contribute to tribal nonprofit organizations and have the complete assurance those contributions will be fully deductible. If that is not a concern, there may be no need to pursue it.

Looking at it from another angle, there is the much larger question of tribal sovereignty as it relates to a state government and to the question of what government body should be handling incorporation matters. If this is also not a concern, again the 7871 option might not be an appropriate route to follow.

Long-Range Outlook for 7871

Whereas the term *501(c)(3)* is currently better known in philanthropy, there is a long-range ongoing effort in Native American philanthropy to elevate the awareness of IRC 7871. The specific goal is to incorporate 7871 into standard granting guidelines among foundations, corporations, and financial-planning institutions.

This toolkit contains a sample IRS ruling a tribe might want to have when communicating with potential donors. While some tribal programs use the nonprofit status without receiving a formal letter ruling, others have found it helpful to have a letter ruling from the IRS to provide to potential donors as an assurance of tax-deductibility for their gifts. If a tribe was not listed in one of the Revenue Procedures published by the IRS in 1983 and 1984, it is required to get a Private Letter Ruling. However, if the tribe is listed, it depends on the facts and circumstances whether a unit of the tribe needs to receive its own ruling. The awareness level of IRC 7871 in Indian Country and in the philanthropy world is varied. Although some foundations, corporations, and donors are familiar with the actual law, some simply do not know that Indian tribes are eligible to receive tax-exempt contributions. Some may not understand the political subdivision aspect of the law (political subdivisions are determined by the power to tax, the power to police, and the power of eminent domain), and some donors are unaware of the opportunity altogether. More Native American tribes and their programs could take advantage of this opportunity. Use of this tax law opportunity will allow Indian Country to access "mainstream" philanthropy more easily, and it will help educate the broad range of people who interface with the philanthropy world about tribal sovereignty.

Most nonprofits file for 501(c)(3) status through a state. Some tribal nonprofits file for 501(c)(3) status through a tribe; in this case, the tribe takes on the role of the state. Sometimes tribes choose to create a 501(c)(3) organization for programs that need to be a separate entity from the tribe. Otherwise, a tribe can set up a restricted fund, which can be reported on in full, without reporting all aspects of the tribe's finances. The maintenance of a 501(c)(3) organization includes specific supervision by the IRS through applications (Form 1023, initially) and reporting (Form 990, on an annual basis). By contrast, a 7871 organization is primarily accountable to its tribal council or the governing board of the tribe. A restricted fund is generally created through a resolution of the governing entity, and it is the responsibility of that governing entity to establish procedures to manage these funds.

Sample 7871 Ruling

DEPARTMENT OF THE TREASURY
INTERNAL REVENUE SERVICE
Office of Indian Tribal Governments

TAX EXEMPT AND
GOVERNMENT ENTITIES DIVISION

April 12, 2006

Jason Smiley, Attorney
Oglala Sioux Tribe-Lakota Oyate Wakanyeja Owicakiyapi
Myrna Young Bear, Board of Director Chairman
P.O. Box 604
Pine Ridge, SD 57770

Dear Mr. Smiley:

This responds to your request for information concerning your tribe's federal tax status, and the issue that has been raised by certain grantors concerning a perceived need for Section 501(c)(3) status. While we have no control over their governing instruments, we can address the issue of Section 501(c)(3) and federally recognized Indian Tribal governments.

Under Section 7871 of the Internal Revenue Code, Congress determined that federally recognized Indian tribes and their subdivisions would be treated like states for certain specified purposes, because tribal governments, like state governments, serve the public within their jurisdictional boundaries, and accordingly should be permitted to devote their limited resources to that end.

There is no provision in the Internal Revenue Code that imposes an income tax on governmental entities or their political subdivisions. Revenue Ruling 67-284 amplifies this issue regarding federally recognized Indian tribes, by affirmatively indicating that they are not subject to federal income tax. Thus, Indian tribal governments do not qualify for exemption from federal income tax as described under Section 501(c)(3) of the Internal Revenue Code, since they are simply not subject to federal income tax.

The Oglala Sioux Tribe is a federally recognized tribe and is listed in Revenue Procedure 2002-64 as an organization that may be treated as a governmental entity in accordance with Section 7871. As such, the tribe's income would not be subject to federal income tax. In addition, the tribe would also be eligible to receive charitable contributions that are deductible for federal income, estate, and gift tax purposes by the donor.

Sometimes governmental units are asked to provide proof of their status as part of a grant application. If your tribe is applying for a grant from a private foundation, the foundation may be requesting certain information from your tribe because of restrictions imposed by the Internal Revenue Code on such foundations under Sections 4945 and 4942 of the Code.

Private foundation grants to governmental units for public or charitable purposes are not subject to these restrictions. Grants to governmental units for public purposes are "qualifying distributions" under Section 53.4942(a)–3(a) of the regulations; and, if they are for charitable purposes, will not be taxable expenditures under Section 53.4945-6(a) of the regulations. Most grants to governmental units will qualify as being for charitable (as well as public) purposes.

Some private foundations require grant applicants to submit a letter from the Internal Revenue Service determining them to be exempt under Section 501(c)(3) and classified as a nonprivate foundation. Such a letter, or an underlying requirement that a grantee be a public charity, is not legally required when the prospective grantee is a governmental unit and the grant is for qualifying (public or charitable) purposes.

The following references may be useful to a grantor in verifying eligibility under Section 7871:

- Revenue Procedure 2002-64 lists Indian tribal governments that are treated similarly to states for federal tax purposes, including Sections 7871 and 7701(a)(40) of the Code.
- Revenue Procedure 84-36 lists subdivisions of Indian tribal governments that are treated as political subdivisions of states for the same specified purposes under the Internal Revenue Code, which are noted in Revenue Procedure 2002-64.
- IRS Publication 78, Cumulative List of Organizations, was recently revised for 2003 to include the following language—"Pursuant to section 7871 of the Internal Revenue Code, Indian tribes and their subdivisions are treated similarly to states and their subdivisions for purposes of section 170(c)(1). See Part II, 'Qualified Organizations,' for additional information on contributions to Indian tribal governments." Part II of Publication 78 provides "Indian tribal governments are treated as states for purposes of deductibility of contributions under section 170(c)(1) of the Code, pursuant to section

7871(a)(1)(A) of the Code. Rev. Proc. 2002-64, 2002-42 I.R.B. 717 contains a list of Indian tribal governments that are recognized by the Internal Revenue Service as tribal governments for purposes of section 7871 of the Code. A subdivision of an Indian tribal government may be treated as a political subdivision of a state for purposes of deductibility of contributions under section 170(c)(1) of the Code if the Service has determined that the entity qualifies as a political subdivision of an Indian tribal government under the requirements of section 7871(d) of the Code."

I believe this general information will be of assistance to your tribe. You may wish to provide a copy to any organization that inquires regarding your federal tax status. This letter, however, is not a ruling and may not be relied on as such. If you have any questions, please feel free to contact Kim Wind at (605) 341-8749, x237.

Sincerely,

John L. Walters
Indian Tribal Government Manager
ID Badge # 41-04101

APPENDIX D

Web Resources

A tremendous amount of information is available on the Internet. The following list is by no means all-inclusive; rather, it is intended to provide you, the organizer of a nonprofit organization, with the resources to start a web search. Keep in mind that the rules governing nonprofits, and indeed the rules governing much of the larger business community, are in transition. Therefore, the sites selected and listed here provide the best starting points for the detailed, up-to the-moment information you will require as you move forward. Familiarize yourself with each of them, follow the internal links, explore the "search" functions, and generally use the sites as working tools.

Internal Revenue Service
www.irs.gov

IRS Website: Nonprofit Section
www.irs.gov/charities/charitable/index.html

Direct Link for Filing IRS Form 990
http://epostcard.form990.org

Small Business Administration
www.sba.gov

National Association of Secretaries of State
www.nass.org

Council of State Governments
www.csg.org

Common Grant Application
www.commongrantapplication.com

U.S. Postal Service Nonprofit Information
http://pe.usps.com/text/pub417/pub417_c3_001.html

First Nations Development Institute—A Resource for Tribal Governments and Foundations
www.firstnations.org

Open Office—A Free Alternative to Microsoft Office Software
www.openoffice.org

Ubuntu—A free, open-source Linux computer-operating system as an alternative to Windows or Macintosh, which is generally easy to download and install and works on any computer
www.ubuntu.org

General Resources
for Nonprofits

General Assistance, Including Board Development and Diversity Training

CENTER FOR CIVIC PARTNERSHIPS
1851 Heritage Lane, Suite 250
Sacramento, CA 95815
Phone: (916) 646-8680
Fax: (916) 646-8660
www.civicpartnerships.org

FOUNDATION CENTER
79 Fifth Avenue/16th Street
New York, NY 10003-3076
Phone: (212) 620-4230
www.foundationcenter.org

NATIONAL MULTICULTURAL INSTITUTE
3000 Connecticut Avenue NW, Suite 438
Washington, DC 20008-2556
Phone: (202) 483-0700
Fax: (202) 483-5233
www.nmci.org

TAPROOT FOUNDATION
National Headquarters
466 Geary Street, Suite 200
San Francisco, CA 94102
Phone: (415) 359-1423
www.taprootfoundation.org

CD Contents

Federal Forms

IRS Form SS-4: Application for Employer Identification Number

Cat. No. 62736F: Instructions for Form SS-4

IRS Form 1023: Application for Recognition of Exemption under Section 501(c)(3) of the Internal Revenue Code

IRS Notice 1382: Complete Form 1023

Cat. No. 46573C: Instructions for Form 1023

IRS Form 8718: User Fee for Exempt Organization Determination Letter Request

Errata Sheet for Form 1023: To Be Used to Complete Parts IX and X

IRS Form 1024: Application for Recognition of Exemption under Section 501(c), (2), (4), (5), (6), (7), (8), (9), (10), (12), (13), (15), (17), (19), (25)—and non-profit other than 501(c)(3)

USPS Form 3533: Application for Refund of Fees, Products, and Withdrawal of Customer Accounts

USPS Form 3624: Application to Mail at Nonprofit Standard Mail Prices

State Forms

Secretaries of State Roster

ALABAMA
AL_Application for Certificate of Existence
AL_Articles of Incorporation
AL_Articles of Amendment

ALASKA
AK_Articles of Amendment
AK_Articles of Incorporation
AK_Establishing a Business

ARIZONA
AZ_Articles of Incorporation
AZ_Cover Sheet for Corporate Filings
AZ_Schedule of Fees for Corporate Filings
AZ_Articles of Amendment

ARKANSAS
AR_Articles of Incorporation
AR_Certificate of Amendment
AR_Doing Business in AR
AR_Fees

CALIFORNIA
CA_Articles of Incorporation
CA_Business Entities Fee Schedule
CA_Certificate of Amendment
CA_Statement of Information_Domestic Nonprofit Corp
CA_Name Reservation Request Form

COLORADO
CO_Articles of Amendment
CO_Articles of Incorporation for a Nonprofit Corporation
CO_Business Resource Guide
CO_Instructions_Amended & Restated Articles of Incorporation
CO_Instructions_Articles of Amendment
CO_Instructions_Articles of Incorporation for a Nonprofit

CONNECTICUT
CT_Certificate of Amendment
CT_Certificate of Incorporation

DELAWARE
DE_Name Reservation Application
DE_Non-Stock Amendment
DE_Non-Stock Corporation

DISTRICT OF COLUMBIA
DC_Articles of Amendment of Nonprofit Corporation
DC_Articles of Incorporation of Nonprofit Corporation
DC_Name Reservation Form

FLORIDA
FL_Nonprofit Articles of Amendment
FL_Nonprofit Articles of Incorporation

GEORGIA

GA_Filing Procedures

GA_Name Reservation Form

GA_Transmittal Information for Georgia Profit or Nonprofit

GUAM

GU_Business License Application

GU_Requirements for Registration

HAWAII

HI_Application for Reservation of Name

HI_Articles of Amendment

HI_Articles of Incorporation

HI_Instructions for Filing Articles of Incorporation

IDAHO

ID_Application for Reservation of Legal Entity Name

ID_Articles of Amendment

ID_Articles of Incorporation

ILLINOIS

IL_Articles of Amendment

IL_Articles of Incorporation

INDIANA

IN_Articles of Amendment

IN_Articles of Incorporation

IOWA

IA_Application for Reservation of Name

KANSAS

KS_Articles of Amendment

KS_Articles of Incorporation

KENTUCKY

KY_Articles of Incorporation

LOUISIANA

LA_Articles of Incorporation

LA_Fee Schedule

MAINE

ME_Articles of Amendment

ME_Articles of Incorporation

MARYLAND

MD_Articles of Incorporation

MASSACHUSETTS

MA_Articles of Amendment

MA_Articles of Incorporation

MICHIGAN

MI_Articles of Amendment

MI_Articles of Incorporation

MINNESOTA

MN_Articles of Amendment

MN_Articles of Incorporation

MISSISSIPPI

MS_Articles of Amendment

MS_Articles of Incorporation

MS_Certificate of Authority

MISSOURI

MO_Articles of Amendment

MO_Articles of Incorporation

MONTANA
MT_Articles of Amendment
MT_Articles of Incorporation

NEBRASKA
NE_Change of Registered Agent

NEVADA
NV_Articles of Incorporation

NEW HAMPSHIRE
NH_Affidavit (Articles) of Amendment
NH_Instructions
NH_Articles of Agreement (Incorporation)

NEW JERSEY
NJ_Nonprofit Information
NJ_Registration Packet

NEW MEXICO
NM_Articles of Amendment
NM_Articles of Incorporation and Registered Agent

NEW YORK
NY_Articles of Amendment
NY_Articles of Incorporation

NORTH CAROLINA
NC_Articles of Incorporation

NORTH DAKOTA
ND_Articles of Amendment
ND_Articles of Incorporation
ND_Nonprofit Instructions

OHIO
OH_Articles of Amendment
OH_Articles of Incorporation
OH_Nonprofit Guide

OKLAHOMA
OK_Certificate of Amendment
OK_Certificate of Incorporation

OREGON
OR_Articles of Amendment
OR_Articles of Incorporation

PENNSYLVANIA
PA_Articles of Amendment
PA_Articles of Incorporation

PUERTO RICO
PR_Articles of Amendment (en Español)
PR_Articles of Incorporation (en Español)

RHODE ISLAND
RI_Articles of Amendment
RI_Articles of Incorporation

SOUTH CAROLINA
SC_501c3 Attachment
SC_Articles of Amendment
SC_Articles of Incorporation

SOUTH DAKOTA
SD_Articles of Amendment
SD_Articles of Incorporation

TENNESSEE
TN_Articles of Amendment
TN_Articles of Incorporation

TEXAS

TX_Certificate of Amendment

TX_Certificate of Correction

TX_Certificate of Formation

UTAH

UT_Articles of Amendment

UT_Articles of Incorporation

UT_Nonprofit Instructions

VERMONT

VT_Articles of Amendment

VT_Articles of Incorporation

VIRGINIA

VA_Articles of Amendment_Name Change

VA_Articles of Amendment

VA_Articles of Incorporation

VA_General Incorporation Instructions

WASHINGTON

WA_Articles of Amendment

WA_Articles of Incorporation

WEST VIRGINIA

WV_Articles of Amendment

WV_Articles of Incorporation

WISCONSIN

WS_Articles of Amendment

WS_Articles of Incorporation

WYOMING

WY_Articles of Amendment

WY_Articles of Incorporation

Sample Nonprofit Documents

Sample Articles of Incorporation

Sample By-Laws

Sample Budget

Sample Mission Statements

Sample Job Description: Executive Director

Sample Job Description: Administrative Assistant

Sample Job Description: Board Liaison

Sample Document Retention and Destruction Policy

Sample Conflict of Interest Policy

Sample Joint Venture Policy

Sample 7871 Ruling

Index

SOFTWARE LICENSE AGREEMENT

YOU SHOULD CAREFULLY READ THE FOLLOWING TERMS AND CONDITIONS BEFORE USING THIS SOFTWARE PRODUCT. INSTALLING AND USING THIS PRODUCT INDICATES YOUR ACCEPTANCE OF THESE CONDITIONS. IF YOU DO NOT AGREE WITH THESE TERMS AND CONDITIONS, DO NOT INSTALL THE SOFTWARE AND RETURN THIS PACKAGE PROMPTLY FOR A FULL REFUND.

1. Grant of License
This software package is protected under United States copyright law and international treaty. You are hereby entitled to one copy of the enclosed software and are allowed by law to make one backup copy or to copy the contents of the disks onto a single hard disk and keep the originals as your backup or archival copy. United States copyright law prohibits you from making a copy of this software for use on any computer other than your own computer. United States copyright law also prohibits you from copying any written material included in this software package without first obtaining the permission of F+W Media, Inc.

2. Restrictions
You, the end-user, are hereby prohibited from the following: You may not rent or lease the Software or make copies to rent or lease for profit or for any other purpose. You may not disassemble or reverse compile for the purposes of reverse engineering the Software. You may not modify or adapt the Software or documentation in whole or in part, including, but not limited to, translating or creating derivative works.

3. Transfer
You may transfer the Software to another person, provided that (a) you transfer all of the Software and documentation to the same transferee; (b) you do not retain any copies; and (c) the transferee is informed of and agrees to the terms and conditions of this Agreement.

4. Termination
This Agreement and your license to use the Software can be terminated without notice if you fail to comply with any of the provisions set forth in this Agreement. Upon termination of this Agreement, you promise to destroy all copies of the software including backup or archival copies as well as any documentation associated with the Software. All disclaimers of warranties and limitation of liability set forth in this Agreement shall survive any termination of this Agreement.

5. Limited Warranty
F+W Media, Inc. warrants that the Software will perform according to the manual and other written materials accompanying the Software for a period of 30 days from the date of receipt. F+W Media, Inc. does not accept responsibility for any malfunctioning computer hardware or any incompatibilities with existing or new computer hardware technology.

6. Customer Remedies
F+W Media, Inc.'s entire liability and your exclusive remedy shall be, at the option of F+W Media, Inc., either refund of your purchase price or repair and/or replacement of Software that does not meet this Limited Warranty. Proof of purchase shall be required. This Limited Warranty will be voided if Software failure was caused by abuse, neglect, accident or misapplication. All replacement Software will be warranted based on the remainder of the warranty or the full 30 days, whichever is shorter and will be subject to the terms of the Agreement.

7. No Other Warranties
F+W MEDIA, INC., TO THE FULLEST EXTENT OF THE LAW, DISCLAIMS ALL OTHER WARRANTIES, OTHER THAN THE LIMITED WARRANTY IN PARAGRAPH 5, EITHER EXPRESS OR IMPLIED, ASSOCIATED WITH ITS SOFTWARE, INCLUDING BUT NOT LIMITED TO IMPLIED WARRANTIES OF MERCHANTABILITY AND FITNESS FOR A PARTICULAR PURPOSE, WITH REGARD TO THE SOFTWARE AND ITS ACCOMPANYING WRITTEN MATERIALS. THIS LIMITED WARRANTY GIVES YOU SPECIFIC LEGAL RIGHTS. DEPENDING UPON WHERE THIS SOFTWARE WAS PURCHASED, YOU MAY HAVE OTHER RIGHTS.

8. Limitations on Remedies
TO THE MAXIMUM EXTENT PERMITTED BY LAW, F+W MEDIA, INC. SHALL NOT BE HELD LIABLE FOR ANY DAMAGES WHATSOEVER, INCLUDING WITHOUT LIMITATION, ANY LOSS FROM PERSONAL INJURY, LOSS OF BUSINESS PROFITS, BUSINESS INTERRUPTION, BUSINESS INFORMATION OR ANY OTHER PECUNIARY LOSS ARISING OUT OF THE USE OF THIS SOFTWARE. This applies even if F+W Media, Inc. has been advised of the possibility of such damages. F+W Media, Inc.'s entire liability under any provision of this agreement shall be limited to the amount actually paid by you for the Software. Because some states may not allow for this type of limitation of liability, the above limitation may not apply to you. THE WARRANTY AND REMEDIES SET FORTH ABOVE ARE EXCLUSIVE AND IN LIEU OF ALL OTHERS, ORAL OR WRITTEN, EXPRESSED OR IMPLIED. No F+W Media, Inc. dealer, distributor, agent, or employee is authorized to make any modification or addition to the warranty.

9. General
This Agreement shall be governed by the laws of the United States of America and the Commonwealth of Massachusetts. If you have any questions concerning this Agreement, contact F+W Media, Inc., via Adams Media at 508-427-7100. Or write to us at: Adams Media, a division of F+W Media, Inc., 57 Littlefield Street, Avon, MA 02322.

We Have
EVERYTHING®
on Anything!

With more than 19 million copies sold, the Everything® series has become one of America's favorite resources for solving problems, learning new skills, and organizing lives. Our brand is not only recognizable—it's also welcomed.

The series is a hand-in-hand partner for people who are ready to tackle new subjects—like you!

For more information on the Everything® series, please visit *www.adamsmedia.com*

The Everything® list spans a wide range of subjects, with more than 500 titles covering 25 different categories:

Business	History	Reference
Careers	Home Improvement	Religion
Children's Storybooks	Everything Kids	Self-Help
Computers	Languages	Sports & Fitness
Cooking	Music	Travel
Crafts and Hobbies	New Age	Wedding
Education/Schools	Parenting	Writing
Games and Puzzles	Personal Finance	
Health	Pets	